PRAISE FOR
SUPPLY CHAIN ETHICS

'Outsourcing and falling sub-contractor rates, child labour and modern slavery, packaging and product waste, carbon emissions etc: we need responsive public policy and responsible corporate strategy. The author provides an in-depth analysis of the ethical challenges along the global supply and value chain and highlights best practices to help governments and corporates find shortcuts towards a more ethical and sustainable business and society.' **Wolfgang Lehmacher, Head of Supply Chain and Transport Industries, World Economic Forum, and author of** *The Global Supply Chain – How technology and circular thinking transform our future*

'In this very accessible book, John Manners-Bell threads together numerous dimensions of the supply chain and demonstrates how embracing the complexity of "people, planet and profit" is the only way to operate now, and increasingly so in the future. His analysis of the implications of this approach shows how there are no longer binary choices to be made, but balances to be struck across ends, ways and means from the board level down to the operating level.' **Robert Palfrey, Managing Director, Minerva Social Risk Management**

'With an overwhelming wealth of examples across industries and regions, Manners-Bell demonstrates how ethics in supply chains go far beyond reducing our carbon footprint to harnessing new value from systemic transformation, from product design to waste disposal. A must-read for any leader seeking success in a low-carbon future.' **Gwyneth Fries, Senior Sustainability Advisor, Forum for the Future**

First published in Great Britain and the United States in 2017 by Kogan Page Limited

2nd Floor, 45 Gee Street	c/o Martin P Hill Consulting	4737/23 Ansari Road
London	122 W 27th Street, 10th Floor	Daryaganj
EC1V 3RS	New York, NY 10001	New Delhi 110002
United Kingdom	USA	India

www.koganpage.com

© John Manners-Bell, 2017

The right of John Manners-Bell to be identified as the author of this work has been asserted by him in accordance with the Copyright, Designs and Patents Act 1988.

ISBN   978 0 7494 7945 9
E-ISBN 978 0 7494 7946 6

British Library Cataloguing-in-Publication Data

A CIP record for this book is available from the British Library.

Library of Congress Cataloging-in-Publication Data

CIP data is available

Library of Congress Control Number:

2016055035

Typeset by Integra Software Services, Pondicherry
Print production managed by Jellyfish
Printed and bound by CPI Group (UK) Ltd, Croydon, CR0 4YY

Supply Chain Ethics

Using CSR and sustainability to create
competitive advantage

John Manners-Bell

KoganPage

CONTENTS

Introduction

The relationship between public policy makers, lobbyists and the logistics and supply industry has been characterized by years of division and mistrust. Anti-globalization campaigners (including those campaigning against the present TTIP negotiations) have ignored the economic benefits that have seen many millions of people across the emerging world lifted out of poverty. Meanwhile, many multinationals have sought to avoid their environmental and social obligations by turning a blind eye to the often degrading and dangerous conditions in which the employees of their remote suppliers work. Governments have sought to influence positive outcomes, as they see it, through regulation and compulsion although in many cases their thinking has not kept pace with the development of new ways of doing business and have been out-of-step with economic reality.

All sides, with a few notable exceptions, have been guilty of a blinkered approach to developing public policy and corporate strategy. The issues are much more finely nuanced than many politicians would have us believe and require a sophisticated response. Likewise managers must recognize that the long-term health of their businesses relies on sustainable environmental and social strategies. Those in charge of public policy as much as those running businesses must realize that positive economic, environmental and societal outcomes are achieved through a wholly integrated business strategy.

A number of artificial choices have been created that no longer make any sense – environmental, societal or economic. For example, despite the best efforts of policy makers, using all the fiscal tools available to them, economic growth has not been decoupled from road freight output. It may indeed be better for authorities to embrace the 'sharing economy', which has the potential to improve the present poor utilization of transport assets. Companies such as Uber and Amazon could, indirectly and unconsciously, achieve more environmental benefits through new business models and technologies than decades of public policy. This will rely on the light touch of regulation rather than the entrenchment of vested interests through government support and protection.

It is not just at this macro-level where similar fine decisions need to be made. Packaging, for example, has attracted the attention of regulators many of whom have seen as their main goal the reduction of 'waste-to-landfill'. This means that single-use packaging has been demonized, although when looking at the overall product lifecycle, it may have lower carbon emissions than a recyclable equivalent.

Nowhere is the link between 'people, planet and profits' more evident than in modern supply chains. Companies are increasingly aware that their businesses are severely at risk from operational disruption and reputational harm if they are not able to identify threats within their outsourced supply chain. If their suppliers are acting unethically towards their employees or undertaking practices that lead to the pollution of their local environment, the consequences to the 'economic owner' of the supply chain can be severe. A number of global retailers found this out to their cost following the disaster at the Rana Plaza industrial complex in Bangladesh.

New thinking and business models

Part I of this book argues the case throughout for a more integrated approach to solving the challenges facing regulators and the business community. It details the latest thinking on the 'triple advantage' of combining ethical, environmental and profit-driven strategies, demonstrating that they cannot be implemented in isolation from one another.

The 'Circular economy', outlined in Chapter 2, offers the potential to manufacturers, retailers and other service providers to achieve this 'triple advantage'. Covering a multitude of innovations, 'circular' supply chains do not only aim for the re-use or recycling of materials, although this is an important part of the ethos; rather, they encourage a shift in thinking by manufacturers from 'product maker' to 'service provider'. For example, high tech manufacturer Philips now enters into long-term contracts with customers to provide lighting services. It has assumed the responsibility for ensuring that buildings are always lit appropriately. This means it is in its best interests to guarantee the longevity of the products it makes, rather than, as has been the case in the past, being rewarded (with new sales) when products fail. This has significant implications for more efficient use of natural resources.

Some circular economy initiatives are strategic and transformative, such as the 'sharing economy' referenced above where asset utilization can be improved. Others, such as designing packaging and product with storage and transportation in mind, can be more easily achieved. None the less, reducing the volumetric size of a product can result in huge savings, just by shipping 'less air'.

The role of technologies in reducing environmental impact has often been underestimated by public policy makers who have preferred a more interventionist approach. In contrast, Chapter 3 looks at the wide range of technological developments, from Transport Management Systems to alternative fuels. It also provides examples of how technologies can be employed with societal benefits, such as the humanitarian use of drones.

The final chapter in this section sets out a new survey by industry consultancy, Transport Intelligence. It looks at, amongst other things, the pressures driving sustainable initiatives, their benefits, how environmental and societal responsibility in supply chains is perceived and future commitment to 'green' and ethical goals.

Public policy and industry response

Part II of the book examines public policy and how this has affected the key transport sectors. 'Top-down' targets have played a major role in driving technological innovations in engine design, for example, although whether these developments would have occurred anyway from the economic pressures on the transport industry is a moot point. Chapter 5 specifically deals with the new targets that have been set at the COP21 summit in Paris, which many people believe will be more effective than previous agreements.

Establishing a Corporate and Social Responsibility department has become an essential element of most companies' response to dealing with ethical and environmental pressures from government and customers. Chapter 6 looks at best practice and sets out the framework for a sustainable corporate strategy, involving the company's management and business ethos; its engagement with society; the treatment of employees and workplace conditions, as well as of course the mitigation of its impact on the environment. The chapter looks at how important total commitment from senior management down is to successful implementation as well as establishing an environmental management system.

One example, specific to the logistics industry, of a 'social investment' is the role companies can play in humanitarian logistics. With global transport and warehousing networks, the world's largest express and logistics companies have a major opportunity to support the work of governmental and non-governmental agencies in terms of disaster relief. Another is volunteering. Companies that encourage their staff to volunteer, sometimes overseas, for a range of good causes benefit from a motivated workforce who in turn gain considerable life skills and experience – another example of a 'triple advantage'.

Chapters 7 and 8 examine two important functions within the supply chain, the development of which is influenced directly by sustainability policies: warehousing and packaging. Both chapters look at how best practice can reduce environmental and financial costs.

Investment in warehousing is growing rapidly not least due to needs of e-commerce, and there is an opportunity to ensure that facilities meet the highest environmental standards. However, impact on local ecologies and societies should not be underestimated.

Regulators need to understand the concept of lifecycle assessments when examining the impact of packaging. The issue is highly complex, as discussed at length in Chapter 8, and policy should be accordingly sophisticated.

As mentioned above, globalization has come under attack from those concerned about conditions of workers and environmental practices in developing countries. The issue has become increasingly politicized in Europe and North America, due to the impact on the workforce in developed markets. Many have argued that economic growth has not resulted in benefits or employment for people whose jobs have been 'exported' to China. The issue played an important part in the US presidential campaign in 2016. Chapter 9 looks specifically at the trans-Atlantic trade deal being negotiated between the United States and Europe that has raised fears and generated widespread protectionist sentiments.

Ethical issues in the supply chain

Part III covers the challenges faced by manufacturers and retailers in ensuring that, 'from cradle to grave', their supply chains meet an acceptable standard from an environmental and ethical perspective.

Chapters 10 and 11 address three main areas of concern: first in upstream supply chains, in particular related to the extraction and processing of raw materials; secondly, in the downstream manufacturing and assembly of components; and thirdly, in the way in which the product is dealt with at the end of its life. Each of these elements has related impacts on the environment and upon society. The best supply chains will mitigate these impacts and even use them to create more value for their shareholders.

Some of the worst environmental and societal problems exist in the mining or extraction of raw materials in Africa, Asia and Latin America where there is little oversight of bad practices. In many regions the use of child labour is frequent and there are no health and safety regulations in place. Some of these mines (for example in the Democratic Republic of Congo) are run for rebel organizations fighting the lawful government. The impact of 'conflict minerals' on companies and societies is dealt with at length in Chapter 10.

The issue of labour practices goes to the very root of supply chain management concepts. For example, the electronics sector is influenced heavily by just-in-time delivery practices as manufacturers strive to reduce inventory. On top of this, cyclical and seasonal demand means that flexible workforces are required to meet the peaks and troughs of demand. Hence low levels of pay are augmented by very high levels of overtime – sometimes as much as 60–100 hours a week to meet the peak requirements. Also, employees are likely to be on short-term contracts or temporary work arrangements.

It is not just consumer electronics where the downstream supply chain problems lie. Some of the most egregious examples relate to the fashion industry, in particular the Rana Plaza incident in 2013 where over 1,100 workers died when the building in which they were working collapsed. Chapter 11 looks at the extent of the problems, at attempts by governments to address some of the issues (including 'modern slavery') and how the best performing companies are dealing with the issue.

The problem here is fundamentally one of lack of supply chain visibility. Most companies in the Western world do care about the provenance of their products – if nothing else they are concerned about the risk of reputational damage or disruption to supply. However, modern supply chains are remarkably complex and many manufacturers and retailers have little knowledge of the practices of their suppliers, and even less their suppliers' suppliers.

While Chapters 10 and 11 examine how manufacturers and retailers can ensure the compliance of their suppliers with their own sustainability objectives, Chapter 12 discusses the potential abuse of power by the 'economic owner' of the supply chain. It looks at how UK grocery retailers have been accused of ethical misconduct in their dealings with suppliers, particularly in the milk sector.

Part III concludes with a discussion of the impact of business models upon logistics workers. E-commerce shipments have grown exponentially over the past decade and this has placed considerable pressure on parcels companies. Many have adopted an owner-driver, sub-contracted model of operations but as the industry has become more competitive, rates paid to sub-contractors have fallen. Many have questioned whether this is sustainable and whether the use of owner-drivers, who have none of the rights of formal employees, is ethical.

Likewise, in the warehouse industry many companies use agencies to recruit low-paid migrant workers. This practice came to light during a House of Commons inquiry into working practices at the Sports Direct distribution facility at Shirebrook. Not only are there implications for the workforce, but consequences for the local communities in the direct vicinity of the facility.

PART I
New Thinking and Business Models

Profit, people and planet – the triple advantage

**THIS CHAPTER WILL FAMILIARIZE
THE READER WITH**

- The concept of 'triple advantage' and how companies are integrating societal and environmental goals within their core business
- The benefits green initiatives can have in cost reduction
- How a 'holistic' approach to sustainability can reduce corporate risk and generate revenue
- A framework for implementing sustainable initiatives at each stage of the supply chain
- Examples of sustainable strategies in action in the retail sector

Routes to supply chain sustainability

The triple bottom line

The concept of 'triple bottom line' ('TBL' or '3BL') was first espoused by business ethics pioneers such as John Elkington in the early 1990s. He asserted that companies have three 'accounts' they need to measure in order to fully understand the overall costs of their business; obviously in terms of financial profitability, but also in terms of societal impact ('people'), as well as their impact on the environment ('planet'). Elkington believed that only by measuring each of these 'accounts' could companies fully assess and then mitigate their impact through changes in corporate behaviour.

The development of the concept came at a time when companies were starting to realize that their practices, and those of their suppliers, could present a profound risk to their brands. Consumers had started to show more of an interest in the provenance of the products they were buying, and global media were able to shine a light on any malpractice that occurred even in the remotest of locations.

There are two main claims by proponents of 3BL: 1) social and environmental performance can be measured objectively to set costs against benefits in financial terms in a profit and loss format; and 2) measuring social performance improves it and in the long term has a beneficial impact on financial performance (Norman and MacDonald, 2003). The triple bottom line concept facilitated the development of some now well-established initiatives such as the 'Fairtrade' movement: organizations that charge a premium to Western consumers, which in turn is passed on to the producers in developing markets. One of the problems with this approach is that it perhaps removes the idea of ethical behaviour from the mainstream – Fairtrade products, for example, comprise a tiny proportion of sales even in the small number of categories they cover.

There is still a long way to go before business investment decisions are truly made on the basis of measuring a triple bottom line. Traditionally financial metrics are used to work out the payback or breakeven period on any investment, looking at measures such as net present value (NPV). Management decisions may then be influenced by considerations of societal or environmental impact, but it is very hard (if not impossible) to factor in the actual costs of all these impacts. In some cases specific costs can be identified (such as those involved in investing in equipment to deal with wastewater). However, intangible costs such as the impact on brand of societal or environmental mismanagement cannot be measured with any degree of certainty (Balraj and Lok, 2006).

The costs that are least likely to be considered are those that economists call 'externalities'. These are costs that are generated by companies but paid for by society as a whole. Within the transport sector, for example, externalities would include the generation of greenhouse gases (GHGs) and other local pollutants (such as diesel particulates) as well as noise pollution, congestion and even the road traffic collisions caused by trucks. How these externalities can be internalized has been a point of public policy discussion for decades, with governments imposing a range of fiscal tools such as fuel duties, levies and tolls upon truck operators. However, many in the industry argue that the amount they pay to governments already outweighs their impact on the environment. What is clear is that arriving at accurate figures to determine the triple bottom line will always be difficult.

This is not to say that 3BL is a purely hypothetical ideal. As will be discussed below, for specific initiatives it is possible to demonstrate that investing in green projects can deliver enhanced profitability. However when it comes to corporations as a whole its application is more difficult. This is one of the reasons why many companies limit their 'green' initiatives to tactical applications only. It is far more challenging for companies to examine their broader impact on the environment or on societies, especially if the results require a fundamental root and branch change to operating models or business plans.

The supply chain sector provides a good example of this (as noted in more detail below). Some of the defining trends of the industry over the past few decades have been centralization of inventory, globalization of supply and just-in-time delivery schedules, which many people believe have had a negative impact on the environment by increasing the transport element of supply chains. However, in terms of environmental initiatives, companies often focus on making their distribution centres greener and their trucks more fuel efficient, rather than addressing the systemic causes of increased carbon emissions in the first place.

A variation on 3BL is 'triple advantage'. This term, used by consultancy Accenture in work undertaken for the World Economic Forum (see below), has been developed due to the challenges faced by the 3BL concept in the scale of its application. 'Triple advantage' may be more limited in its ambition – it does not seek to measure a corporation's entire value based on financial, environmental and societal performance. However, it provides a useful system by which to define, categorize and, crucially, more easily measure the value created by the implementation of tactical initiatives.

Why is 'sustainability' important in supply chains?

As will become clear from this book, the term 'sustainability' should be regarded in its broadest sense. The World Business Council for Sustainable Development defines the trend towards sustainability as 'forms of progress that meet the needs of the present without compromising the ability of future generations to meet their needs' (WBCSD, 2016).

Hence sustainability relates not just to the environment or to the people involved or affected by the process of business (positively or negatively) but to the economic resilience of all companies involved in manufacturing, sourcing, moving and selling goods. This is fundamental since, as a concept, it embraces the idea of 'the triple bottom line' or 'triple advantage' as referred to above. Although sustainability is sometimes used as a shorthand term for the act of mitigating environmental or societal impact, sustaining profitability is of equal importance in the long term.

Many companies have adopted sustainable policies for a number of reasons. For a significant number, the idea of 'green logistics' started off as a public relations exercise: to be seen to be doing 'the right thing'. This approach is sometimes referred to as 'greenwash'. A view persisted that having a Corporate and Social Responsibility (CSR) department meant that a 'box has been ticked' and that CSR existed as a 'necessary evil' that was at best an irrelevance to the company's primary aim of making money, and at worst a source of cost and a waste of management time.

A survey by consultancy Insight argued in 2008 that 'when companies take action, they are typically taking the easy route of reputation and brand protection on green messaging' (McKinnon *et al*, 2012). This view has now become increasingly outdated as companies recognize that commercial efficiency savings can have environmental benefits and vice versa: 'green and gold' benefits. For instance, managing the provision of lighting more efficiently within a warehouse reduces not only electricity bills but also the facility's carbon footprint. Likewise there are many examples in the transport industry where driver training, investment in new engines, making trailers more aerodynamic and improved route planning reduce fuel costs and consequently GHG emissions.

There are broader benefits as well. In a study by consulting company Accenture for the World Economic Forum (WEF, 2015) it was highlighted that sustainability is becoming more important to companies for a range of reasons:

- The issue is of increasing consequence to their customers (whether individuals or other businesses).

- Younger customers in particular are becoming more sensitive to the environmental and societal practices of the companies from which they buy their goods and services.

- The issue is on the agenda of many governments around the world (cf the UK's modern slavery legislation). There is the belief that if businesses are not able to put their own houses in order they will be compelled to do so by regulation.

- Some natural resources are becoming scarcer, leading companies to become more concerned about the longer-term sustainability of supply and the more efficient use of materials and reuse and recycling of end-of-life products.

In *Green Logistics* (McKinnon *et al*, 2012), Professor Alan McKinnon writes that, 'It seems... that those firms that most effectively apply logistics best practice in terms of economic efficiency and customer service are also the best placed to green their logistics operations.' However, he goes on to point out, 'This does not necessarily mean that applying commercial best practice in logistics automatically minimizes its environmental impact.' This is because the company rarely has to bear the full cost of its commercial decisions on the environment, ie the increased frequency of transportation and its reduced efficiency caused by implementing just-in-time strategies.

Table 1.1   Supply chain initiatives and their environmental impact

Supply Chain Initiative	Consequence	Environmental Impact
Supply chain focus	Management competence	Green and social benefits
Reduced inventory holding	Fewer goods manufactured	Lower resource exploitation
'Right first time'	Fewer goods manufactured	Lower resource exploitation
Centralization of inventory	Fewer warehouses	More modern, greener warehousing
Centralization of inventory	Increased transport route kms	More carbon emissions
Just-in-time	Lower vehicle size/more frequency	More carbon emissions

Even in the case of JIT and centralization, there is conflicting evidence that in fact the dis-benefits of modern supply chain practice may be overplayed. Studies by McKinnon and Woodburn (1996) and Kohn and Huge-Brodin (2008) have contended that centralization of distribution networks can bring about benefits in terms of consolidation of loads; see Table 1.1. In the case of 'triple advantage', those companies with the most mature supply chains, including higher levels of visibility, stronger relationships with suppliers and a management that understands the issues involved, are the best placed to initiate and implement sustainability programmes.

'Triple advantage' in the supply chain sector

Supply chain management concepts were originally developed with one goal in mind: to optimize business value by ensuring that product reached the end-user in the most effective way possible. The adoption of supply chain practices has undeniably resulted in massive economic benefits, both in the emerging and the developed world. It has provided more consumer choice, economies that are more resilient to recessionary pressures, as well as improved living standards for many millions of people in poverty-stricken regions.

However, the gains have not been completely without cost. As discussed above, at a tactical level at any rate, JIT supply chains can be heavy and inefficient users of transport services due to the trade-off between the high cost of inventory ownership and the low (financial) cost of transport. On occasion this can result in what could be described as sub-optimal operational (and environmental) decisions such as the more frequent use of smaller vehicles.

Many have argued that the classical inventory/transport trade-off is in fact artificial as it doesn't take into account transport's external costs such as the effect of carbon emissions on the environment. Political pressure and lobbying have made many manufacturers, retailers and logistics companies more aware of the impact of their businesses on the environment, and carbon reduction measures are now an integral part of most companies' strategic development plans.

The third factor that companies need to take into account if they are to create truly sustainable supply chains is becoming increasingly important – that of the societal impact of their businesses. There have been growing calls for companies to demonstrate that they implement ethical policies when it comes to the conditions in which their suppliers' employees work. No longer is it morally acceptable for manufacturers to outsource production or for retailers to purchase goods from suppliers without having full visibility of these issues.

That the CSR dimension is critical to supply chain has been evidenced by the huge reputational damage caused by catastrophes such as the Rana Plaza factory collapse in Bangladesh in 2013. Over 1,100 people died in the disaster, implicating a number of international retailers whose goods were being produced in unsafe conditions.

There have been many other examples of corporate behaviour that has fallen well short of standards thought appropriate in the West. These range across a huge number of different issues and include:

- the use of child labour in consumer electronics assembly plants;
- the sourcing of 'conflict minerals';
- incidences of suicide due to supplier employee mistreatment;

- toxic lead paint used on toys;
- deforestation by suppliers;
- improper handling and disposal of toxic and hazardous materials.

A tripartite approach to supply chain management is critical to ensure long-term sustainability, although striking a balance between each of the core 'pillars' – economic viability, environmental accountability and social responsibility – will be challenging (see Figure 1.1). Destroying value in the supply chain by burdensome government regulation is not necessarily welcome and nor, on its own, is it the answer.

A smarter solution lies in convincing senior management that increasing the visibility of supply chains in order to audit the corporate behaviour of their suppliers can provide them with the capability to make smarter sourcing decisions, especially in the case of a supply chain disruption. An opaque supply chain may not only hide unethical behaviour but also creates high levels of vulnerability and fragility from unknown risks.

Governments and non-governmental organizations (NGOs) have an important role to play in facilitating the development of these pillars. Companies can be nudged towards best practice and in an ideal world a partnership approach can successfully bring about positive results to all constituents. In China, for example, consumer electronics manufacturer Apple is now working alongside the Fair Labor Association, a network of socially responsible companies, to ensure that the working practices of its main supplier Foxconn conform to a globally acceptable standard.

A combined corporate and governmental approach has also worked elsewhere in the developing world. High-tech manufacturers and governments have worked together in East Africa to create a reverse logistics solution, thereby reducing the amount of product being dumped and minimizing harm to the environment and human health (see Chapter 10).

What is clear is that economic, environmental and societal issues are bound tightly together, interwoven in deeply dependent relationships. In order to ensure a long-term, sustainable future for global supply chains, companies must build collaborative, multi-stakeholder approaches to creating value that don't impact on the environment

Figure 1.1 The three pillars of triple advantage

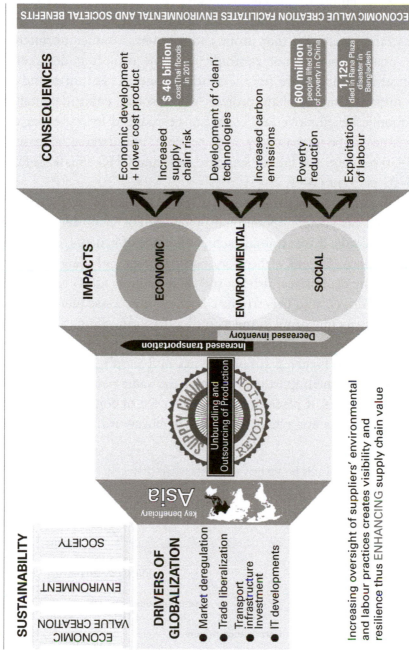

SUSTAINABILITY

ECONOMIC VALUE CREATION | ENVIRONMENT | SOCIETY

DRIVERS OF GLOBALIZATION
- Market deregulation
- Trade liberalization
- Transport infrastructure investment
- IT developments

Asia
key beneficiary

SUPPLY CHAIN REVOLUTION
Unbundling and Outsourcing of Production

Increased transportation
Decreased inventory

IMPACTS
ECONOMIC
ENVIRONMENTAL
SOCIAL

CONSEQUENCES

Economic development + lower cost product

Increased supply chain risk
$ 46 billion cost Thai floods in 2011

Development of 'clean' technologies

Increased carbon emissions

Poverty reduction
600 million people lifted out of poverty in China

Exploitation of labour
1,129 died in Rana Plaza disaster in Bangladesh

ECONOMIC VALUE CREATION FACILITATES ENVIRONMENTAL AND SOCIETAL BENEFITS

Increasing oversight of suppliers' environmental and labour practices creates visibility and resilience thus ENHANCING supply chain value or have a negative impact on people's wellbeing. In many cases the problem goes to the very heart of corporate supply chain strategy. There is a failure of 'joined up thinking' as regards the three goals of profitability, environmental and social awareness. What many companies fail to realize is that profit and socio-environmental outcomes are complementary, not contradictory. The project undertaken by consultancy Accenture for the World Economic Forum found that by initiating supply chain projects where social, environmental and economic benefits overlap, costs can be reduced by 9–16 per cent, revenue can be increased by 5–20 per cent, brand value increases by 15–30 per cent, and labour standards rise and GHG emissions fall by 13–22 per cent (WEF, 2015).

The smartest companies see that there is much to be gained from adopting sustainable operational practices. For instance, companies that undertake driver training achieve a range of benefits. Vehicles are driven more efficiently, therefore cutting costs and increasing profits. A more economical driving style also reduces GHG emissions, is safer for drivers and pedestrians or cyclists and consequently reduces the risk to a company's brand as well as insurance/litigation costs.

The best-in-class companies go a step further and adopt a 'holistic' approach; see Figure 1.2. For logistics and supply chain companies this provides the opportunity to enter the same peer group as many of its customers. It places it on the tender list of companies to whom sustainability is not a 'take it or leave it' buzzword. Companies such

Figure 1.2   Towards best practice in sustainable strategies

as Unilever live and breathe sustainability and they are only willing to work with suppliers that take the same approach.

Of course there are difficulties to be overcome before the concept of triple advantage is understood and adopted by all companies; one of the primary challenges for proponents is making a compelling business case. Results of the UN Global Compact-Accenture CEO Study on Sustainability showed that the inability to quantify the commercial benefits of improved societal and environmental practices was one of the main reasons why they were not being adopted.

Another issue is the lack of transparency in many global supply chains characterized by outsourcing. In many cases management may not know that problems exist within their supply chains (although this is increasingly no excuse to auditing suppliers and their practices in lower tiers of the supply chain). A further challenge is the fear of many companies that being a first mover in adopting best practice may put them at a competitive disadvantage in terms of cost. Improving pay and working conditions may, for example, create short-term cost increases before the longer-term benefits (in terms of reliability of supply and quality) are experienced. This is especially the case in sectors or markets where there is little regulation and no compulsion across the board to implement improvements.

Those companies that differentiate their businesses on the basis of cost are least likely to be adopters of 'holistic' triple advantage strategies. Instead they will focus on the efficiencies to be gained from better use of resources. The importance of this should not be understated. It will mean that sustainability strategies and practice will be limited to those functions where there is an obvious business case with immediate benefits. Longer-term benefits to companies, societies and the environment may end up being ignored.

Businesses that differentiate their products and services on the basis of brand and/or quality are more likely to invest in the longer-term benefits of triple advantage. If they already operate with industry-leading profit margins, this gives them the confidence to take more risks with initiatives that can enhance their perception in the market, brand equity and appeal to consumers with higher personal spend, for example.

CSR gaining in importance in Asia

The focus on sustainable logistics is no longer the preserve of European or North American companies but is becoming more evident in the emerging world. In its supply chain rankings, Gartner notes two Asian companies that have embraced sustainability practices. Ranked number two in the listing, the pallet pooling initiative of Chinese consumer electronics company, Lenovo, was highlighted. Officially launched in 2013, the programme began with the collection of used pallets from carriers' facilities in Hong Kong and then reused in Lenovo's distribution centre in Shenzhen. It was estimated that this would reduce about 640 $MTCO_2e$ (million metric tons of carbon dioxide equivalent) per year. As a result, the company now plans to expand this practice to eastern China and to the rest of the world.

Pallet-pooling is just one of several such initiatives Lenovo is implementing. It also supports the incorporation of Green Freight Asia Network practices. This network consists of private companies working to increase the fuel/CO_2 efficiency and to lower the air pollution of freight transportation in the Asia-Pacific region.

Huawei, ranked number five in this year's Gartner listing, also implements measures to reduce its carbon footprint through logistics optimization and innovative packaging. Other logistics activities it pursues include utilizing the efficiency of regional warehouses to save warehouse space; increasing the proportion of direct shipments from supply centres outside of China; reducing the environmental impact of transhipments and developing multi-modal transport solutions such as sea-air, air-land and air-sea.

Although such logistics practices adopted by the likes of Lenovo and Huawei are not immediately observed by consumers, there is an impact on the environment and as more companies adopt such measures, practices such as these will become the norm for the logistics industry.

A framework for triple advantage

The reasons why many companies are now pursuing sustainable supply chain strategies are varied. Some do so in order to mitigate risks by complying with regulations, others to gain efficiency improvements. However, for an increasing but significant proportion, bottom-line benefits and an increase in brand equity are becoming the most important factors. The decision by senior management to develop a strategic approach to sustainable supply chains can only

Table 1.2   Triple advantage – a framework for best practice

A. Product design	i. Packaging reduction
	ii. Circular economy – design for maximum recyclability (both product and packaging)
	iii. Reduce weight and size of product
B. Sourcing	i. Raw material and components – use of alternatives from sustainable suppliers
	ii. Use of non-conflict minerals
	iii. Establish supplier environmental and ethical audits
	iv. Fair labour policies
	v. Source from micro (local) suppliers
C. Production	i. Assessment of JIT supply chain management concepts on workers, environment and suppliers
D. Warehousing	i. Smart and green warehousing – best practice
E. Transport and Distribution	i. Innovating to make transport and distribution more carbon efficient
	ii. Impact of pollution on environment and people
	iii. Use of intermodal strategies
	iv. Labour practices and sub-contracting in the transport industry
	v. De-speeding the supply chain
F. End-of-life Recycling	i. Environmentally and ethical disposal of goods
	ii. Re-use of materials

SOURCE WEF (2015)

be put into effect by determining a tactical approach to creating sustainability within individual supply chain processes. In Table 1.2 the supply chain is deconstructed into constituent parts, which provides a useful framework for analysing best practice.

European Retail commitment to sustainability

European retailers have joined together in an organization called the Retail Forum for Sustainability to confirm their commitment to the circular economy (see Chapter 2). Their objective is to act at every lifecycle stage where they can exert influence or have a positive impact (REAP, 2016):

- Sustainable sourcing: within this category there are some ambitious commitments for both product and raw material certifications. A number of the retailers have set targets as high as 100 per cent certified from sustainable sources for fish, seafood, palm oil, paper or wood.

- Product design, labelling and certification, including implementing eco-design packaging projects, phasing out hazardous chemicals and a goal to ensure plastic material used in a select product group is 100 per cent renewable.

- Greener operations and distribution, including decreasing greenhouse gas emissions, installing solar panels and specialist heating and cooling systems that reuse the air emitted.

- Consumer and employee information, including the introduction of new communication campaigns to further highlight to consumers the ways of living more sustainably, staff training programmes, more effective labelling, and inviting consumers to participate in activities on sustainable living and introducing repair workshops.

- Food waste prevention, including the collection of used cooking oils, increasing partnerships with charities to donate food and using produce that is not appropriate for sale in a more efficient manner.

- Reuse and recycling, including reducing the amount of waste sent to landfill and increasing the reuse of technical equipment arising from remodelling or closure of stores in order to extend the lifetime of products and prevent waste.

As part of the programme, they have also published commitments to reach a number of sustainability targets (Retailers' Environmental Action Plan). According to the Retail Forum, these 'will lead to concrete, clear and measurable actions that will be monitored and transparently reported'. Those relating to their logistics operations include the following.

Colruyt Group (Belgium)

By 2018, roll out production and use of sustainable hydrogen for powering material-handling equipment ('pallet jacks') in its Dassenveld distribution centre. The retailer will order 200 more fuel cells in order to expand the number of pallet jacks running on hydrogen. An indoor filling station will be installed.

El Corte Inglés (Spain, Portugal)

Across its retail and warehouse facilities, focus on energy efficiency and emissions reduction to achieve 20 per cent reduction in energy per square metre by: replacing conventional bulbs by low consumption LED bulbs; replacing conventional transformers by electronic transformers; and reducing permanent lighting in low-transited areas by automatic movement sensor switches.

Co-operative Group

Reduce direct GHG emissions by 50 per cent by 2020, compared to 2006.

Ikea (multi-country)

By 2016, reduce carbon emissions from the transport of goods by 20 per cent (compared to 2011) and 30 per cent (compared to 2012).

Lidl (multi-country)

By 2017, train staff in distribution centres to sort waste and initiate a waste collection system thereby helping to reduce the amount of residual waste by approximately 50 per cent and simultaneously increase recyclables. Use only recycled paper as raw material for the production of own-brand food product packaging.

Marks & Spencer (multi-country)

By 2020 procure 70 per cent (32 per cent in 2015) of cotton from sustainable sources (Fairtrade, organic or Better Cotton Initiative). Maintain zero waste to landfill (100 per cent recycled) from M&S stores, offices and warehouses in the UK and Ireland. Improve energy efficiency in M&S-operated UK and ROI stores, offices and distribution centres by 50 per cent per square foot by 2020.

Metro Group (multi-country)

Phase out PVC packaging by 2018; 100 per cent FSC certified beverage cartons by 2018.

Tesco (multi-country)

Reduce CO_2 emissions per square foot of stores and distribution centres by 50 per cent by 2020, compared with 2006. Reduce carbon emissions per case of goods delivered by 25 per cent by 2020 compared with 2011.

CASE STUDY   Ethical outdoor clothing manufacturer Patagonia

Even companies that promise to pursue the highest environmental and ethical standards can sometimes be caught out by a lack of awareness of supplier practices. US outdoor clothing company Patagonia is one such business with the strap line, 'Cause no unnecessary harm.' It was established by an environmentalist, Yvon Chouinard, who has written books on sustainability in business.

Rapid expansion led to a disconnect between the company's marketing messages and the reality of using extended, global supply chains reaching deep into developing markets. For example, according to a report in *The Wall Street Journal,* investigations by animal welfare campaigners found a number of abuses in its supply chain relating to the treatment of geese (providing the feathers for filling materials) and sheep at a South American ranch (Phillips, 2016).

The issue relating to wool was particularly damaging. A campaign group had shot footage of sheep being mutilated during shearing on a farm that was part of a major collective providing material to Patagonia for its underwear, hats and sweaters. Additionally, a Taiwanese supplier was found to be allowing 'brokers' to charge migrant workers thousands of dollars to gain placements at its factory, a practice considered by many to amount to a form of modern slavery. These practices were discovered by an internal audit, showing at least that the company was living up to its moral responsibility as the 'economic employer'.

Recognizing the problems and the impact they would have on its reputation, Patagonia undertook a number of remedial steps:

- It employed a livestock handling company to audit the farms of its wool suppliers in South America.
- It ended its contract with the collective where the problems originated, choosing instead to 'near-source' from farms based in the United States.
- New standards for the treatment of sheep in its supply chain were put in place.
- In Taiwan, it has worked with suppliers to pay back the workers who were affected (about 5,000 staff).
- It worked with an independent organization, Verité, to identify wages issues and health and safety violations.

- It reduced the number of first-tier suppliers in its textile supply chain (from 108 to 75) so that it could exert more control and gain more visibility.
- It has undertaken more audits of Tier 2 suppliers (175 textile mills).
- It has set employment standards for its suppliers.

The problems have had an economic impact on the company. When it severed its contract with the wool growing collective, several lines of its products were affected, resulting in a loss of sales. It is far more difficult to assess the damage to its ethical reputation, which will take a longer time to rebuild. Management are banking on their customers showing loyalty to the brand due to the honest way in which they have responded to the crises and the fact that they are doing more to root out problems in their supply chains than many of their competitors.

Summary

This chapter has examined how leading companies are increasingly integrating societal, environmental and business targets within a holistic corporate strategy. Instead of aiming solely for compliance with government targets, many leaders are going much further, recognizing that sustainability must form part of their companies' DNA. Only through this approach can they realize benefits from enhanced brand equity, more customer engagement, a motivated workforce and decreased levels of risk. Part of the problem with modern supply chains is the high level of outsourcing. Economic owners (the major branded manufacturers or retailers that control the supply chain) may have little visibility of the practices of lower-tier suppliers, but ignorance is no longer a defence, as consumers expect increasingly high ethical standards.

Key points

- Companies should measure the costs of their societal and environmental impact and set them against their profitability.

- Modern supply chains are not necessarily harmful to the environment despite seemingly sub-optimal.

- Younger consumers are becoming more discerning in their choice of product, with ethical considerations increasingly important.

- There are opportunities to improve sustainability and save costs at each stage of the supply chain.

- Commitment to environmental goals is no longer a Western preserve – it is becoming increasingly important in Asia.

- Supply chain complexity and lack of visibility means that even companies that have strong ethical policies can be harmed by the practices of their suppliers.

References

Balraj, K and Lok, A (2006) *Capital Budgeting and Corporate Responsibility,* Jack Graduate School of Business, UWI, Trinidad & Tobago

Kohn, C and Huge-Bronin, M (2008) Centralized distribution systems and the environment, *International Journal of Logistics,* **11** (3), pp 229–45

McKinnon, A C and Woodburn, A (1996) Logistical restructuring and freight traffic growth: an empirical assessment, *Transportation,* **23** (2), pp 141–61

McKinnon, A C, Browne, M and Whiteing, A (2012) *Green Logistics: Improving the environmental sustainability of logistics,* Kogan Page, London

Norman, W and MacDonald, C (2003) Getting to the bottom of 'triple bottom line', *Business Ethics Quarterly,* http://www.businessethics.ca/3bl/triple-bottom-line.pdf

Phillips, E (2016) Patagonia's balancing act: chasing mass-market appeal while doing no harm, *Wall Street Journal,* 17 August, http://www.wsj.com/articles/patagonias-balancing-act-chasing-mass-market-appeal-while-doing-no-harm-1471426200

REAP (2016) Commitment to the Circular Economy by REAP signatories, June, http://ec.europa.eu/environment/industry/retail/pdf/Retail%20Forum%20A3.pdf

Savitz, A and Weber, K (2006) *The Triple Bottom Line: How today's best-run companies are achieving economic, social and environmental success – and how you can too,* Jossey-Bass, San Francisco, CA

WBCSD (2016) World Business Council for Sustainable Development, http://www.wbcsd.org/Overview/About-us

WEF (2015) *Beyond Supply Chains: Empowering responsible value chains,* World Economic Forum/Accenture, Geneva

White, G (2015) All your clothes are made with exploited labor, *The Atlantic,* 3 June, http://www.theatlantic.com/business/archive/2015/06/patagonia-labor-clothing-factory-exploitation/394658/

Supply chains in the 'circular economy'

THIS CHAPTER WILL FAMILIARIZE THE READER WITH

- The concept of the 'circular economy' and the 'circular supply chain'
- How the 'sharing economy' will lead to higher levels of product utilization and reduce the pressure on natural resources
- 'Performance-based logistics' strategies that transform business models and customer experience
- The importance of designing products that will enable them to be reused and recycled
- The prospects for landfill mining and reclamation
- How 3D printing will affect the supply chain

What is a 'circular supply chain'?

Highlighted amongst the initiatives identified in the Accenture/World Economic Forum research referenced in Chapter 1 (WEF, 2015) is the increasingly popular concept of the 'circular economy'. This term refers to maximizing the use of reused and recycled materials in new products thereby reducing waste to a minimum. This requires a concerted effort by designers to develop products that can be made of reclaimed materials and ensuring that these materials can themselves be used in other products at their end-of-life. The circular economy is seen as an alternative to existing 'linear' economies where products, materials and components are discarded when their usefulness comes to an end, also known as 'take, make, waste'. In the latter model the value of materials reduces to nothing over the lifetime of the product in which they are integral; in the circular economy, design at the outset ensures that these materials retain some of their value, so it is economically viable to reuse them in one function or another.

In a traditional manufacturing process 'virgin' materials are typically used and there is the assumption of cheap and easily accessible energy. External costs of disposal and the wider environmental dis-benefits generated throughout the manufacturing process are borne by society and not the producer or the consumer. This approach is looking outmoded, not least due to the increase of alternative business models being developed as part of the 'sharing economy'.

The circular economy also has the advantage that it encourages manufacturers and retailers to look beyond production and sales to engage more closely with their customers in terms of product use. It also decouples the growth of their company from the sourcing and use of natural resources.

Disadvantages of linear economies

- Wasteful of materials and excess capacity.
- Vulnerable to volatile commodity prices.
- Exposed to imports of resources and energy supply.
- Vulnerable to dwindling natural resources.
- Threatened by policy makers seeking to internalize external environmental costs.

Lacy and Rutqvist (2014) identify five business models that could be adopted by companies to shift their businesses to a 'new paradigm':

1 Circular supply chain: shift to the use of secondary materials for new products as an alternative to 'virgin' resources.

2 Recovery and recycling: recover value at end of life.

3 Prolong product life.

4 Sharing economy, eg Uber and Airbnb.

5 Shift from the sale of products to selling access to products.

While the first three of these innovations could be related directly to materials, the last two involve development of new markets and ways of doing business. For example, the authors say that 80 per cent of products kept in the typical home are only used on average once a month. The sharing economy means that new platforms are being developed to better utilize these assets by matching latent supply with demand. The best known examples are Uber and Lyft (the use of cars and time) and Airbnb (the use of spare room space). By using these assets more efficiently fewer cars or homes/hotels need to be built, meaning that fewer resources are required in the first place. At the same time, consumers and micro-entrepreneurs are able to save and/or make money, leading to economic growth (decoupled, as mentioned earlier, from resource exploitation).

New technologies have enabled transaction costs to be reduced while at the same time matching supply and demand. It works best when consumers have an expensive and under-utilized asset. They are then able to rent out access to this asset with a software application providing a range of transaction-facilitating services such as advertising its availability; letting prospective customers know its location (through GPS); providing social network feedback on the trustworthiness and customer service of the supplier; and handling the billing. All these services may have existed in one form or another prior to the onset of the 'sharing economy'; however, they were often too inefficient or expensive to make the exercise worthwhile for customer or supplier.

Sharing cars

A car – with the exception of a house – is the most expensive purchase most people make in their life time. Despite this, for a large proportion of the time it remains either in a driveway or car park, unused. This inefficient use of capital makes personal mobility highly exposed to disruption from the 'sharing economy'. In the United States there have been a number of start-ups that have entered this space. Zipcar, Relayrides, Car2Go, Lyft and Uber all allow people to improve the utilization of their vehicles.

According to the consulting company PWC, this phenomenon is having several impacts on driving and driving behaviour – many beneficial. For instance, the 'millennial generation' (those born around the turn of the century) are less likely to drive – a cheap and highly available mobility option is open to them. They also are less likely to see the car as a status symbol compared with earlier generations (PWC, 2014).

This is also having benefits for social problems such as drink driving and presumably vehicle collisions. In terms of opportunity costs, driving is becoming more expensive. If you are being chauffeured in an Uber car, for example, you are able to text or do e-mails, a far more productive use of time than just driving a car.

The sharing economy has major implications for the vehicle manufacturing industry, as purchasing a car is becoming just one of a number of options in the personal mobility market. How the major manufacturers react to the additional competition will frame the future of the industry over the coming century. It may be that they themselves enter the market to facilitate ride sharing, for instance. In the long term it would seem self-evident that improving the utilization of vehicles means that fewer vehicles are required. An obvious first step for many corporations that have large fleets of cars, often sitting unused during the day, would be to mimic the car sharing applications and allow staff to use any spare vehicle.

'I think the biggest change that we're seeing here is that people are choosing to buy mobility as opposed to just buying a car,' states Shelby Clark, CEO of Peers.org. The trends towards this type of behaviour would inevitably see the dwindling importance of the industry in terms of both logistics and supply chain services.

The shift from manufacturing products to 'selling access' to them is a transformational concept, but one that is increasingly common in some niche sectors. The move means that consumers would lease goods through a 'product as a service' model with the manufacturer taking on responsibility for the total cost of ownership. As in the auto sector, this would mean that manufacturers take more interest in longevity, reliability and reusability. As Lacy and Rutqvist (2014) say, 'Performance trumps volume, durability tops disposability, and companies have an opportunity to build new relationships with consumers.' Perhaps as important for the manufacturers, it also means that there is a way of reducing commoditization of products through adding value.

One of the most developed sectors in this respect is defence and aerospace, which for years has practised 'performance-based logistics' (see the box below). It is now being joined by high-tech manufacturers, such as those providing server capacity, and other sectors such as lighting. Although these sectors are by no means insignificant, the greatest gains will be achieved if the model gains traction in the 'big ticket' slow-moving consumer goods market. If manufacturers took over the responsibility for maintaining white goods such as ovens, washing machines and fridges, a substantial impact would be made on waste goods. At the moment, replacing these types of appliances is often easier and cheaper than having them repaired, reinforcing the idea of a 'throw away' society – something alien to earlier generations. In fact, the modular components used in the manufacture of these appliances in many cases makes repair uneconomic – a state of affairs that obviously benefits the manufacturer in terms of new product sales.

Aerospace and high-tech performance-based logistics

One of the latest trends supply chains are presently experiencing is the move towards performance-based logistics (PBL). This concept rewards suppliers for the amount of time that a product is working – up time – rather than paying them for parts and maintenance when a product is down. Although very simple and rational, this is completely at odds with the normal way in which many markets work. For instance, most printer manufacturers make money not from the printers themselves but from highly expensive toner cartridges. The same is true in the automotive sector to a degree. The bottom line is that the manufacturer of a product gets remunerated when that product is out of service or broken.

It is this counter-intuitive business model that some major manufacturers (most notably in the defence and aerospace sectors) are trying to reverse. Contracts are being signed where remuneration is based on capability and availability. Where either is not in place, the supplier is penalized. This is the ultimate 'win-win' scenario – both parties are rewarded when a product works. Another way of looking at this is that the approach turns a product into a service (a piece of machinery into a capability). When the service is provided, value is created and the supplier is paid. The most relevant example in the high-tech sector is the provision of servers. In some cases the manufacturer will own and maintain the server on behalf of the customer. It is therefore their responsibility to ensure that it functions 24/7.

However, even though PBL sounds logical, it may be some time before it becomes more widely adopted. It would need a shift in mindsets and the reworking of the business economics of not only spare parts but entire product plans largely because, as mentioned earlier, many companies make the majority of their profits from the after sales service they deliver. Costing this back into the initial sales price would be very unpopular among manufacturers, and unless they were forced to do so by major clients (such as the US Department of Defense, which has huge buying power) there would be considerable resistance.

PBL is now being adopted by other sectors such as lighting. For example, in 2013 Philips Lighting entered into a new relationship with municipal authorities in Washington DC. Instead of buying new LED lights from the company, authorities opted to use Philips' 'Lighting as a service' offering, which gave them access to the new technology without the need to pay for upfront costs. Philips upgraded 13,000 light fixtures in Washington's car parks and at the same time provided a 10-year maintenance contract. The company is paid from the $2 million saving expected to be made from the implementation of more energy-efficient light bulbs. Software alerts the company when bulbs need to be replaced. This type of service obviously means that Philips benefits financially from the reliability of its own products as it has a vested interest in ensuring that its LEDs last as long as possible.

Table 2.1 Ten opportunities for the circular economy

Food and beverage	Value capture in bio-refineries Reduction of avoidable food waste
Construction and real estate	Industrialized production and 3D printing of building modules Reuse and high value recycling of components and materials Sharing and multi-purposing of buildings
Machinery	Remanufacturing and new business models
Plastic packaging	Increased recycling Bio-based packaging
Hospitals	Performance models in procurement Waste reduction and recycling

A white paper on the sector by the Ellen MacArthur Foundation (2015) sets out 10 circular economy opportunities in five sectors; these are shown in Table 2.1. The report claims that in Denmark, where research was undertaken, 10–15 per cent of building materials are wasted, and food waste amounts to 80–90 kg per person per year. These could be reduced to less than 1 per cent and 40–50 kg per capita per annum respectively by 2035 if a circular economy was achieved. Conservatively this would lower Denmark's CO_2 footprint by 2.5 per cent in terms of million tonnes, increase jobs by 0.4 per cent and add 0.8 per cent to the Danish economy by 2035. More ambitious targets would lead to a reduction in CO_2 of 6.9 per cent, create 0.6 per cent more jobs and add 1.4 per cent to the Danish economy by 2035.

Interestingly, the authors believe that 3D printing and industrialized production of building modules could create the greatest annual value in terms of the potential economic impact of circular economy opportunities (33 per cent of the total). However, they recognize that the technology is not yet available at the required scale to deliver these benefits. Should the technology come to maturity, this would have significant impact on the logistics sector and will be discussed at more length below.

According to another report (London Waste and Recycling Board, 2015), the circular economy could bring London benefits of at least £7 billion 'every year by 2036'. This not only refers to products but also to construction projects for example, where there are opportunities to reuse existing materials.

The secondary materials market

The increased use of 'secondary materials' – that is, materials that have been used once and can be used again – would have a major impact on the supply chain industry. In theory the resources that are presently invested in the movement of primary goods around the world (for example, ores and other extracted materials) would be transferred to the global movement of waste. However, whereas these days large volumes of bulk goods flow in an east-west direction, this may change as the origin of secondary materials (recycled textiles, building materials, plastics and consumer electronics) would be in Europe or North America.

In fact the movement of waste is already of major importance to the logistics industry. Containers that would have returned empty to ports of origin in Asia are often filled with recycled material, utilizing lower 'back haul' rates. However, although there are some benefits from this trade, this hardly qualifies as 'circular' as original equipment manufacturers (OEMs) still work on a linear basis: they do not integrate recycled secondary materials into their new products, instead relying on virgin materials.

The market has other problems. It is highly volatile, susceptible to a range of market conditions such as the price of raw materials (obviously if their cost is low, the attractiveness of secondary material inputs diminishes); the cost of back haul and the demand by container shipping lines; trade restrictions (such as the Chinese government's Green Fence Operation – GFO – that blocked the import of contaminated waste products) and a lack of supply chain transparency. There are also ethical questions over the 'informal' recycling and reprocessing that takes place in Asia (primarily China). In some cases villages have become overwhelmed with the sheer volume of waste leading to environmental, public health and societal problems. Many of the locations where this activity takes place have very lax laws, which raises questions about the morality of exporting Europe's or North America's waste problems to societies that are least able to cope with them. However, it is a major employer in economies that lack significant industry: one estimate suggests that 0.5 per cent of the urban population works in the informal recycling sector – around 20 million people (Wilson *et al*, 2013).

There are technical issues as well which OEMs will need to address to ensure cyclicality within their manufacturing processes. They will need to design or incorporate materials that can be reused in the next generation of products. At present much of the plastic scrap that is reprocessed in China, for instance, is of poor quality and of limited use. There is also little visibility where this particular secondary material ends up and the proportion of primary materials that are substituted. This means that although waste and recycling supply chains exist already, they could be described as 'sub-standard' (Velis, 2015).

Secondary plastics market

According to research undertaken for the International Solid Waste Association (Velis, 2014), the annual volume of trade in waste plastic products around the world is 15 million tonnes. Although a large figure, this represents less than 5 per cent of new plastics production. The biggest importer is China, with flows of waste plastics mainly emanating from Europe, which is responsible for almost half of exports of plastics collected for recycling. Despite China generating a lot of its own plastic waste (it manufactures around 40 per cent of all the world's plastics), there is a demand in the country for the high quality plastic recyclates produced by European manufacturers.

There is also a link with economic growth. Following the recession of 2008–9, the price for high quality waste plastic bottles fell from £260–330 per tonne in November to £130–150 per tonne in December. Investment in recycling projects was put on hold, before the prices eventually recovered to their former levels in May 2009.

One of the major risks to the demand for European plastic recyclates is that China develops its own higher quality products that it will be able to use in its own recycling industry. This will mean that there is less demand for European secondary materials, impacting on the global trade. This could ultimately mean that more plastic ends up in European landfill sites or is incinerated in energy from waste (EfW) plants. Although the latter may not be environmentally unfriendly (there are many views on this, for and against), it would still encourage plastics manufacturers to pursue a linear model, using virgin raw materials. Part of the solution will be the development of more local reprocessing plants, which would also limit the industry's exposure to the Chinese market.

The same report shines a light onto recycling practices in the UK. It is estimated that:

- 73.7 per cent of post-consumer plastic waste was disposed of in landfills;
- 7.4 per cent was recovered via EfW;
- 18.9 per cent was collected for recycling;
- around 70 per cent of plastics collected for recycling were exported.

Although industrial waste is almost entirely recycled, it is far more difficult to use post-consumer plastics, not least due to the requirement to sort the various types of co-mingled polymers.

So what happens when the plastics are reprocessed in China? The demand for plastic recyclates has continued apace due to the growth of the country's petrochemical industry. The Government has made a political priority of reducing the market's reliance on imports of 'feedstock' (plastic scrap) and consequently has developed domestic recycling networks. Volumes of the former are out-pacing those of imports, which again creates a challenge for the sustainability of the global market. However, domestic recycled plastics are often of poor quality, which makes them more difficult to recycle at their end-of-life. This means not so much of a 'circular economy' as a 'delayed' linear model. There is very little visibility of the conditions in which the recycling takes place but there are concerns that the manufacture of lower grade plastics could have health implications for workers as well as increase the risk to public health. There are also concerns that much of the plastics could be burnt in energy generation plants without air pollution controls (unlike EfW plants in Europe).

So, it would seem that there is a considerable way to go before a true 'circular economy' exists in the plastics sector. Implications for the logistics and supply chain industry include the following:

- The development of a domestic recycling market in China could hinder the growth of a true global supply chain in plastic scrap.

- Shipping lines may lose back haul business as China's domestic recycling industry develops.

- A large proportion of low quality recyclates may end up in energy generating plants rather than as inputs for new product – limiting the potential for 'circularity'.

- Visibility of recycling supply chains is very limited (especially in China).

- If a circular economy does develop, there will be implications for the movement of bulk goods around the world and consequences for shipping lines.

Landfill mining and reclamation (LFMR)

There are presently countless landfill sites around the world containing enormous volumes of discarded waste. This has led some in the reclamation industry to look at the possibility of 'mining' some of these sites to reclaim materials that still have a residual value. This is far from straightforward – as evidenced by the fact that there are still very few projects on-going.

However, research looking at the feasibility of an LFMR project in Belgium concluded that it was technologically possible to recover materials both for recycling and EfW uses. One of the problems is dealing with the build-up of gases in landfills, although the report considered that this challenge could be overcome. More difficult than extraction was the task of sorting material for reclamation from that destined for incineration. Although waste separation machinery has improved significantly in recent years, its application to underground sources of waste is untested.

Another major problem with LFMR is that older sites are often poorly documented, which means it is difficult to establish what is contained within the landfill. This may mean that it could contain hazardous materials (such as asbestos) or that the materials have no commercial value. The uncertainty impacts on the projected revenues any mining projects could realize. There is also the issue that materials in older landfill sites are likely to have been contaminated or degraded, impacting upon their value.

In terms of the impact on the environment, landfill mining could be regarded as counter-productive. Many local communities may be wary of the consequences of disturbing an old site due to the possibility of uncovering toxic waste as well as the noise, additional truck movements, etc. However, there could be an environmental value to removing pollutants from an area that could suffer long-term ecological harm if they were left untouched.

In research commissioned in a report for Zero Waste Scotland, a number of hypothetical scenarios were developed to explore the economic case for LFMR (Warren, 2014). These looked at the feasibility of using waste for energy recovery on site; using refuse-derived fuel (RDF) on site; selling the cleaned site for development purposes and reusing construction materials in that development. Metals recovered from the site would be sold as scrap. The research concluded that there was little scope for using recovered plastics due to the high cost of reprocessing and so they should be used as RDF.

The research found that there could be a borderline financial case for LFMR if energy recovery occurred on site, but overall the conclusion was that many projects would struggle for financial viability. This may change in the coming years as costs of waste sorting and reprocessing fall, demand for land development increases and virgin raw materials diminish and become more expensive. Until then it seems that LFMR will have little material impact on supply chains.

Building product design into the supply chain

A fundamental supply chain sustainability issue for manufacturers and retailers is the design of the products they are making or sourcing/selling. For example, if products can be made lighter or smaller this can have significant impact on their carbon footprint. In some sectors this has been occurring as a result of technological developments and is unrelated to an overt 'green' strategy. Consumer electronics have been getting smaller and lighter for some time, leading to lower logistics costs. iPods and smartphones have been at the forefront of this miniaturization revolution. Flat screen televisions and computer monitors take up only a fifth of the space of the traditional (now largely superseded) cathode ray tube (CRT) equivalents. It has been estimated that Dell was shipping 25 million pounds in weight of CRT monitors in the mid-2000s. This dropped to 7 million pounds when it introduced flat panel monitors, requiring only one third of the previous number of containers (Jindel, 2008).

The miniaturization of electronics products has had a significant impact on the air cargo sector, which of course has the highest levels of GHG emissions of any mode. According to Fred Smith, CEO of FedEx, electronics account for about half of all air cargo volumes, which is why the trend is particularly hard felt in terms of revenues (Smith, 2014). The falling price of technology has also had an impact, meaning that it makes more sense for many shippers to look at lower cost (and lower GHG emissions) sea freight. While this is bad news for the air cargo sector, it has certainly had a major impact on carbon footprints within the high-tech sector. This has been one of the drivers behind the retirement of many older, less fuel efficient aeroplanes, as air cargo operators seek to minimize their costs and make their offering more competitive.

In addition to this, components are becoming lighter. This is particularly the case in the automotive and aerospace industries where, for reasons of fuel efficiency, there are very good reasons to keep vehicles and aeroplanes as light as possible. The Boeing Dreamliner, for example, is around 20 per cent lighter than its predecessor (Jindel, 2008).

Looking to the future, 3D printing has the potential to reduce component weights even further by using lightweight but exceptionally strong materials. By being able to build light, 'porous' structures, additive manufacturing can create high tensile strength without the weight associated with normal manufacturing techniques.

3D printing in the aerospace sector

In the transport industry, the development of additive manufacturing (3D printing) has a twofold impact. First, the weight of parts being moved through supply chains is reduced (and in some cases eliminated); secondly, the reduced weight of vehicles and aeroplanes results in lower carbon emissions.

3D-printed parts are already being used in Airbus's commercial jetliner product line – including the wide body A350 XWB, the single-aisle A320neo and the A300/A310 range. Some 2,700 plastic parts have been produced by 3D printing for the A350 XWB programme, with Airbus also working with the European Aviation Safety Agency (EASA) to get regulatory approval for titanium components produced by the technology. The aircraft manufacturer is also using 3D printing to produce out-of-production spare parts for its A300/A310 range.

According to high-tech manufacturer EOS, 3D printed 'intelligent' lightweight structures manufactured using laser sintering processes combine high strength with a weight reduction of 40–60 per cent. The material savings also translate into more flexibility in design and engineering. As a result, aeroplanes consume significantly less fuel and emit less carbon dioxide.

In a joint project run by EOS and Airbus's parent company, EADS, additive manufacture of hinge brackets was shown to reduce the consumption of raw materials by 75 per cent. The optimized design of the engine cowling hinge showed the potential to reduce weight per plane by approximately 10kg, using titanium powder rather than steel. Over the lifetime of a plane, replacing this component alone would have a substantial impact on CO_2 emissions. Both companies are looking at where else 3D printing could also be used.

Summary

The 'circular economy' is increasingly being adopted as an alternative to existing 'linear' economies where products, materials and components are discarded when their usefulness comes to an end. This will have important consequences for the design of products and the supply chains required to return them to useful purpose. The 'sharing economy' phenomenon, where ownership of capital-intensive assets such as cars, is replaced by 'access' will have a profound impact on the exploitation of natural resources. Other business trends and technological developments, such as performance-based logistics and 3D printing, will also have a positive effect in mitigating environmental impact.

Key points

- Linear economies based on 'take, make, waste' principles are increasingly being replaced by 'circular supply chains' underpinned by the reuse and recycling of materials.

- 'Sharing economies', which allow consumers access to assets such as cars, will increase utilization and reduce wasteful use of natural resources.

- Companies are increasingly opting for performance-based logistics services, whereby manufacturers commit to the maintenance and upkeep of the products they supply, providing an incentive to maximize utilization.

- Products are increasingly being designed with logistics in mind – minimizing volume and weight to reduce transport and storage costs as well as reducing carbon emissions.

- 3D printing will play an increasingly important role in this respect.

References

Ellen MacArthur Foundation (2015) Delivering a circular economy: a toolkit for policy makers, www.ellenmacarthurfoundation.org

Jindel, S (2008) How the iPod is killing air freight, *Traffic World,* 13 October

Lacy, P and Rutqvist, J (2014) *Waste to Wealth: The circular economy advantage,* Palgrave Macmillan, Basingstoke

London Waste and Recycling Board (2015) London: The circular economy capital, www.lwarb.gov.uk

PWC (2014) The Sharing Economy, pwc.com/CISsharing

Smith, F (2014) State of the international air cargo industry, Speech to International Aviation Club of Washington, DC

The Economist (2013) The rise of the sharing economy: On the internet, everything is for hire, 9 March

Velis, C A (2014) *Global recycling markets – plastic waste: A story for one player – China,* International Solid Waste Association, Globalisation and Waste Management Task Force, ISWA, Vienna

Velis C A (2015) Circular economy and global secondary material supply chains, *Waste Management & Research,* **33** (5), pp 389–91

Warren, K and Read, A (2014) Landfill mining: goldmine or minefield? Ricardo-AEA, https://waste-management-world.com/a/landfill-mining-goldmine-or-minefield

WEF (2015) *Beyond Supply Chains: Empowering responsible value chains,* World Economic Forum/Accenture, Geneva

Wilson D C, Velis C A and Rodic, L (2013) Integrated sustainable waste management in developing countries. Proceedings of the ICE, *Waste and Resource Management,* 166, pp 52–68

The role of supply chain technologies

03

THIS CHAPTER WILL FAMILIARIZE THE READER WITH

- The importance of technology in creating supply chain efficiencies and reducing the impact of logistics on the environment
- Which type of technologies are perceived as being the most beneficial
- The range of alternative fuels and which are likely to be most readily adopted across the industry
- The new entrant truck manufacturers and the competition they face from existing players
- The role of drones in a humanitarian context
- How technologies can be used to create supply chain visibility for suppliers' ethical and environmental practices

Technology is an important tool in reducing environmental and societal impacts by supply chain and logistics companies, as indicated by responses to a survey undertaken by industry consulting company, Ti (see Figure 3.1). However, in some regards its role has been overlooked due to the fact that in many cases the benefits are indirect, ie the primary role of most supply chain technologies is to create operational efficiencies, which subsequently play a positive role in reducing carbon emissions or create visibility, which then allow companies to make better societal decisions (Ti, 2016).

Figure 3.1 Do you consider technology an important tool in mitigating environmental impact?

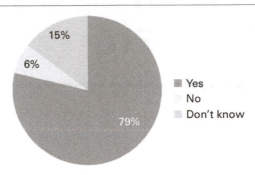

The term 'technology' covers software applications as well as developments in mechanical, chemical and electrical engineering. Respondents to the Ti survey, for example, pointed to improvements in engine efficiency and 'smarter' fuels. Within the warehouse sector, improvements in pervious concrete, which prevents run off, were mentioned. Others indicated that e-shipping documents had considerably reduced unnecessary use of paper. Overall, 79 per cent of respondents said that technology was an important tool in mitigating environmental impact.

One less obvious benefit brought by technology is the ability it gives companies to 'measure and manage'. One respondent commented, 'One of the main challenges is to understand the current level of impact on environment. Technology in this respect enables businesses to baseline their current picture in order to start to drive year-on-year improvements.' Another logistics executive put it more bluntly: 'Technology will be essential to enforce and control.'

Referring specifically to software applications, when asked which type brought the most benefits, 45 per cent indicated transport management systems, while 31 per cent stated supply chain planning software (see Figure 3.2). Warehouse management systems were perceived to have few green benefits, despite the efficiencies they create within the warehouse environment.

Technology also gives companies the ability to calculate their carbon footprint. As one respondent put it, 'Our technology gives us the opportunity to calculate what the emission is per shipment, specifically per trade lane, and also on a customer level. Knowing this gives us the opportunity to discuss improvement levels with our global customers.'

Figure 3.2   What type of technology do you consider brings the most environmental benefits?

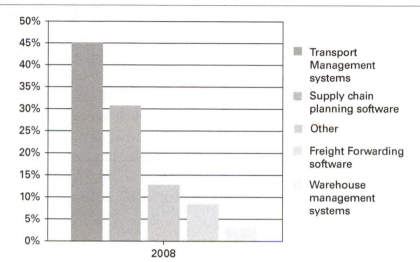

Of those who measure their carbon footprint, two thirds said that they managed the process in-house, sometimes using their own software, while the remainder looked to outside consultants and software houses. Many said that this initiative was only just in development.

Transport management systems (TMS)

TMS technology is a very good example of how systems designed to create operational efficiencies benefit the environment. Typically they:

- Reduce the distance travelled by vehicles (optimized route planning).
- Select the most fuel efficient roads to use (ie choosing between less congested primary routes and shorter, more congested residential streets).
- Create better utilization of vehicle payloads by planning more efficient collections and deliveries.
- Enable an operator to schedule back hauls thereby increasing vehicle utilization.
- Allocate appropriate vehicles to each route.
- Dynamically update driver and management on traffic congestion and suggest alternative routes.

A further opportunity for users of TMS is the ability to consolidate multiple individual shipments into full loads, thereby optimizing flows of goods to individual customers or locations. This can even influence modal choice, with lower cost options being used. For example, when Korean consumer goods manufacturer LG implemented a TMS in the United States it aimed to be able to increase 'load fill' rates by 3 per cent and reduce transportation cost by 4 per cent. With over 700 truck-load movements a day, this would be a considerable saving. In fact the company was able to reduce transport and distribution costs by 8 per cent as well as improve its customer delivery reliability to between 98 and 99.2 per cent. According to ARC Advisory Group, TMS users can achieve average freight savings of 8 per cent (ARC, 2016).

CASE STUDY   UPS – using TMS to reduce carbon and costs

Operating a large-scale parcels network in the United States and around the world, express operator UPS has recognized that increasing its operational efficiencies through the development of sophisticated TMS technology is a critical competitive advantage.

UPS claims that its recently developed On-Road Integrated Optimization and Navigation (ORION) routing system reduces the distance driven by its drivers by 100 million miles annually. The company included all its US routes by the end of 2016 and global routes outside the United States will be deployed after 2017. The implementation will result in a 100,000 metric ton reduction in CO_2 emissions. The company expects additional benefits including annual savings of 10 million gallons of fuel and more than $300 million on final United States implementation.

UPS's ORION routing system uses data from customers, drivers and vehicles to calculate the most efficient route, taking into consideration all scheduled package delivery and pick-ups. UPS began implementing ORION routing in 2012 after 10 years of development work.

'We have realized a reduction of 6 to 8 miles driven per route, resulting in significantly lower fuel use and related lower vehicle emissions,' said Mitch Nichols, UPS senior vice president of transportation and engineering. Dynamic routing is planned for a future version to enable more efficient routing changes during the drivers' day.

The TMS has also gained in importance due to omni-channel strategies being employed by retailers. This has added additional levels of complexity within the distribution process and the reduction in shipment size has increased costs. It is more important than ever to maximize efficiency. 'Green' agendas also require shippers and logistics companies to minimize their carbon emissions, which of course the use of TMS allows.

Alternative fuels

Governments around the world have invested heavily in the concept of alternative fuel strategies with the aim of replacing some or all carbon-based fuels with sustainably produced options. Using alternative fuels in engines designed for petrol-based fuel is not straightforward. For example, if bioethanol makes up more than a certain percentage of the fuel by volume, its corrosive nature means that engine components must be replaced (McKinnon *et al*, 2012).

Biofuels

Biofuels (fuels derived from organic matter or animals) are becoming increasingly important as a replacement for traditional diesel, bunker fuels for ships or aviation gas. However, they only account for about 3 per cent of the total volume of fuel used, the remaining 97 per cent being carbon-based.

There are two main types of biofuels: biodiesel and bioethanol. Biodiesel is made from plant or animal oils, the main source of which varies from region to region depending on crops that suit local growing conditions. In North America, soy bean oil is preferred while in Asia the greatest source is palm oil. In Europe, rape seed oil is most popular. Bioethanol is produced from any feedstock that contains sugars such as starch. This means that crops as diverse as wheat, corn, willow and sugar cane can be used.

There are problems with the sustainability credentials of biofuels. First, studies have shown that although carbon monoxide, hydrocarbons and sulphur dioxide emissions can be reduced, other pollutants such as nitrogen oxides and volatile organic compounds (VOCs) increase. Evidence on carbon dioxide emissions is ambiguous depending on the lifecycle assessment (LCA) used. Obviously there are considerable carbon emissions involved in the growing, harvesting, production and transport of biofuels.

Hydrogen

Hydrogen has the potential to be a completely clean form of energy. Electricity is produced from the chemical reaction between hydrogen and oxygen, leaving only water vapour as the waste residue. This is very much a technology in development; it is favoured particularly for use in urban environments due to the lack of pollutants.

However, hydrogen is not the answer to all pollution problems. The element has to be produced and, depending on the energy source used (coal or gas for example), there could be high levels of carbon emissions involved.

CASE STUDY   Truck manufacturers compete to offer 'next generation' trucks

Manufacturers have yet to agree on a single technology for the next generation of trucks. United States-based start-up manufacturer Nikola Motor Company has opted to develop a hydrogen powered truck which it claims will have zero emissions. It says it will be able to achieve this goal because it plans to build its own solar farms to produce the clean energy required to generate the hydrogen from electrolysis of water. It will also develop its own network of 50 hydrogen stations across the United States. Each truck will have a range of 1,200 miles. The company says that in addition to the hydrogen cell, each truck can be powered by a 320-kilowatt lithium ion battery although the hydrogen cell will be the main source of power. Other claims made by the manufacturer include:

- trucks will have half the operating costs of diesel equivalents;
- 15 minute refill time;
- 1,000 horsepower;
- 20 mpg.

The launch date of the first vehicle was December 2016 and in August 2016 the company said that it already had $3 billion in pre-orders.

Rival company, Tesla, meanwhile, has opted for all-electric, using the technologies it has developed for its cars. Details on what the new 'Tesla Semi' will look like are sparse but plans have attracted scepticism as critics believe the batteries required will be too big and heavy and the range of each truck will be very low (perhaps under 200 miles). Although Tesla states that a model will be launched by 2017, more realistic prospects could be by the end of the decade. With a Tesla Semi potentially costing up to double that of an orthodox truck, the operational savings would have to be considerable over a long time period to make the economics work.

Wrightspeed, another US company, is further ahead of the game. It already has working prototypes in operation powered by natural gas turbines. The company has entered into an agreement with a New Zealand bus company to re-power its engines.

Daimler Trucks is perhaps best placed to deliver a new generation of trucks. With its proven track record as one of the world's most successful vehicle manufacturers, its ambition to launch a range of 'eTrucks' by the beginning of the next decade must be taken seriously. Based on an existing model, the conventional drivetrain has been replaced by an electrically driven rear axle with electric motors directly adjacent to the wheel hubs. The power is provided by a battery pack consisting of three lithium-ion battery modules. The range of the truck is up to 200km, long enough, the company says, for intra-urban deliveries.

BMW already deploys a fully-electric truck to move goods between distribution facilities. The vehicle has a range of 62 miles and can be charged in three to four hours. According to the company, it will save 11.8 tonnes of carbon dioxide a year compared to its diesel equivalent.

Natural gas (NG)

Natural gas is a more mature technology than some of the others discussed above. However, in terms of environmental credentials it has the downside that it is considered to be a fossil fuel and 'unclean'. Methane (one of the most frequent gases used) has a global warming potential of 21 times that of carbon dioxide (McKinnon *et al*, 2012). Liquefied Petroleum Gas (LPG) and Compressed Natural Gas (CNG) are other forms, but they too are fossil-based.

That is not to say that natural gas does not have its advantages. There are around 220,000 medium and heavy duty trucks powered by NG in the world, their popularity driven by low emissions of nitrogen oxides and particulates. They are also quieter than equivalent diesel-powered engines, which makes them well suited to urban deliveries in particular.

Electric vehicles

The main challenge facing electric van and truck manufacturers is that the batteries required to power freight-carrying vehicles are relatively large and heavy. At the same time the range of electric vehicles is low (up to 250 miles) which means that they can only be used for niche sectors, such as city logistics. Hybrid vehicles, which use a combination of diesel fuel and electric, have become widely adopted.

The advantage of electric vehicles is that there are virtually no emissions from the exhaust pipe, which again makes them suited to urban areas. They are also very quiet. However, in terms of carbon emissions, the sustainability of electric vehicles is directly related to the type of fuel used to generate the electricity that charges the batteries. If power stations supplying the grid are oil- or gas-based, vehicle emissions are in effect being transferred upstream. If the ultimate power source is either nuclear or from renewables, electric vehicles become much more sustainable.

Tesla and other auto manufacturers are investing huge sums in battery technology and it seems inevitable that in the next five years it will become feasible for even the largest trucks to be powered by electricity. Until then, electric vehicles will probably be restricted to urban deliveries, although given the growth of cities and mega-cities, this is an important sector in its own right.

CASE STUDY   Express parcels companies and green technologies

The global express parcels companies have been at the forefront of developing and implementing new technologies to mitigate their environmental impact and of course reduce their fuel costs. These companies have some of the largest private fleets in the industry due to the number of package delivery vans and consequently the initiatives they undertake have significant impact.

Since 2005, FedEx has improved total fleet miles per gallon within the United States by 14.1 per cent, saving over 53 million gallons of fuel or approximately

472,700 metric tons of carbon dioxide emissions. Its goal is to increase savings to 20 per cent by 2020. The company also operates one of the largest fleets of commercial hybrid trucks in North America, consisting of more than 329 hybrid-electric trucks, and operates 19 all-electric trucks in Los Angeles, London and Paris.

UPS is also expanding its hybrid-electric fleet and in 2015 purchased 125 new technology hybrid-electric delivery trucks. The new trucks provide significant fuel economy equivalency gains – up to four times the fuel economy of a diesel powered vehicle, compared to a 10 to 15 per cent improvement with previous hybrid designs. They rely on a small internal combustion engine and lithium ion battery to deliver a 50–60-mile per day range. UPS states that it operates one of the largest private alternative fuel fleets in the United States, with more than 5,088 alternative fuel and advanced technology vehicles. This includes all-electric, hybrid electric, hydraulic hybrid, CNG, LNG, propane, biomethane and lightweight fuel-saving composite body vehicles. By the end of 2017, UPS anticipates logging 1 billion miles from its alternative fuel fleet.

DHL has also taken many initiatives to enhance the efficiency of its fleet. Out of approximately 92,000 road vehicles deployed worldwide, 13,500 vehicles have been enhanced with about 22,500 technical modifications. These include telematics, engine tuning and speed limiting measures, aerodynamics and alternative drive systems. It uses biodiesel, LPG and bioethanol fuel alternatives, although these represent just 2 million kg out of a total of nearly 450 million kg. DHL has recently undertaken an initiative to deploy 141 electric vehicles in Bonn by 2016, resulting in decreased CO_2 emissions of over 500 tons per year.

The 'Internet of Things' and telematics

The 'Internet of Things' (IoT) is a term used to encompass the use of sensors, technology and networking to allow buildings, infrastructures, devices and additional 'things' to share information. The efficiencies created will be an important factor in companies' efforts to reduce their carbon emissions.

Fleet and asset tracking is one capability that IoT can provide and many logistics operators have already installed new tracking technology across their fleets of vans, trucks, trailers and intermodal containers. Tracking technology can deliver continuous, real-time information on the location and load status of each trailer and container, often using solar or cellular power. This allows companies to pinpoint the exact location of empty containers and trailers, making the planning and dispatch process more efficient while reducing drivers' wasted time and empty miles.

The increased use of sensors and vehicle telematics allows logistics managers to gather data daily on the mechanical performance of vehicles and behavioural patterns of drivers. This includes vehicle speed, direction, braking, performance of the engine and mechanical components. This can be used to improve driver behaviour, reducing wear on vehicles and fuel consumption (thereby reducing CO_2 emissions). This results in the improved maintenance of vehicles, less downtime and fewer breakdowns.

Sensors are not just being introduced to the road freight industry. Aircraft engine manufacturers have been capturing engine performance data in flight for years. This data is constantly being transmitted to the manufacturers so that any variation from expected norms generates an alert. This information is then used to trigger specific inspections at the next point the aircraft lands, along with the appropriate recommendations for resolving the issue such as having a replacement part available at the airport, which is installed before the plane is allowed to continue.

This regime is well established and has resulted in enormous gains in reliability, a reduction in flight delays due to engine problems, and improved engine efficiency in terms of jet fuel use. The engine manufacturers (eg Rolls Royce, GE, and Pratt & Whitney) now have massive amounts of data that is constantly analysed for improvements and greater insight into how the next generation of engines can be made more efficient and effective. Every flight continues to add to these data stores and is only part of the data that is now being captured from the numerous systems on board aircraft.

Autonomous vehicles

The phenomenon of 'autonomous driving' (otherwise known as 'driverless vehicles') is set to revolutionize the global logistics industry. With technology giants such as Google and vehicle manufacturers such as Mercedes Benz investing heavily in the concept, it is only a matter of time before fully autonomous vehicles are seen on roads around the world. Cars and trucks will be able to communicate with the road infrastructure, other vehicles and a range of technology platforms (including those monitoring traffic), which will create huge efficiencies. Not only will this result in environmental advantages due to a reduction in carbon emissions, but there will be huge social benefits from a reduction in accidents, injuries and deaths.

Autonomous road vehicles are under development by almost all major manufacturers. They believe that the efficiencies the technology will deliver will come in the form of:

- reduced fuel consumption – the computer will drive the vehicle more fuel efficiently;
- reduced emissions – for the same reason;
- 100 per cent connectivity and location services, which allow for 'perfect' route planning;
- diagnostic services, which ensure correct maintenance and fewer breakdowns;
- emergency braking will ensure fewer accidents, gaps between vehicles will be adhered to;
- routes can be re-planned around known areas of congestion;
- accidents caused by human error (through tiredness, for example) will be considerably reduced and eventually eradicated.

One of the greatest benefits will be the reduction in congestion. German authorities predict that truck transport volume will increase by 39 per cent by 2030 unless something is done to limit numbers of trucks (Newbold, 2016). Construction of new roads is unpopular from an environmental perspective, and many countries in Europe don't have the money available to make the sort of investment required. Major trunk road networks in Western Europe have barely grown in the past decade, so it becomes essential to utilize existing road capacity more efficiently and new technologies can aid in this goal.

It is increasingly possible to 'harvest' a huge amount of data from vehicles, both cars and trucks, which if analysed in a proper and timely way will result in efficiencies, mostly related to the avoidance of congestion. This data can be generated either by traffic authorities (such as municipalities or highway agencies), by private companies that provide information to users on speed of traffic, or more recently mobile applications that allow individuals to log incidents as they observe them. The latter can theoretically mobilize thousands of drivers who act as monitors of traffic situations in areas that no other organization could reach.

With vehicles having the capability to interact, not only with other vehicles around them, but also with highway infrastructure, a lot more data will be generated. Embedded sensors in everything from transport infrastructure, through to smart devices on board the vehicles themselves, will be generating the data which then has to be assimilated and processed, with the resulting conclusions fed back into the system.

With vehicles being able to communicate with each other, there is also the possibility of 'platooning'. Trucks (and even eventually cars) will be able to travel in convoys along the motorway, drafting the vehicle in front. According to the US Department of Environment, this can create fuel cost savings of 8–11 per cent (Lammert *et al*, 2014).

Unmanned aerial vehicles (UAVS)

New technologies can bring new opportunities to address logistics challenges; this is definitely the case for Unmanned Aerial Vehicles or, as they are more popularly known, drones. The usefulness of drones to undertake mainstream logistics deliveries is certainly up for debate. However, in certain circumstances and environments there is no doubt that they can come into their own. In remote regions, for example, where existing road infrastructure is weak or non-existent, they can provide an essential resource, travelling long distances across difficult terrain to deliver critical shipments. Consequently their utility has been recognized by aid agencies and health organizations as a way of delivering medicines and other potentially life-saving materials or equipment.

The case study opposite highlights how a partnership between global express company UPS and an aid agency resulted in drones being integrated within an effective solution to medical emergencies.

CASE STUDY   Supplying vaccines by drone

In 2016, UPS announced a partnership with Zipline, a California-based robotics company, and Gavi, the Vaccine Alliance, to explore using drones to transform the way life-saving medicines such as blood and vaccines are delivered around the world.

According to the World Health Organization, Africa has the highest rate in the world of maternal death due to postpartum haemorrhaging, which makes access to life-saving blood transfusions critically important for women across the continent.

Delivering these vital supplies to people in remote areas can be extremely difficult, particularly when the product has a limited life span. UPS saw the need for an innovative solution to ensure critical medical resources reached their recipients quickly and without damage. Partnering with Zipline and Gavi, UPS helped to develop a plan involving the use of drones to deliver vital medical supplies to rural areas of Rwanda. The public-private partnership combines the global logistics expertise, cold chain and healthcare delivery from UPS with Zipline's national drone delivery network and Gavi's experience in developing countries focused on saving lives and protecting health in the most remote places of the world.

While the project is initially focused on the delivery of blood supplies, the plan is to expand Rwanda's national drone network to include vaccines, treatments for HIV/AIDS, malaria, tuberculosis, and many other essential and lifesaving medicines.

The launch of the initiative was funded by an $800,000 grant from the UPS Foundation. Each year, The UPS Foundation's Humanitarian Relief & Resilience programme assists with more than 200 global humanitarian shipments. UPS has also leveraged healthcare industry expertise for safely storing, transporting and distributing pharmaceutical and medical supplies.

Following a successful trial, the Rwandan Government will deploy drones to make up to 150 deliveries per day of life-saving blood to 21 transfusion facilities located in the western half of the country. Rwanda's drone delivery operation is expected to save thousands of lives over the next three years and could serve as a model for other countries.

Using technology to create supply chain visibility for societal impact

Technology is not just used to mitigate environmental impact. A number of software tools allow companies to improve the oversight of their suppliers, enabling them to identify any breaches of ethical practice and the risks that this could cause. This is increasingly important for companies, given the legislation passed in recent years related to modern slavery, conflict minerals and anti-bribery and corruption. It is now a requirement to demonstrate to authorities that steps have been taken to audit supply chains. 'Compliance risk' is now an important part of running a multinational company.

The complexity of modern supply chains means that creating a database of suppliers (supply chain mapping) and ensuring that workflow procedures are followed are crucial. According to supplier management company Achilles, companies already spend a large amount on managing information about their suppliers: $60 billion in 2015. However, in many cases this information does not cover many essential issues such as health and safety or bribery and corruption policies.

Supplier management groups build and manage communities of manufacturers, retailers and their suppliers. They provide customers with the assurance that the suppliers they use comply with a range of regulations and meet the requirements of sustainable sourcing strategies tailored to the needs of individual sectors. As part of their services many offer customers online procurement platforms. These enable customers to choose suppliers based on a range of metrics, such as ethical and environmental credentials as well as quality standards, bribery and corruption, insurance and legal, financial and health and safety. By storing all the relevant information about the suppliers in a single database, customers can understand more fully supply chain risks at a multi-tier level and take action appropriately. It also demonstrates a level of 'due-diligence' to authorities to show that customers are taking all appropriate steps to comply with the relevant legislation. There exists an electronic data trail that can protect a customer's interests.

According to Achilles, currently just 51 per cent of manufacturers regularly audit their tier-one suppliers. In another survey undertaken by the Chartered Institute of Purchasing and Supply, 72 per cent of British supply chain professionals have no visibility of their supply chain beyond the second tier (Achilles, 2014). Undertaking supply chain mapping and subsequently auditing the ethical and environmental practices of the suppliers can only be facilitated by a fully automated system of questionnaires and case notes. Working with a defined set of suppliers allows customers this level of supply chain visibility. However, gaining visibility (and accessing the levels of information needed to populate supplier mapping software) relies heavily on the 'buy-in' of the key economic owners within a supply chain structure (the main Tier 1, Tier 2, etc suppliers). In many vulnerable parts of the world, this requires audits to be undertaken by experienced professionals on the ground.

Summary

The role technology plays in reducing the impact of logistics operations on the environment can be overlooked. However, the efficiencies that have been achieved through transport management systems have been incalculable and new developments in sensor technology and telematics will continue to deliver benefits. Autonomous vehicles, connected within the Internet of Things, will also reduce congestion and lead to fuel use reduction through opportunities for 'platooning'. Several competing alternative fuels are being developed and although not competitive against fossil fuels at the moment, they have the potential to transform the industry in the near future. The commercial use of drones is debatable, but in certain conditions (such as in a remote and difficult environment) it is becoming clear that they can provide an essential humanitarian service. In terms of ensuring supply chain visibility, technology platforms are now being used to reduce 'compliance risk', providing a tool for supply chain managers to assess the ethical suitability of suppliers.

Key points

- Transport management systems have been highly effective in reducing unnecessary vehicle mileage, and new technologies will increase the benefits through dynamic routing.

- Autonomous vehicles connected through sensor technology will reduce congestion and increase fuel efficiencies.

- Massive investment by existing truck manufacturers as well as new market entrants will lead to the development of viable alternative fuel vehicles in the near future.

- Drones can be used for humanitarian purposes, such as the delivery of drugs, in the appropriate environment.

- Express parcels companies, due to their large fleets, have been at the forefront of the adoption of new, cleaner technologies.

References

Achilles (2014) Is modern slavery being factored into supply chain risk assessments? http://www.achilles.com/en/about-achilles/industry-insights/1242-is-modern-slavery-being-factored-into-supply-chain-risk-assessments

ARC (2016) Proven ROI Drives Market Growth, ARC Advisory Group, http://www.arcweb.com/market-studies/pages/transportation-management-systems.aspx

Lammert, M, Duran, A, Diez, J, Burton, K and Nicholson, A (2014) Effect of Platooning on Fuel Consumption of Class 8 Vehicles Over a Range of Speeds, Following Distances, and Mass SAE, *International Journal of Commercial Vehicles,* 7 (2), doi:10.4271/2014-01-2438

McKinnon, A C, Browne, M and Whiteing, A (2012) *Green Logistics: Improving the environmental sustainability of logistics,* Kogan Page, London

Newbold, R (2016) Five Driving Forces behind Driverless Trucks, http://www.inboundlogistics.com/cms/article/five-driving-forces-behind-driverless-trucks/

Ti (2016) Sustainable supply chains, Transport Intelligence, www.ti-insight.com

Sustainable supply chains survey

04

THIS CHAPTER WILL FAMILIARIZE THE READER WITH

- The importance of the environment to a company's strategy and the main pressures behind implementing a sustainability policy
- The main benefits managers perceive to accrue from good environmental and ethical practice
- How widespread is the adoption of formal environmental policies and how effective they are perceived to be
- The extent to which environmental compliance is made part of the tendering process and who is expected to pay
- The impact any future economic slowdown would have on environmental strategies

It is very rare these days for any manufacturer, retailer or logistics company to ignore the importance of sustainability to its company. Even if the commitment to mitigating environmental and societal impact is motivated by corporate self-interest or at the very least the desire to avoid damage to its brand, the issue is at least being taken seriously.

How seriously, of course, is another question and that is why surveys on the matter are so important to gauge trends. For example, has the global economic downturn which started in 2008 had a long-lasting impact on supply chain managers' attitudes towards sustainability? Are the drivers of green supply chain management strategies the same now as they were in the mid-2000s?

Transport Intelligence, the industry consulting company, first surveyed the industry in 2008 and followed this up with a further survey in 2016. The results make for some interesting reading (Ti, 2016).

Importance to corporate strategy

Overall there has been some change in the importance managers attach to the environment; see Figure 4.1. In 2008, 87 per cent of respondents thought that the environment was either 'important' or 'highly important' to their companies' strategies. This had fallen to 79 per cent in 2016, which is perhaps surprising as it might have been expected that more companies would regard sustainability as a fundamental consideration in their business models. There was an increase in the proportion of respondents who considered the environment as 'highly important' but the most significant growth occurred in the category of respondents who regarded the environment as 'neither important nor unimportant'.

Delving deeper into respondents' attitudes (Figure 4.2), a large majority indicated that they considered business needs should be balanced with environmental initiatives. Almost a fifth of those

Figure 4.1 How important is the environment to your company's strategy?

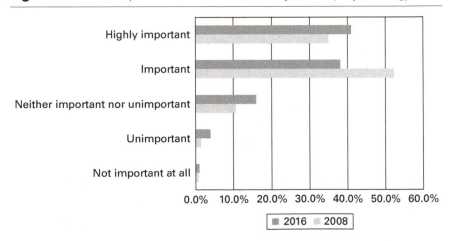

Figure 4.2 Which of the following statements most closely describes your personal views on 'green' issues?

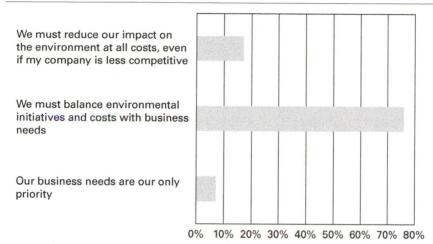

We must reduce our impact on the environment at all costs, even if my company is less competitive

We must balance environmental initiatives and costs with business needs

Our business needs are our only priority

0% 10% 20% 30% 40% 50% 60% 70% 80%

surveyed thought that green initiatives should take priority over the needs of their company, although only a very small proportion considered that the business needs were the only priority.

In 2008 when a similar question was asked, significantly fewer respondents believed that their company should reduce its impact on the environment, even if that meant it was less competitive (10 per cent in 2008 compared with 17 per cent in 2016). This suggests that, on a personal level, people are starting to take the issue more seriously. The survey also looked at altruistic corporate behaviour (Figure 4.3). Almost two-thirds (64 per cent) of respondents judged that their

Figure 4.3 Has your company spent money on an environmental initiative that has no direct commercial benefits?

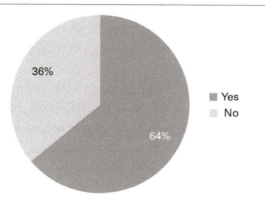

36%

Yes
No

64%

company had undertaken an environmental initiative for no commercial value. This represented a significant increase from 2008 where only 44 per cent of those surveyed could identify such initiatives.

The main pressures driving logistics policies

As discussed in Chapter 1, it is not easy to identify the core reasons behind the corporate adoption of ethical and environmental policies and initiatives. There is often a mixture of drivers, ranging from the philanthropic to the self-serving. This was highlighted by McKinnon in *Green Logistics* (McKinnon *et al*, 2012) in his review of 'rhetoric and reality'. In many respects the driver is not necessarily the key issue: a positive outcome is more important. However, for those with an interest in sustainability it is useful to understand the thinking behind management decisions and attitudes.

Respondents to Ti's survey were asked to list the key pressures behind their companies' sustainability policies (Figure 4.4). The results suggest that the main reasons were compliance with government and customer requirements rather than any altruistic motives, these two categories occupying the top two positions. This was followed by the pressure to reduce transport costs in third position.

In *Green Logistics*, McKinnon says that most supply chain surveys 'rather curiously' omit to make explicit reference to the need to protect the environment. Ti's survey addresses this omission. It would seem that although being 'green for the sake of being green' is not the most motivating factor – ranking only fourth and significantly below the top two factors – it is still very important. As McKinnon points out, 'the most fundamental of all green objectives should be to maintain a physical environment that can support a high level of economic activity in the longer term'.

The 'need to reduce risk' appears near the bottom of the scale. At some level, there seems to be a disconnect between increasing levels of supply chain risk, which of course includes meteorological events such as flooding, hurricanes and typhoons (all of which may be related to global warming) and sustainable policies.

Figure 4.4 What do you believe are the main pressures driving your sustainable supply chain and logistics policies?

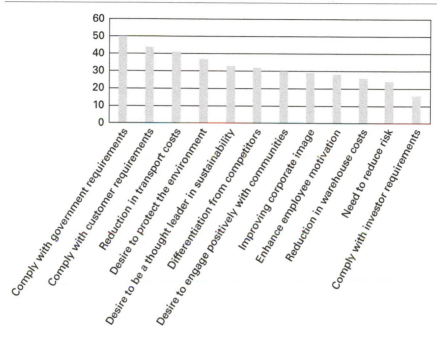

'Comply with investor requirements' is by far the least frequent response. Although anecdotal evidence suggests that for the manufacturers, retailers and logistics providers this is an growing issue, it would seem across a more balanced survey of the industry that this does not play a major part in managers' decisions.

The main benefits of implementing a sustainable supply chain and logistics strategy

The next question in the survey looked at the main benefits that managers believed would accrue from implementing a sustainable supply chain and logistics strategy. The top two answers were 'improve brand image' and 'improve profitability' (Figure 4.5).

Figure 4.5   What do you believe are the main benefits of implementing a sustainable supply chain and logistics strategy?

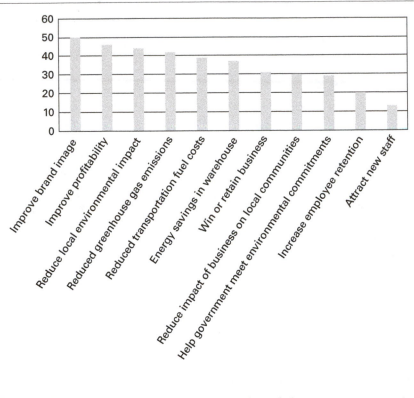

This reinforces the theme from the results of the previous question, which suggested that respondents were looking for direct benefits from a 'green' policy. In this case these benefits are achieved primarily through building brand equity as well as financial.

Although complying with government regulations was identified as the main pressure, interestingly, 'helping government meet environmental commitments' appeared low on the list of benefits. It would suggest that companies have not necessarily bought into government and inter-government policy, but perhaps, rather begrudgingly, comply with regulations out of necessity. It is also apparent that companies see comparatively few advantages in terms of retaining and attracting new staff accruing from their implementation of a sustainable business model.

Effectiveness of formal environmental policies

The next two questions of the survey were designed to identify the proportion of companies that had implemented a formal environmental policy and, if so, how effective this policy had been.

It seems that companies are increasingly recognizing that a structured approach to environmental management is important in demonstrating their credentials to stakeholders. Just under three-quarters of respondents stated that their company had a formal environmental policy. Indicating the importance companies are now placing upon the issue, in 2008, when Ti undertook its first survey on the environment, the equivalent response rate was 64 per cent.

Figure 4.6   Does your company have a formal environmental policy?

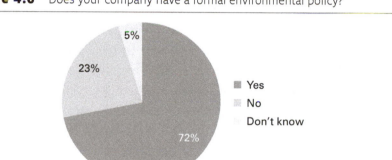

Figure 4.7   How effective is your environmental policy in the adoption of more sustainable working practices?

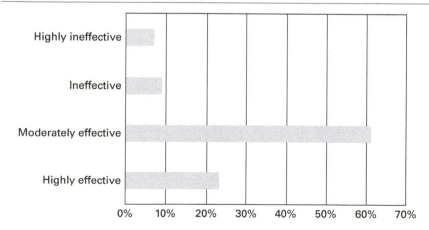

The majority of respondents (61 per cent) thought that their environmental policies were 'moderately effective', perhaps not a total endorsement of the work of their CSR departments but positive none the less. Only 23 per cent thought that they were 'highly effective'; this is perhaps an area of concern, at least in how the work of the CSR department is perceived internally. However, overall it seems that CSR departments are believed to be doing a good job, with only 16 per cent indicating that their environmental policies were either 'ineffective' or 'highly ineffective'.

Measurement of impact on the environment

One of the most positive conclusions that can be drawn from comparing the survey in 2016 with its predecessor in 2008 is the increased number of companies measuring their impact on the environment. As mentioned in Chapter 1 and elsewhere, only by measuring impact can it subsequently be managed. Without a set of baseline metrics it is impossible to track improvements and/or assess whether targets are being met.

As Figure 4.8 shows, the number of companies measuring environmental impact (eg, carbon footprint) has increased from 34 per cent of those surveyed to 64 per cent. The numbers of managers who didn't know if their company had some type of measurement scheme in place fell from 21 per cent to 7 per cent, perhaps suggesting that environmental initiatives are being better communicated across companies.

Figure 4.8   Does your company measure the impact of its business on the environment?

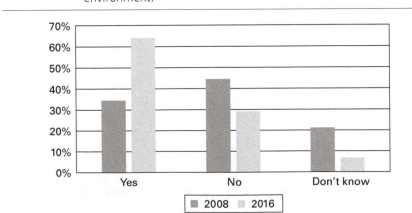

Environmental impact and suppliers

A set of questions within the survey examined how companies perceived and handled the issue of sustainability in the context of outsourcing. Given the ongoing trend of unbundling and outsourcing production and logistics, this is of growing importance to the industry. Although many operational and commercial aspects of doing business can be outsourced, the moral responsibility for societal and environmental impact should not be amongst them. In fact the vast majority of respondents agreed in this respect. Just under three-quarters stated that they saw it as their responsibility, with only 12 per cent disagreeing (Figure 4.9).

The degree of sustainability of suppliers' operations is very important to outsourcing companies, according to the results of the survey (Figure 4.10). Three-quarters of respondents stated that it was either 'very important' or 'reasonably important'. This is slightly at odds with the response to a previous question, where sustainability's role in winning or retaining business was downplayed as a benefit. Clearly it is expected by customers, although perhaps the advantage of a green or ethical approach is not as 'front of mind' as other benefits.

One of the ways in which companies can ensure that their outsourced suppliers comply with a set of environmental standards is through the selection process (Figure 4.11). According to the survey, 68 per cent of respondents stated that they had made environmental compliance part of the tendering procedure.

Figure 4.9 Do you consider the impact which your suppliers have on the environment and societies to be your responsibility?

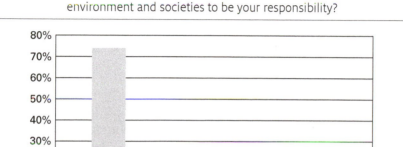

Figure 4.10   When awarding a contract, how important is the environmental compliance of your suppliers?

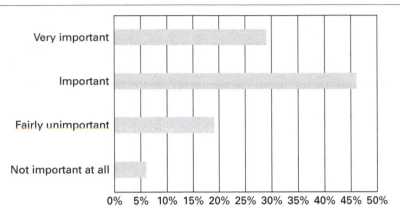

Figure 4.11   Do you make environmental compliance part of your tender documents when contracting out or buying services?

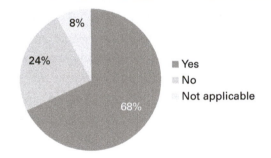

Figure 4.12   Do you consequently make provision for extra costs?

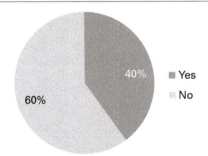

When it came to whether the outsourcing company was prepared to pay for the sustainable compliance it was insisting upon, there was a positive response (Figure 4.12). The majority (60 per cent) of respondents replied that they expected the supplier to pay – perhaps not as large a proportion as might have been expected. However, it does show that economic owners are pushing costs onto their suppliers and these costs must be absorbed.

The importance of sustainability to business activities

The next part of the survey looked at how important sustainability is to operational efficiency. As Figure 4.13 shows, it is seen as a significant driver to adopting more efficient processes within a business: 75 per cent of managers surveyed believed that it was either 'reasonably important' or 'very important'. This compared with 74 per cent in 2008, a similar proportion.

In terms of the implementation of a sustainable warehousing strategy, there seems to be little consensus. Managers were asked to select an option that best fitted their views, as shown in Figure 4.14.

In 2016, as in 2008, the most frequently chosen option was, 'I am happy to pay more in an initial investment if running costs are lower,' although the gap had narrowed considerably with the second most frequent selection, 'The "green" alternative must cost no more than a traditional warehouse.' Significantly the greatest increase from 2008 was the choice of, 'I am happy to pay more to gain environmental benefits.' The proportion of those willing to pay more for green benefits rose by 12 percentage points from 16 to 28 per cent. It is

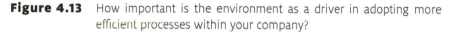

Figure 4.13 How important is the environment as a driver in adopting more efficient processes within your company?

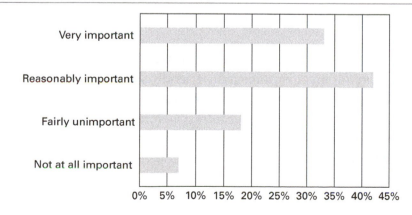

Figure 4.14 If you were to select a more environmentally friendly distribution centre over a traditional alternative, which of the below most closely matches your views?

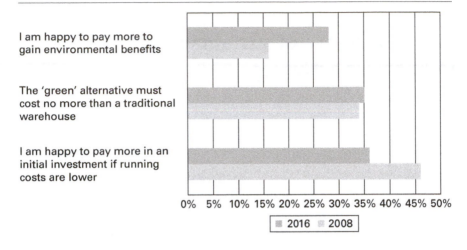

noticeable that the proportion of those who felt that green warehousing should cost the same as traditional warehousing stayed at about the same level between 2008 and 2016.

Future commitment to the environment

Just how committed would supply chain and logistics managers be to the environment if there were another economic downturn? There has always been the suspicion that sustainability as an issue drops down the corporate priority list when making profits gets harder. Managers were asked whether their attitudes would change in the event of another recession; the results are shown in Figure 4.15.

About a quarter of respondents indicated they would be willing to pay more for an environmentally-friendly alternative, slightly less than the proportion who said that, in such a scenario, they would look for the cheapest services or infrastructure. However, the majority chose a third option, which stated that they believed investment in environmental initiatives would bring operational efficiencies and lower costs.

Figure 4.15 In the event of an economic slowdown, would you continue to invest in or pay more for more environmentally-friendly services or infrastructure?

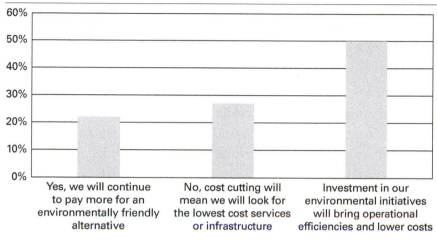

Summary

The results of the 2016 survey and comparison with the 2008 results convey a positive view of the response of the logistics and supply chain sector to the social and environmental challenges it faces. Undoubtedly progress has been made in many areas. For instance, the number of companies measuring their impact on the environment has grown significantly over the period; managers would be happy to pay more for environmentally-friendly warehousing; the vast majority think that their suppliers' practices are also their responsibility; and that overall they think their company has effective sustainability policies in place.

It is also encouraging, in some respects, that companies see the potential benefits of sustainability in terms of brand image and profitability. This shows that many are buying into the concept of triple advantage outlined in Chapter 1. However, the survey also suggests that the main reasons for adopting sustainable policies are still government regulation and pressure from customers rather than from internal, commercially-led initiatives. It is also of concern that the 'headline' importance of the environment to companies' overall strategies (Figure 4.1) has diminished over the years. This may be due to the difficult economic climate and the operational challenges many in the industry face.

Key points

- The perceived importance of the environment as a business issue has lessened slightly for logistics and supply chain managers over the past eight years, although the number of companies that have participated in sustainable initiatives without direct benefit has increased.

- The main reasons for introducing sustainable policies were compliance with government regulations and customer requirements rather than to protect the environment per se.

- Attracting and retaining employees were the least important reasons.

- The majority of respondents agreed that the behaviour of their suppliers was ultimately their responsibility and that environmental compliance when awarding a contract was important.

- A majority of respondents (61 per cent) thought that their environmental policies were 'moderately effective'.

- In the event of another economic slowdown, most logistics and supply chain managers would continue to invest in green initiatives due to the operational cost savings they are expected to bring.

References

McKinnon, A C, Browne, M and Whiteing, A (2012) *Green Logistics: Improving the environmental sustainability of logistics,* Kogan Page, London

Ti (2016) Sustainable supply chains, Transport Intelligence, www.ti-insight.com

PART II
Public Policy and Industry Response

Government policy and industry response to climate change

05

THIS CHAPTER WILL FAMILIARIZE THE READER WITH

- The reasons why governments have targeted the transport and logistics industry with environmental legislation
- The latest intergovernmental targets agreed at the COP21 summit in Paris and how these will be met by business
- The European Union's strategy for reducing carbon emissions and other pollutants
- How the transport industry impacts on the environment
- Responses to the issue by the road, sea, air and rail sectors

Although modern supply chain management concepts have been fundamental to economic development, they have also been criticized due to fears about their impact on the environment. In particular the green lobby has highlighted 'just-in-time' (JIT) deliveries not least because they have led to the more frequent movement of less efficient vehicles.

It is well established in supply chain theory that the extra cost created by the greater number of delivery journeys and the use of smaller, less efficient vehicles is more than offset by the reduced costs in inventory holding. However, critics believe that this trade-off only works as external costs to the environment are not fully passed on to the consumer. These include the social costs of higher levels of pollution and noise as well as the environmental costs of greenhouse gas emissions. Consequently, governments throughout the world have seen it as their role to regulate the market and levy taxes on companies in order to cost some of the externalities back into the supply chain. For example, the fuel duty escalator was used in the United Kingdom to artificially inflate the price of petrol and diesel with the avowed intent of reducing the number of vehicle-miles. As well as penalizing users of road freight, governments and regulators have also sought to promote less-polluting modes of transport such as rail, which was also placed at a disadvantage by the flexibility and reliability required by JIT.

IKEA, one of Europe's largest shippers and a major user of rail services, estimates that transporting goods by rail reduces carbon dioxide emissions by 70 per cent compared to transporting the same amount of goods by road. In addition particle emissions are less than half and the level of hydrocarbon emissions is less than 20 per cent of that for road transport. However IKEA's distribution system is very much the exception to the industry and its ability to regard rail as a credible alternative to road is helped by its relatively unique distribution needs and management ethos.

Pressure on governments to act more decisively has increased over recent years, not least because the issue of climate change has become more urgent. This chapter sets out the reasons why the transport and logistics industry has become a target for government action and the extent of the problem.

COP21 intergovernmental summit

The 21st Session of the Conference of Parties (COP21) took place in Paris in December 2015 with the aim of agreeing a new set of environmental targets. It was a high level meeting of government ministers from almost 200 countries and was largely regarded as the successor to the Kyoto Protocol. The latter 1997 agreement set emissions targets for a number of developed countries but was largely regarded as a failure when the United States pulled out and others failed to comply. COP21, in contrast, managed to achieve agreement between all the countries involved. It established targets to limit the growth in global temperatures to below 2 degrees above pre-industrial levels and 'endeavour' to limit them to just 1.5 degrees.

There was also agreement to attempt to limit greenhouse gas emissions to levels that can be absorbed by trees, soils and oceans by 2050–2100. Developed countries would provide financial support to poorer ones for them to adapt to climate change and ensure that they developed their economies in sustainable ways. The deal sets the level of support at $100 billion a year by 2020 with increases by 2025. One of the criticisms made by climate change activists was that only elements of the deal are legally binding. There will be an assessment of progress in 2018 followed by five yearly reviews. With only voluntary caps on emissions it remains to be seen how successful the agreement is in practice.

Every country was invited to submit its own plan setting out how it intended to cut emissions. The United Kingdom's submission is contained in the 'UK's Sixth National Communication and First Biennial Report under the United Nations Framework Convention on Climate Change', published by the Department of Energy and Climate Change in December 2013 (DECC, 2013). Officially it is described as, 'published under Article 12 of the United Nations Framework Convention on Climate Change (UNFCCC), under Article 7 of the Kyoto Protocol and under decision 2/CP.17 of the Conference of the Parties under the UNFCCC'. Within the report the UK Government highlights the transport policies and measures it has already taken:

- LGV policies (EU new LGV CO_2 emissions targets: 175g CO_2/km by 2017 and 147g CO_2/km by 2020; and complementary measures):
  - mandatory CO_2 emissions targets have been implemented for new passenger cars and new light commercial vehicles registered in the EU; these are driving innovation from vehicle manufacturers and their suppliers
  - negotiated using a mixture of voluntary agreements and regulatory measures on an EU basis.

- HGV policies (low rolling resistance tyres and industry-led action to improve efficiencies):

  - EC Regulation 661/2009 sets minimum requirements and introduces labelling for the rolling resistance, wet grip and external rolling noise of tyres for both light and heavy goods vehicles.

There have been other industry initiatives such as:

- The Freight Transport Association's Logistics Carbon Reduction scheme, a voluntary scheme to record and report reductions in CO_2.
- A Low Carbon Truck and Infrastructure trial to encourage the use of alternative fuels.
- The development of low carbon technologies.
- Encouragement of modal shift from road to lower carbon alternatives negotiated using a mixture of voluntary agreements and regulatory measures.
- Biofuels policy (8 per cent by 2020).

The European Commission's Renewable Energy Directive (2009/28/EC) (RED) requires the United Kingdom to source 15 per cent of its overall energy, and 10 per cent of energy used in transport, from renewable sources by 2020. The related Fuel Quality Directive (FQD) requires fuel and energy suppliers (principally those providing fuel and energy for land-based transport) to reduce the lifecycle GHG emissions per unit energy (GHG intensity) of the fuel/energy they supply by 6 per cent by 2020. The RED and FQD have both been transposed into UK law (2011 and 2013 respectively) (see Chapter 3 for more on alternative fuels). According to the Government, their key initiatives are:

- improving the fuel efficiency of vehicles;
- reducing CO_2 tailpipe emissions of road vehicles;
- reducing the fossil fuels content of road transport fuels;
- encouraging behaviour change.

Looking at projections to 2030, the Government believes that GHG emissions will reduce significantly despite an increase in transport output. The reason for this is the increased efficiency of vehicles and engines, as well as the increased use of alternative fuels. Domestic transport emissions (including passenger vehicles) are expected to drop by 12 per cent in 2030. Shipping and aviation are not included in these calculations due to their international nature and the difficulty of attributing them to any one nation. The United Kingdom's contribution to aviation GHG emissions is expected to fall in any case due to the capacity constraints on its airport network. Even though the UK Government has now made a decision to expand Heathrow it will be many years before the additional runway is built (if ever).

Following COP21 a number of major businesses came together to contribute towards meeting what is termed the 'business-determined contribution' (BDC). To meet targets, global GHG emissions would have to be limited to 42 billion metric tonnes in 2030. It has been estimated that on current trends, emissions would actually be 61 billion tonnes by that date, leaving a large excess that will have to be addressed if targets are to be met. Governments have committed to contributing 6 billion tonnes towards this required reduction, but business will have to provide the majority. Given existing commitments, businesses are already expected to reduce output by 4.2 billion but further reductions will be required.

EU environmental policy

Governments around the world take a keen interest in transport due to the level of emissions this sector is responsible for. In the EU, the transport sector is only second to the energy sector, emitting 24.3 per cent of GHGs compared to energy's 29.2 per cent. As can be seen from Figure 5.1, road transport is the dominant sub-sector, accounting for 72 per cent of emissions, dwarfing those emanating from sea and air.

Figure 5.1   GHG emissions by mode and sector

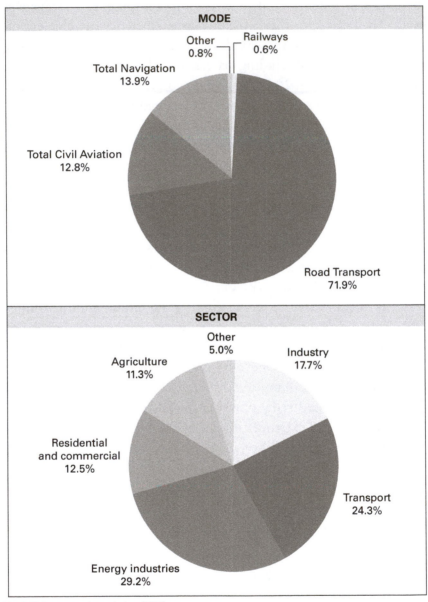

SOURCE European Commission (2012)

Over the years, the EU has put in place a range of policies to reduce emissions from the sector:

- Aviation has been included in the EU Emissions Trading System (ETS) (see below).

- A strategy has been developed to reduce emissions from cars and vans, including emissions targets for new vehicles.

- A strategy has been implemented for reducing heavy duty vehicle fuel consumption and CO_2 emissions.

- A target to reduce the greenhouse gas intensity of fuels is in place.

- Rolling resistance limits and tyre labelling requirements have been introduced and tyre pressure monitors made mandatory on new vehicles.

- Public authorities are required to take account of lifetime energy use and CO_2 emissions when procuring vehicles.

At a strategic level, the European Commission has published its ideas for the future of transport, entitled, 'Roadmap to a Single European Transport Area – Towards a competitive and resource efficient transport system'. The report's core principles are to, 'break the transport system's dependence on oil without sacrificing its efficiency and compromising mobility'. This has led the EC to suggest that:

> new transport patterns must emerge, according to which larger volumes of freight and greater numbers of travellers are carried jointly to their destination by the most efficient (combination of) modes. Individual transport is preferably used for the final miles of the journey and performed with clean vehicles. (EC, 2011)

In other words the EU thinks both freight and passenger traffic should largely be based on rail and sea transport, with road only used for local journeys. This would require an increase in the level of multimodal traffic. As the report says, for trips of more than 300km, 'multimodality has to become economically attractive for shippers. The EU needs specially developed freight corridors optimized in terms of energy use'.

As well as earlier initiatives foreseen in a 2001 White Paper, such as boosting rail and maritime connections for long distance freight transport, the EC believes that additional instruments will be needed to achieve these objectives. They include:

- a freight logistics action plan;

- intelligent transport systems to make mobility 'greener' and more efficient;

- an action plan to boost inland waterways;
- an ambitious programme for green power in trucks.

The transport policy outlined in the review builds upon the 2001 White Paper. It includes actions to create a competitive European railway network through liberalization, technological innovation and interoperability of equipment and investment in infrastructure.

One key change of tone in its latest policy document is that the Commission has recognized that road freight is essential to the working of any modern economy; it has moderated its opposition to trucks on environmental grounds. Nevertheless it states that it intends to create 'Green Corridors' that are 'co-modal'. The Commission also restated its wish to create 'Motorways of the Sea', which it hopes will play an important role in restructuring long-distance freight transport in Europe and improving its sustainability.

The EC favours rail and wants to create a European freight network that will provide a better quality of service in terms of journey times, reliability and capacity. However, it does not control significant transport budgets, which remain firmly in the hands of the national governments. In a key state such as France the national rail freight organization (Fret SNCF) is in crisis and losing market share rapidly, while in the United Kingdom passenger volumes are increasing so fast that rail freight will have difficulty challenging for future capacities. Complex multi-country dynamics will make a pan-European approach difficult to implement.

US environmental policy

Europe is not the only region to be concerned with the impact of road freight on the environment. A whole raft of legislation exists in the United States that regulates the emission of GHGs and other pollutants, especially those that have an impact on health. The industry is regulated by the Environmental Protection Agency (EPA) whose job it is to enforce federal law as well as provide the latest research on environmental risks.

In the United States, trucks have already reduced fuel consumption by 50 per cent since the 1970s. In 2004, the EPA launched SmartWay, a public-private programme designed to help the transportation industry become more efficient and reduce emissions. It involves large and small trucking companies, rail carriers, logistics companies, commercial manufacturers, retailers and other federal and state agencies. Specifically, SmartWay Transport programmes claim to lower emissions of carbon dioxide (CO_2), nitrogen oxides, and particulate matter (PM). Since 2004, SmartWay Partners report:

- saving 144.3 million barrels of fuel;
- $20.6 billion in fuel costs saved;
- eliminating 61.7 million metric tons of CO_2;
- eliminating 1,070,000 tons of nitrogen oxides;
- eliminating 43,000 tons of PM.

Tighter regulations had been proposed by the Obama administration to limit CO_2 emissions even further, and if they had come into effect this would have inevitably had a major impact on the US trucking sector. Larger trucks would have been obliged to improve their fuel efficiency by up to 40 per cent, with the largest vehicles increasing their miles per gallon from 5 or 6 in 2015 to 9 mpg in 2017. However, given the new Trump administration's attitude to climate change, these new regulations must be in doubt.

Logistics' impact on the environment

The transport industry contributes to global warming as a result of greenhouse gas emissions such as carbon dioxide and nitrogen oxides released during the combustion of fossil fuels. These gases provide additional layers in the earth's atmosphere, gradually allowing less and less radiation through, and subsequently heating up the earth. This is what many believe has led to a noticeable change in climate patterns.

CO_2 is the most important greenhouse gas due to the high levels released around the globe and the length of time it resides in the atmosphere. Nitrogen oxides produce ozone but reduce the concentration of methane within the atmosphere. Ozone increases dominate the effects on methane and lead to more gases in the atmosphere. Nitrogen oxides mainly contribute to over-fertilization of the subsoil and groundwater (eutrophication). In addition, nitrogen oxide emissions are partly responsible for ground-level ozone and thus for summer smog.

Water vapour's effect on global warming is contested; when released from aircraft engines it forms 'contrails' which are thought to warm the earth's surface and contribute to the formation of cirrus clouds, which may have warming effects. However, this impact is scientifically uncertain and many scientists think the opposite. 'Contrails' can actually block the sun's rays, and when aircraft movements are reduced or cease (such as in the immediate aftermath of the 9/11 terrorist activity) ground temperature was believed to rise. Both sets of views are very speculative.

Hydrocarbons are classified as methane and non-methane hydrocarbons. Methane is a greenhouse gas, but is only of very minor importance in the transport sector. Non-methane hydrocarbons and nitrogen oxides together contribute to the formation of ground-level ozone, and are thus a cause of summer smog.

Total dust/soot particulates are a severe health hazard. Soot particulates, which are produced by diesel combustion, are now regarded as a cancer risk. They represent the major component of the total dust emissions from diesel vehicles. In the case of electrically-powered vehicles, on the other hand, dust emissions are produced during power generation and distribution. While most dust emissions are dissipated into the atmosphere at great height (eg power plant stacks), the distance travelled by airborne diesel soot particulates from their source of emission to the human who inhales them is much shorter.

Sulphur dioxide is the main cause of forest dieback and the acidification of subsoil and groundwater. Sulphur dioxide can also lead to respiratory diseases.

Summary of environmental impacts

Carbon dioxide emissions:	Greenhouse gas – climate change
Nitrogen oxide emissions:	Eutrophication, summer smog, eco-toxicity, human toxicity
Non-methane hydrocarbons:	Human toxicity, summer smog
Dust emissions:	Human toxicity, summer smog
Particulate soot emissions:	Human toxicity, summer smog
Sulphur dioxide emissions:	Acidification, eco-toxicity, human toxicity

Transport factors impacting the environment

There are many factors that determine the level of environmental impact of freight transport, the key one being the choice of transport mode: truck, rail, inland waterways, ship or aircraft. Even within the individual transport systems, there are considerable differences due to the vehicle technology, the capacity of the transport as well as other factors. For example, in the case of a truck, the key influencing factors will be the vehicle size (and thus the maximum permissible load), the capacity utilization level and the technical standards for the reduction of exhaust emissions (Euro standards).

Traction

With rail transport, the type of traction utilized determines environmental impact levels. With electric traction, environmental impacts are produced entirely at the power station whereas the largest percentage of emissions is produced with diesel traction during the actual transport of the goods, as is the case with trucks. In addition the trailing load of a freight train is yet another key factor influencing environmental impact levels (per transported unit of quantity).

Transport network

Each mode of transport is restricted to one specific transport network. However, the road network tends to be denser than a rail network or a network of inland waterways. As a result, shipments travelling by rail or water are in some cases forced to take a roundabout route, which increases the transport distances covered and thus the environmental impacts.

Vehicle capacity and utilization

Each mode of transport has a maximum loading capacity defined by the weight or the volume of the shipment. Whether the limiting factor is weight or volume depends on the type of cargo being shipped. In the case of dense goods such as coal or steel, a good level of vehicle capacity utilization is achieved on the basis of weight, so it is not unusual for the environmental impact per transported net ton for these types of goods to be lower than for lighter goods, such as household goods or clothes. In the case of the latter, although vehicles might be full in terms of volume, the full utilization capacity in terms of weight may not be achieved.

Pre-supply chain energy use

Energy consumption and emissions in freight transport not only occur during the actual shipment, but also at a much earlier stage in the processes leading up to the supply of transport services. In the case of electrically-powered rail transport vehicles, for example, the emissions are produced entirely in the pre-supply chain. To identify environmental impacts of a shipment and to make any comparison between different transport modes this energy pre-supply chain would need to be taken into account.

In some countries, Switzerland for example, the majority of the country's power production is based on hydro-electric generation, so electrically-powered rail transport services produce no emissions. In other countries, a large percentage of electric power is generated with coal or other fossil fuels.

Topography

In some countries, topography is also a factor in the environmental impact of transport. In road transport, significant differences in energy consumption and emissions can occur: for example, the steeper the gradients encountered on the roads, the greater the fuel consumption will be.

Road freight

While road transport emissions in Europe fell by 3.3 per cent in 2012 (EC, 2012), they are still 20.5 per cent higher than in 1990. The European Commission asserts that transport is the only major sector in the EU where greenhouse gas emissions are still rising. However despite the headline figures, trucks and buses are responsible for only about a quarter of CO_2 emissions from road transport in the EU and for some 6 per cent of total EU emissions. Most come from cars and light vans, responsible for 15 per cent of overall emissions. The four main environmentally damaging chemicals to be released from diesel engines are carbon monoxide, nitrogen oxides, hydrocarbons and particulates.

There has been ongoing legislation related to van and lorry engine specifications that has impacted on emission levels. According to the European Environment Agency, new cars and vans registered in Europe in 2014 were on average 2.5 per cent more efficient than in 2013. A new van sold in 2014 emitted on average 169.1 grams of CO_2 per kilometre, already below an EC 2017 target of 175 grams. Manufacturers still have to reduce emissions further to meet the target of 147g CO_2/km by 2020 for vans.

Efforts to reduce pollutants from the engines of diesel vehicles have been orchestrated by the European Commission through a number of regulations, the most recent being Euro 5 and 6 standards. The latest standard, Euro 6, came into force in 2014 and prevents the sale of new vehicles that do not conform to its provisions. Regulations are particularly aimed at reducing the levels of nitrogen oxides and particulates. Vehicle manufacturers started to introduce new engines that conformed to Euro 6 from 2012 and claim that performance is similar to earlier engine types. However, they are more expensive, which has added an extra burden to road freight operators.

To give an idea of how vehicle emissions have improved over the years, a Euro 0 engine of 1991 origin had the same level of emissions as 34 Euro 4 equivalents. However, although the 'Euro' initiatives have improved air quality – a health priority – the same cannot be said for carbon emissions. The European Commission aims to reduce CO_2 emissions to around 60 per cent of its 1990 level by 2050 and in 2014 it published a White Paper looking at how this could be achieved.

About 25 per cent of road transport emissions result from what the EC terms Heavy Duty Vehicles (HDVs) and these levels have increased in line with economic activity. CO_2 emissions grew by about 36 per cent between 1990 and 2010, surprising given the progress made in air quality. The EC believes that CO_2 emissions will be about 35 per cent greater than 1990 levels in both 2030 and 2050, helped by improved fuel efficiency of HGVs. However this is far in excess of its published goal. The EC believes further improvements can be made through:

- technical improvements to engines and transmissions;
- improved aerodynamics;
- tyres; and
- lighter construction materials.

On its own, improved aerodynamics on long-haul tractor-trailer vehicles can reduce annual fuel consumption by 6,000 to 7,000 litres, which leads to the elimination of 20 metric tonnes of CO_2. Aerodynamics can be improved by minimizing tractor-trailer gaps, adding side skirts and keeping tarpaulins tight. Improving driver techniques such as reducing idling time, smoother braking and acceleration and using optimal gearing can save 5 per cent of fuel. In addition, the EC believes that road freight operators have a role to play in reducing emissions through:

- improved fleet management;
- better driver training;
- better vehicle maintenance; and
- improved capacity management through technology solutions.

In the long term the Commission is working on developing intermodal networks as an alternative, or at least a complement, to existing road networks. It is also promoting the use of cleaner fuels to reduce GHG emissions, such as natural gas and biomethane. It has suggested increasing tax on the CO_2 element of fuels. Specifically, the Commission would like to see Member States adopt the following provisions:

- HGV truck driver tests to include eco-driving requirements.
- Road-user charging, which promotes the polluter- and user-pays principle.

- A carbon foot-printing initiative to provide more information on the CO_2 impact of freight transport.

- Increased levels of cabotage to make the road freight industry more efficient.

Restructuring road freight networks

According to a World Economic Forum report into supply decarbonization, significant steps can be taken to abate emissions through improvements in transport network efficiency (WEF, 2009). The report estimates that 24 per cent of goods vehicle/kms in the EU are running empty and when carrying a load, vehicles are typically only 57 per cent loaded as a percentage of maximum gross weight. The report also estimates that the total abatement potential across the sector globally could be 124 mega-tonnes of CO_2 per year. Of this, around 30 per cent may be due to the potential to improve economic transaction sizes in freight movements.

Shipping

The World Shipping Council claims that sea freight is the world's most carbon-efficient mode of transport, requiring 10g of CO_2 to carry 1 ton of cargo 1 kilometre. This compares with 21g for rail and 59g for road. Shipping accounts for just 2.1 per cent of the world's CO_2 emissions and liner shipping accounts for around a quarter of the total.

For example, a ton of freight shipped from the Port of Melbourne in Australia to the Port of Long Beach in California, a distance of 12,770 kilometres (7,935 miles), generates fewer CO_2 emissions than the same cargo moved by truck from Dallas to Long Beach, a distance of 2,307 kilometres (1,442 miles). Another way of looking at the comparison between modes is that an entire container voyage from China to Europe is equivalent in CO_2 emissions to about 200 kilometres of long-haul trucking in Europe. This means that, for most goods that can be delivered using slow-moving freight, there is no real green benefit to moving production to Europe.

However, in the past, the shipping industry gained a very bad reputation for polluting both the air and sea. Until regulations came into force in the 2000s, highly noxious heavy bunker fuels were used to power ships, resulting in high levels of emissions including sulphur oxides, nitrogen oxides, particulate matter and carbon dioxide. The pollution was worst on heavily congested sea lanes or in ports and, to reduce threats both to the environment and to human health, the International Maritime Organization (IMO) established a number of legally-binding international treaties. Some governments have wanted to impose tighter restrictions on shipping lines, establishing, for example, annual fuel consumption limits or operational energy efficiency standards. However, this has been actively opposed by many parties in the industry who believe that the wide range of commercial and operational conditions in which ships are required to operate would make such an arrangement impossible to administer.

Emission levels have been helped by the trend to much larger shipping vessels. Shipping Consultants, Drewry, asserted that average ship sizes have increased by 40 per cent in the five years up to 2013, resulting in a 35 per cent drop in round-voyage emissions on a per slot basis. As well as greater economies of scale, ships are also using less fuel in real terms. This is through a combination of 'slow steaming', more efficient engines and better ship design. Since 2007 Maersk says it has achieved a 25 per cent reduction in CO_2 emissions per container.

CO_2 emissions are not the only focus of shipping lines and governments. Sulphur emissions have seen particular policy emphasis. Europe and the United States have implemented regulations that limit emission levels and Hong Kong has introduced port rebates for cleaner shipping lines. This has been backed up by a threat to ban the use of high-sulphur fuels due to pollution problems in the port. Vessel design has seen progress in the recent past. Talks at the IMO brought about an Energy Efficiency Design Index (EEDI). In 2011, energy efficiency standards applicable to newly-built ships became legally enforceable.

Air pollution is just one issue facing the industry. Another is vessel discharges, such as ballast and bilge water, 'grey' and 'black' water (sewage). This can also include accidental spills of oil and fuel. There are international regulations that should in theory control these types of emissions and the World Shipping Council has created sets of guidelines for responsible practices.

A further environmental problem is the use of antifouling compounds on ships' hulls. These are important to prevent the build-up of barnacles and slime, thus indirectly reducing CO_2 emissions by minimizing resistance to movement through the water. However, they can contain biocides that are harmful to the marine environment. One such biocide, tributyltin, was banned in 2008 due to its impact on non-target species and its persistence.

Air cargo

Modern aircraft have high fuel efficiencies and manufacturers have made the most significant advances in fuel efficiency of any transport sector in order to drive down costs. Direct emissions from aviation account for about 3 per cent of the EU's total GHG emissions, which is equivalent to 13 per cent of emissions of the transportation sector (EC, 2012). The large majority of these emissions come from international flights. It is, of course, difficult to attribute which emissions relate to cargo and which to passengers, as in most cases cargo is carried on scheduled passenger flights; with or without cargo, each flight would have generated a certain amount of emissions.

By 2020, global international aviation emissions are projected to be around 70 per cent higher than they were in 2005 even if fuel efficiency improves by 2 per cent per year. The International Civil Aviation Organization (ICAO) forecasts that by 2050 they could grow by a further 300–700 per cent.

For optimum fuel efficiency, aircraft need to be light, have low drag, and fuel needs to have high energy content per unit volume/ weight. Some alternative fuels that are being considered include:

- synthetic liquid fuels – being manufactured in South Africa by SASOL;
- biojet fuel – a soya derivative;
- ethanol fuel – only useful for short haul flights;
- hydrogen – fuel cells are gradually being developed for aircraft.

Since 2012 emissions from all flights from, to and within the European Economic Area have been subject to the EU Emissions Trading System

(EU ETS), which the EU describes as the 'cornerstone' of its climate change policy. Airlines receive tradeable allowances covering a certain level of CO_2 emissions from their flights per year. The EU ETS works on the 'cap and trade' principle where a 'cap', or limit, is set on the total amount of GHGs that can be emitted by an organization. This limit is gradually reduced over time. An airline can buy 'emission allowances' or 'off-sets', which are generated by emission-saving projects around the world that allow it to go above its emissions cap. Exceeding its cap would attract large fines.

The theory behind what could be considered a well-meaning but bureaucratic and complex mechanism is that it gives value to each tonne of emissions and encourages airlines to take steps to become more energy efficient. The EU also believes that it creates a major driver of investment in clean technologies and low-carbon solutions, particularly in developing countries that generate the 'emission allowances'.

The ETS scheme was highly controversial and many non-EU airlines and governments threatened not to comply. This led to a watering down of the provisions, exempting international long-haul flights. China said the ETS rules would have cost its airlines $123 million in the scheme's first year. The system is still in its early days and it is difficult to identify how successful it is for the intra-European flights to which it still applies.

Rail and intermodal

Railways have the capacity to move large volumes of goods in one single journey, with significantly lower carbon emissions, and thus fuel costs, in comparison to movement by road. Consequently it has been part of many governments' environmental strategy to encourage a road to rail migration of volumes.

The European rail and intermodal sector has been re-energized over the past decade by a series of region-wide market reforms that have allowed access for private operators from a range of different backgrounds. A market that was previously dominated by state-owned incumbents has become increasingly competitive with shippers now offered services from shipping lines, freight forwarders, intermodal operators as well as the national rail giants.

As part of a long-standing plan to revitalize the rail industry in the European Union, in January 2007 all EU rail freight lines were opened up to competition. Up until then only international freight services, which represented approximately half of the total market for the rail transport of goods in Europe, were liberalized. The European Commission is hoping that rail freight will now attract new investors and customers by offering services that are more adapted to the needs of the market. The main hope is that the railways will steadily increase their market shares.

However, many rail freight customers still believe that there is a long way to go before the railways offer an acceptable service. National rail operations in Europe are perceived to be more expensive, less flexible and unreliable, with a distinct lack of customer focus which only the private sector will be able to provide.

As far back as 2004 the association of Europe's railway supply industry, UNIFE, called on the European Commission and Member States to increase their investment in rail 'as an essential part of a competitive and sustainable transport system for Europe' with the emphasis on sustainability and reflecting the green issues that were becoming more prevalent. One view, mainly held by the incumbent rail operators, is that attempts at liberalization have brought no new volumes and have split existing business between more operators, harming rail's ability to compete with road. They believe that as a result they are losing their dominant positions and liberalization has led to the destruction of the existing system of cooperation between all the European railway networks and companies. Such a view is undoubtedly based on self-interest, although that is not to say that the European rail structure that has been adopted is working particularly well.

In the United States the rail and intermodal sector has many advantages over its European counterpart. A true single market exists across the country, which allows the industry to take advantage of its competitive advantage over road – efficient and economic movement of containers or bulk goods over long distances. In the United States an intermodal train emits only 6.8 pounds of carbon emissions for every 100 ton miles, compared to a truck, which emits 19.8 pounds. The Association of American Railroads asserts that one ton of goods can be moved 479 miles on a single gallon of fuel. Freight rail fuel efficiency improved by over 100 per cent between 1980 and 2014, measured in terms of ton-miles per gallon.

CASE STUDY   WEGO Couriers and ICRF: connecting parcels with rail services

WEGO is a carbon-neutral courier service. It provides sustainable and cost-effective 'last mile' delivery solutions using zero emissions vehicles. WEGO has depots in Nottingham, Derby, Leicester, Sheffield and London and uses electric vehicles, load-carrying bicycles and high speed trains.

In 2011 WEGO Couriers entered into a partnership with InterCity RailFreight (ICRF) to facilitate deliveries by high speed train that are faster and greener than existing road-based couriers. It pioneered the reintroduction of sending parcel-sized freight consignments by passenger train, having developed the necessary operational, safety and security systems. This service links the Midlands to London 70 times a day, providing cost-effective and green same-day and premium overnight deliveries of time-sensitive consignments and e-commerce. It integrates with WEGO's zero carbon first/last mile courier services to transport items direct into the centre of London.

This operation is currently unique in the UK and its expansion is being championed at government and local authority levels as an effective means to reduce urban congestion and pollution. Consignments include ultra-time-critical tissue samples destined for testing laboratories, and fresh seafood for London restaurants.

WEGO and ICRF have proved that using passenger trains can work; the partnership provides a practical and viable low-carbon alternative to trucks and vans travelling into city centres. At the same time, it has also demonstrated that the service provides an effective route to market for regional SMEs. An example of this is its Cornish services, which it operates in conjunction with Great Western Railway.

ICRF's planned high speed shared user freight trains are attracting significant interest from large retailers, e-tailers and carriers that have recognized the huge potential to overcome increasing city centre delivery restrictions and pollution controls; the new solution meets e-commerce challenges while satisfying increasingly stringent environmental targets. This development will enable the partnership to further plan the 'first and last mile' not only to deliver better resource utilization, but also to fully utilize zero carbon transport, such as the WEGO cycle logistics and electric vehicles. The joint aim is to expand into other UK cities to provide a viable alternative to standardized delivery methods.

Summary

Governments around the world have renewed their commitment to increasing the sustainability of their economies with a range of new targets that they hope will limit global warming and lessen the impact of climate change. At the same time, they recognize that this cannot come at the expense of economic development and new ways of thinking will be required to solve this problem. Many initiatives have been implemented in the road, sea, air and rail sectors to lessen environmental impact, some of which have been government led. Others have come from within industry, a by-product of companies seeking to make their own operations more efficient and increase their overall competitiveness.

Key points

- The Paris intergovernmental summit, COP21, held in 2015, managed to achieve agreement to establish targets to limit the growth in global temperatures.

- Increased levels of efficiency created by technological innovation in the transport sector will help governments reach these targets.

- The road freight industry has high potential to increase its efficiency – the World Economic Forum estimates that 24 per cent of goods vehicle/kms in the EU are running empty. Technology developments will help.

- Despite the environmental benefits of using rail, many shippers still prefer the flexibility and speed of road. Liberalization of the European rail market has helped but it still faces many challenges.

- The shipping industry has become much less carbon-intensive due to the introduction of larger vessels; however, it still has a bad reputation for other forms of pollution.

- The airline industry in Europe has become more regulated through the EU Emissions Trading System. It is still too early to identify how successful the scheme has been in reducing carbon emissions.

References

DECC (2013) *UK's Sixth National Communication and First Biennial Report under the United Nations Framework Convention on Climate Change,* Department of Energy and Climate Change, London

EC (2011) *Roadmap to a Single European Transport Area: Towards a competitive and resource efficient transport system,* European Commission, Brussels

EC (2012) Reducing emissions from transport, European Commission, http://ec.europa.eu/clima/policies/transport/index_en.htm

WEF (2009) *Supply Chain Decarbonization: The role of logistics and transport in reducing supply chain carbon emissions,* World Economic Forum/Accenture, Geneva

Implementing a CSR strategy

THIS CHAPTER WILL FAMILIARIZE THE READER WITH

- The role Corporate and Social Responsibility departments have in implementing a sustainable business strategy
- A multi-level approach that brings together management and strategy, employees and workplace as well as impact on the environment and communities
- Environmental Management Systems and how they can be implemented
- Ethical investors and the role they play in influencing many supply chain strategies
- Integrating sustainable standards within the contract tendering process
- The activities many logistics operators undertake in humanitarian logistics

The business case behind CSR

For many of the world's largest logistics companies, the requirement to develop sustainable businesses in terms of environmental and societal impact is now a fact of life. Managers and employees are, after all, human beings and the value sets most people adhere to in everyday life are not somehow suspended when they start running or working for a company. Business is a sub-set of society and consequently the values of the society in which companies operate are reflected in the goals and aspirations of businesses as well as the people who work for them.

This may be a rather philosophical point but most businesses do not need restraining from a range of unethical or environmentally deleterious practices by government regulation. At the very least Google's motto of 'Do the right thing' would seem to be a reasonable starting point. Indeed, as Mariam Al-Futery, Communications and CSR Director of the logistics company, Agility, commented in a presentation at Transport Intelligence's 2014 Conference in Singapore, 'Who doesn't want to do good things?' This seems to be a far more positive foundation on which to build a responsible business and stems from a confidence in the goodness of human nature.

As discussed at length in the first chapter, acting responsibly is good for business as it not only protects companies' reputations but also motivates employees, builds strong relationships with customers, not to mention in many cases delivering lower costs and in some cases creating additional revenue. In some locations, such as in developing countries, it can deliver a competitive advantage as a way of differentiating global from local businesses. This is not to say that implementing a sustainable business model is not challenging. Issues which those in charge of CSR policies face include:

- fear within management of adding cost;
- a divergent management focus;
- lack of prioritization;
- complexity;
- operational challenges.

Agility highlights three main lessons it has drawn from its experiences:

1 Aim higher than the law when it comes to fair labour. This is especially the case in developing markets where there is little employee protection provided by the government. Failing to be a responsible employer can lead to a major reputational disaster not least to the global nature of media and lobby groups should shortcomings be identified.

2 Add environmental impact to time and cost considerations in supply chain planning. This includes introducing new initiatives such as consolidating goods-in-transit and repacking to reduce packaging weight, number of pallets and dead space on vehicles, ships or planes.

3 Collaborate on social investments to increase scale of contributions. This includes humanitarian logistics (see below).

CSR policies and practice

Environmental and societal impacts have become a major issue for all companies involved in the supply chain and logistics industry for many reasons, including:

- pressure from governments (such as targets to reduce carbon footprints);
- pressure from customers through the tendering process;
- 'green and gold' efficiency savings; and
- well-meaning intentions.

The survey in Chapter 4 provides an insight into these pressures and their relative importance as perceived by supply chain managers.

As a result of these imperatives, businesses have embraced a host of green initiatives. In some instances these have been driven by specific regulation, although companies increasingly understand the need to act voluntarily to stave off more draconian action by legislators. The responsibility for such green initiatives, and environmental policy as a whole, often resides with a CSR department. As will be discussed later in this chapter, this is not necessarily wholly positive if it results in sustainability becoming 'siloed'. However, if the ethos of sustainability is adopted throughout the company, with the CSR department acting as a facilitator, the result can be a positive engagement with a wide range of stakeholders including communities, customers, employees, investors, government, suppliers and the media.

The relationships forged with each one of these constituents should be regarded as two-way. Inevitably companies must be influenced by the value sets of their stakeholders, but they also have the opportunity to positively influence the behaviour of those stakeholders. For example, commercially customers are able to insist on their suppliers acting in a sustainable way. Likewise, employers can encourage their staff into healthier lifestyles (by providing cycle-to-work schemes, for instance). Communicating with stakeholders has become essential to the sustainability process and an important part of the CSR department's role. It enables the company to:

- Demonstrate to investors that business risks are being mitigated.
- Show governments that rules are being complied with.
- Build trust with communities, neighbours and, if applicable, NGOs.
- Motivate employees by increasing their involvement and 'buy-in' to green agendas.
- Win and/or retain business and ensure customer loyalty.
- Inform the wider community of its achievements through the media, enabling it to retain control of its key messages.

For large companies, corporate responsibility is a complex subject. The concept can embrace a wide variety of issues and communicating progress to stakeholders is clearly important. Companies invest a lot of time and money in drawing together all their initiatives into a coherent communications strategy. The constituent parts of a coherent CSR strategy, such as that employed by global logistics company DHL, fall into the following four categories.

1 *Management and business ethos*

- Procurement and supplier management
- Compliance
- Code of conduct
- Resilience

At a corporate level, all businesses have to comply with government regulations on the way in which they engage, inter alia, with the environment, their suppliers, their employees and the communities in which they are embedded. In addition to a layer of regulatory requirements, companies often aim to achieve best practice and abide with codes of conduct/guidelines they feel are in their long-term interests.

Multinational companies have to face the challenge of developing a consistent, corporate-wide ethos of high quality behaviour and performance. This must take into account stakeholder expectations as well as, where necessary and feasible, adapting business models. Part of establishing high standards of behaviour is a commitment to global agreements such as the UN Global Compact, including anti-corruption measures, and the UN Global Goals for Sustainable Development.

Ensuring that suppliers meet the same standards of behaviour as the contracting company is increasingly important given the high levels of outsourcing in the logistics and supply chain industry. Whether suppliers are contract manufacturers based remotely in Asia, or whether they are sub-contracted owner-driver couriers working in Europe, there is an obligation for them to adhere to the same levels of performance as their customer's own employees. Likewise (although this is not emphasized in many company's CSR communications), the contracting company has a moral obligation to uphold its own standards of behaviour in its dealing with a sub-contracted company.

Developing resilient organizational and operational structures within the company and identifying supply chain and logistics risks that threaten the business is critical in an increasingly unstable world. Environmental and humanitarian disasters have become a part of doing business on a global level and those companies that are able to respond to these threats with the greatest agility are those that will out-perform their competitors. Having a 'play book' that can be rolled out in response to a supply chain threat is an important part of a resilience strategy.

2 Employees and workplace

- Workforce structure
- Remuneration

- Diversity
- Employee relations
- Occupational health and safety

Although societal and environmental considerations fit easily under the umbrella of CSR initiatives, many companies may consider internal issues, such as human resources, remuneration and employee relations as a separate matter. In particular many would consider that staff remuneration is not a 'corporate responsibility' in the sense that pay levels are largely driven by the market rather than by a corporate desire to improve standards of living in an economy.

However, this is not a view held by all companies. DHL, for example, asserts that it views diversity and the role of women in the workplace as important parts of its CSR policy (DHL, 2015). In its CSR report, it states:

> We see great strength in the diversity of our workforce and the potential in each and every one of our employees. Ours is a working environment that opposes any form of discrimination. The objective of our diversity management is to increase diversity awareness at all levels of the company and to reinforce employee commitment to conduct based on respect and a sense of personal responsibility.

DHL established a 'Diversity Council' in 2014 which convenes twice a year to discuss issues such as regional labour market trends and women in management.

It is possible to measure companies' progress towards goals that have been set in this category through a number of KPIs. Companies are able to:

- Undertake employee opinion surveys to track engagement and motivation.
- Measure the number of accidents to ascertain the effectiveness of training in occupational health and safety.
- Measure the number of sick days taken and employee turnover to gain an insight into staff morale.
- Measure the number of women employed to ensure appropriate representation in the workforce and management.

3 Society and engagement

- Volunteering
- Refugee aid
- Disaster relief
- Educational opportunities

Employee volunteering is an important part of many logistics and supply chain organizations' CSR policies. It is a very clear example of the mutual benefits social engagement can bring about. Volunteers can use the skills and experiences they have developed in their career for initiatives or projects in their local communities or to support colleagues' communities in other parts of the world, including disaster relief efforts.

The volunteers themselves benefit from a life-enhancing experience that allows them to put something back into communities as well as gaining an understanding of different social, cultural or ethnic groups. Projects that involve cleaning up the local environment or planting trees are very popular.

From the company's perspective, the employee gains experience and maturity as well as potentially a new set of skills that can be leveraged in the business. It also acts as a way of motivating staff, enhancing employee retention and gaining loyalty.

CASE STUDY   Volunteering for Transaid

Transaid is a UK-based international development organization that works to improve the health and life-chances of communities in Africa by leveraging expertise and experience of the transport and logistics industry. This includes driver training to reduce the number of accidents on Africa's roads, but also involves managing projects that help with the delivery of healthcare and medicines as well as with the minimization of post-harvest food losses.

Transaid works with partner companies in the United Kingdom to facilitate volunteer programmes in support of its initiatives. An example of this is a project in 2016 which involved the secondment of a United Kingdom operations manager from Yusen Logistics to the Industrial Training Centre (ITC) in Zambia, supporting the centre in its aim of reducing the traffic fatalities in sub-Saharan Africa through professional HGV, PSV and forklift truck training. The specific role undertaken by the volunteer involves helping the ITC:

- to standardize training materials;
- to identify areas of improvement in the teaching, scheduling and planning of training activities;
- in processing the project's data.

A further volunteering project involved the secondment of a Field Training Manager to the National Institute of Training (NIT) in Tanzania to implement a comprehensive education programme to raise the teaching standards of forklift truck driving instructors. The work, which forms part of Transaid's Professional Driver Training Project, included teaching a group of 11 forklift instructors how to safely demonstrate machines to their students, as well as how to put together comprehensive lesson plans.

In 2012, Pullman Fleet Services sent two mechanics to Zambia to deliver technical training on trucks, including delivering advanced diagnostics training on Transaid's trucks to eight motor vehicle lecturers at Zambia's Industrial Training Centre in the nation's capital, Lusaka. More people than ever are dying on Zambia's roads, with 1,400 fatalities in 2010. In July 2012, a high-profile truck crash killed 11 people in the country, prompting the editorial board of the *Times of Zambia* to call for better awareness of road safety throughout the country. At the same time the Road Traffic Safety agency has collected evidence suggesting the situation can be measurably improved by training efforts such as the one undertaken by Pullman Fleet Services on behalf of Transaid.

4 Environment

- Measuring emissions
- Technology innovation
- Routes and network efficiency
- Energy management

Companies in the supply chain and logistics industry recognize that the very nature of their business has a negative impact on the environment in terms of pollution, greenhouse gas emissions, noise and congestion. In addition, transport and warehouse companies have a high media and public profile, which makes them an easy target for criticism. Therefore a coherent environmental policy, including communication, is essential to demonstrate that they are taking steps to reduce their impact. Of course, it is also important to ensure that business can be seen to be acting voluntarily, which will limit scope for politicians to impose more burdensome (and potentially unnecessary) regulations.

Setting quantifiable targets is key to stimulating action and measuring success. For example, DHL has set a target to reduce its greenhouse gas emissions for every letter, parcel, tonne of freight and square metre of warehouse space by 30 per cent by 2020. This target applies to its sub-contractors as well. It claims to have already made a carbon efficiency improvement of 25 per cent compared to its baseline of 2007. It uses a Carbon Efficiency Index (CEX) as its main KPI, with emissions resulting from fuel and energy consumption being assessed in relation to transport and warehousing services provided. Greenhouse gas emissions are calculated using a methodology in accordance with EN16258, the European standard for the calculation of greenhouse gases in logistics.

As well as an internal focus on carbon reduction, many logistics companies offer their customers climate-neutral, carbon-reduced and environmentally-friendly products and services. They can also offer consultancy services that help meet environmental targets.

Other company policies can show the crossover between good business practice and good environmental management. For example, innovation, network efficiencies and the development of advanced technologies to minimize greenhouse gas emissions, energy consumption and noise, particularly from aircraft and vehicle fleets, have positive impacts on the bottom line.

CSR: whose responsibility?

One of the criticisms of establishing a department dedicated to corporate and social responsibility is that it can lead to responsibility for environmental and societal impacts being abrogated by other parts of the company. However, as companies that demonstrate best practice have shown, responsibility actually starts in the boardroom and should permeate the entire organization. A clear commitment by the chief executive can imbue the company with a clear vision that can then be executed by managers and employees alike.

Management should be clear about their individual responsibilities from a legal and ethical perspective:

- CEO – sets the targets, standards and vision for the company as a whole and ensures that progress is made in achieving the corporate goals.

- Company Secretary – understands the legal requirements and ensures they are complied with.

- Finance Director – ensures that investments in environmental initiatives not only provide a return on investment but also satisfy the needs of increasingly ethical investors.

- Logistics Director/Manager – ensures that operations are in line with environmental objectives and that a plan is in place to mitigate or deal with environmental incidents.

- HR Director/Manager – ensures that staff have sufficient training and are clearly motivated to meet environmental targets.

Employees themselves, of course, have a high degree of responsibility for their own actions. They are, in many cases, best placed to identify efficiency savings, spot environmental breaches or hazards and suggest improvements. As employees are also likely to be part of the local community they are an essential bridge between the business and local residents acting as ambassadors. However, the CSR department, headed up by a senior manager with a clear portfolio, is still an important asset. The manager and department become responsible for implementing, managing and measuring the impact of green or social initiatives, but only in conjunction with other functions and divisions.

Leading from the top: Paul Polman and Unilever

Paul Polman, CEO of Unilever, is an excellent example of a senior manager who has driven change within his organization and implemented a clear social and environmental strategy. As he says on his personal website:

> As CEO of Unilever, my personal mission is to galvanize our company to be an effective force for good. We have an ambitious vision around

decoupling growth from our environmental footprint and at the same time increasing positive social impact through our Unilever Sustainable Living Plan. We actively seek collaboration with other companies who share a common purpose in driving that systemic change.

In 2010, soon after he became CEO, he implemented the Sustainable Living Plan. It set out ambitious targets to double revenues while at the same time halving the impact of its products on the environment. As well as this there were targets to improve the nutritional quality of its products, develop its supply chain to integrate more smallholders, and source sustainable raw materials.

His bold agenda has differentiated his company from other competitors in the consumer manufacturing industry. In an interview in *The Guardian* he claimed:

I don't think our fiduciary duty is to put shareholders first. I say the opposite. What we firmly believe is that if we focus our company on improving the lives of the world's citizens and come up with genuine sustainable solutions, we are more in synch with consumers and society and ultimately this will result in good shareholder returns. (Confino, 2012)

CASE STUDY CEVA's commitment to sustainability

CEVA Logistics is a global logistics provider with worldwide warehousing, freight management and distribution capabilities. Corporate and Social Responsibility is viewed by the company as 'part of its DNA', according to Chief Commercial Officer, Hakan Bicil. By aiming to create a culture of deep-rooted sustainability within the company, from CEO to warehouse operative, Bicil believes that the company gains a 'corporate advantage' which it is then able to turn into what he describes as an 'indirect' competitive advantage creating positive profitability and additional value for the customer.

Occasionally this involves some difficult decisions, and CEVA Logistics will not drop its standards to win business that doesn't fit in with its overall CSR commitment. For example, the company has stepped away from tendering for certain distribution and warehousing contracts that don't comply with its policies on sustainability.

There is a growing number of global leaders in manufacturing and retailing who share CEVA's approach, especially in the European, North American and Middle Eastern markets, although the level of commitment in other parts of the world is not as broad. There are others that still regard CSR as a 'box-ticking' exercise but to those who place value on sustainability, CEVA Logistics is able to provide solutions such as its Carbondex® service. This provides detailed information on the transportation options available for the customer such as the type, age and fuel efficiency of the plane on which a consignment is being flown. Customers then have the choice of flying their shipment by the least carbon-emitting alternative.

Measuring the success of CSR policies is very important to the company. It employs a range of KPIs to track progress and these metrics are designed specifically for what it terms its business 'clusters'. For example, its range of KPIs for its operations in Vietnam will be very different for those in developed economies such as Dubai, the United Kingdom or the United States.

CEVA's employees are a major part of its commitment to sustainability. The company has an 'on-boarding' process that conveys the corporate values and inculcates a sense of environmental and social responsibility within each employee. This has wider benefits as, by training and educating staff, ethical and environmental values are disseminated throughout society as a whole, especially in more developing markets. By helping individual employees, the overall community benefits. By such positive initiatives, the company creates a virtuous cycle, as stronger societies create more robust economies leading to growth benefits and a better trained and more capable workforce. CEVA's approach varies depending on the local culture and geography, allowing local management to develop models that work best for the specific market conditions.

While CEVA's management assumes responsibility for establishing a strong value set within the company as a whole, a high level of expectation is placed upon individual employees. Creating a culture in which 'bottom up' initiatives are encouraged and rewarded is of critical importance to the company. Bicil stressed that CEVA's commitment to sustainability – from its shareholders to its employees – was not just part of a corporate strategy to gain a competitive advantage; rather the importance it places on ethics and the environment runs through the entire fabric of the organization. Of course, its deep-rooted commitment to sustainability will undoubtedly strengthen the company as well as its value proposition.

Environmental Management Systems

An Environmental Management System (EMS) has been defined by the US Environmental Protection Agency as 'a set of processes and practices that enable an organization to reduce its environmental impacts and increase its operating efficiency'.

For many companies, especially SMEs, an EMS can be undertaken internally without external accreditation, but for larger companies it is becoming more important as a way of demonstrating their green credentials. An EMS is designed to manage a company's 'cause and effect' on the environment. Steps should be undertaken to understand how its activities interact with the environment and what this means in terms of impact. Consequently actions can be taken to mitigate these effects.

Ten steps to developing an EMS

1 Define organization's goals for EMS

The first step in EMS planning is to decide why you are pursuing the development of an EMS. Are you trying to improve your environmental performance (eg, compliance with regulations or prevent pollution)? How should the project scope be defined? (What is the 'organization' that the EMS will cover? One location or multiple locations?)

2 Secure top management commitment

One of the most critical steps in the planning process is gaining top management's commitment to support EMS development and implementation. Management must first understand the benefits of an EMS and what it will take to put an EMS in place.

3 Select an EMS champion

The choice of project champion is critical. The champion should have the necessary authority, an understanding of the organization, good project management skills and have top management support.

4 Build an implementation team

A team with representatives from key management functions (such as engineering, finance, human resources, production and/or service)

can identify and assess issues, opportunities and existing processes.
A cross-functional team can help to ensure that procedures are practical and
effective, and can build commitment to and 'ownership' of the EMS.

5 Hold a kick-off meeting

Once the team has been selected, hold a kick-off meeting to discuss the
organization's objectives in implementing an EMS, the initial steps that
need to be taken and the roles of team members. Follow up this meeting
with a communication to all employees.

6 Conduct preliminary review

Conduct a preliminary review of your current compliance and other
environmental programmes/systems. Evaluate your organization's
structure, procedures, policies, environmental impacts, training
programmes and other relevant factors.

7 Prepare a budget and schedule

Based on the results of the preliminary review, prepare a project plan and
budget. The plan should describe in detail what key actions are needed,
who will be responsible, what resources are needed, and when the work
will be completed.

8 Secure resources

The plan and budget should be reviewed and approved by top
management.

9 Involve employees

Ownership of the EMS will be greatly enhanced by meaningful employee
involvement in the development process. Employees are a great source
of knowledge on environmental and health and safety issues related to
their work areas as well as on the effectiveness of current processes and
procedures.

10 Monitor and communicate progress

As you build the EMS, be sure to regularly monitor your progress against
the goals and project plan, and communicate this progress within the
organization.

SOURCE Adapted from Environmental Protection Agency (EPA, 2016)

Within this broad project outline, there will be many more specific action points at various stages of the plan. Some of the most important of these are:

- Identify (and if possible quantify) the environmental risks of the business.
- Document processes to follow in the event of environmental incident (such as fuel spillage or pollution leak).
- Undertake training sessions.
- Put in place processes to record water usage, fuel usage, energy usage and waste production.
- Write an Environmental Management Manual including management procedures.
- Identify legislation that may regulate environmental processes.
- Identify goals for environmental improvement.
- Produce an action plan to achieve goals.

Within the logistics sector, the distribution centre has a large environmental impact due to its role as a node within the supply chain. The confluence of people, goods and transport means that risks of pollution, noise, waste, societal impact and contamination can be significant without proper management. To mitigate these risks, they need to be identified and managed. In particular an EMS will be critical to identifying the level of significance of a risk. These outcomes can be categorized as those that:

- breach legislation;
- have a significant financial consequence;
- produce demonstrable harm to the environment (including those involving the intervention of agencies or emergency services);
- result in concerns to customers, investors or insurers;
- result in complaints from the local community;
- harm the reputation and brand of the company.

External certification

In Europe there are two main standards to which companies can become accredited. Both allow companies to demonstrate to their customers and their suppliers that they are at the forefront of environmental practice. Although there is no legal necessity for a company to implement an EMS or indeed have their EMS certified externally, it is becoming increasingly important in terms of corporate strategy and positioning.

ISO 14001

The International Standard Organization's ISO 14001 sets out the criteria for an environmental management system which, once implemented by a company or other entity, can be measured by external accreditors. The ISO claims that the standard 'can provide assurance to company management and employees as well as external stakeholders that environmental impact is being measured and improved'.

The standard was first issued in 1996 and around 300,000 companies have so far been certified. The standard was renewed in 2015 with a focus on long-term sustainability and 'bringing environmental performance into the strategic day-to-day business of the organization'.

EMAS

The EU Eco-Management and Audit Scheme (EMAS) is a management tool developed by the European Commission for companies and other organizations to evaluate, report on and improve their environmental performance. It claims to be more rigorous than ISO 14001 as it includes a full regulatory compliance audit.

Environmental action plan for the local environment

Due to the potential impact of a distribution centre on its immediate neighbourhood, operators should, without fail, put in place a local environmental action plan that takes into account not only the impact on the local ecology but also on local residents. For this reason plans to mitigate the effect of the day-to-day running of the centre or contingency plans are essential. This may involve collaboration on a risk assessment or emergency action plan.

A local environment impact mitigation plan should include:

Land and water contamination	eg, minimize grey water run-off and develop contingency plan in the event of flooding.
Air pollution	eg, reduce idle running of truck engines on site.
Noise pollution	eg, consider timing of vehicle movements, engine idling, construction of bunds.
Visual intrusion	eg, consider screening and greening the building/car parks with trees and shrubs.
Industrial odours	eg, minimize emissions/maintain drains.
Waste and recycling	eg, proper disposal of pallets, oil, tyres and other industrial refuse.
Health and safety	eg, ensure that proper training is carried out to meet all the regulations of storage, especially if hazardous materials are kept on site.
Personal transport policy	eg, encourage alternative transport options to limit the number of car movements, especially at shift change-overs.

As well as the local environment, companies should put in place plans to reduce their impact at a global level. This includes: greenhouse gas emissions reduction, water use reduction, green energy generation and reuse and recycle initiatives.

Ethical investors

Financial investors are often overlooked in terms of the influence they have on a company's ethical behaviour, but they are becoming more important as some take a more activist role. Many funds now seek to differentiate themselves by their emphasis on investments that have a clear moral position. For some, this is a principled decision; for others the driver is lower returns from traditional investments due to the present economic and financial situation.

Another major factor is the risk associated with investing in companies that may breach environmental or humanitarian regulations. On the positive side, there is also the belief that those companies with strong social and environmental governance are those most likely to perform well operationally, out-performing less sustainable companies on the stock exchange.

According to DHL's Corporate Responsibility report, 42 per cent of its share capital is held by investors who have signed up to the Principles for Responsible Investment (PRI) initiative. One of its aims is to promote the reporting of non-financial key performance indicators (KPIs) to provide increased transparency (DHL, 2015). Paul Polman, CEO of Unilever, has acknowledged the difficulty that he has in convincing mainstream City investors of the effectiveness of his new, holistic approach to designing a business model around ethical and environmental principles. He believes that CSR is regarded by most as a side-line to the real business of making money.

As mentioned above, one of the problems with CSR is that it is, in many respects, 'self-awarding'. Best practice involves setting targets (such as carbon reduction) but in most cases the company will do its own assessment, undertaking the measurement and announcing its successes. In a survey by CDP Climate Disclosure, it found that 79 per cent of companies set carbon reduction targets. Of 173 reported, only 141 (80 per cent) were correctly reported with all details provided (start date, end date, base year emissions, scope, proportion of scope covered by the target and decrease rate). As the organization commented, 'Without all the correct details, it is difficult to accurately assess the achievability and ambition of these targets' (CDP, 2014). Consequently it is challenging for ethical investors to identify which companies they should include in their portfolios and which they should avoid.

A more effective way of providing independent assessment is the use of third-party rating agencies to assess progress and achievements. Investors see a listing on a sustainability index as an important part of their decision on whether to engage with the company. DHL (2014) commented:

> For our company these ratings primarily have a strategic significance. We consult them when we review the direction of our Corporate Responsibility activities and use them as a benchmark comparison. Rating agencies have a place among those stakeholders... we intend to deepen the dialogue with them.

FTSE4Good and Dow Jones Sustainability Indices (DJSI) were established to meet the needs of ethical investors as a benchmark for the growing market for socially responsible investment funds. There are a number of thresholds of minimum standards that have to be met in order to be included in the indices; for example, UK retailer Tesco was initially excluded from the first FTSE4Good index as it failed to publish a CSR statement. Admittance to the Index is also based on how well a company engages with its stakeholders. Other ratings agencies include Sustainalytics, CDP Climate Disclosure, MSCI and Corporate Responsibility Prime.

Investors and rating agencies

Ecclesiastical Investment Management (EIM) was one of the first companies to develop ethical and responsible investment in the UK and it has developed a comprehensive socially responsible investing policy across a range of funds. EIM's approach involves screening in the stock selection process, as well as engagement with companies.

EIM uses Sustainalytics' research to support its company engagement activities as well as to identify companies involved in products deemed controversial such as gambling, tobacco, and animal testing. Company and sector Environmental, Social and Governance (ESG) reports as well as monthly controversy alerts are analysed and included in EIM's integrated methodology, helping the firm to better understand corporate risk and opportunity and to pinpoint engagement topics.

Sustainability: a growing factor in tenders

The dominant supply chain partners (eg, the grocery supermarkets in the retail sector or the vehicle manufacturers in automotive) have been able to use their leverage to ensure that their suppliers commit to a wide range of sustainability measures. In fact, first-tier providers are being asked to pick up the cost for much of the responsibility for cutting CO_2 emissions, in much the same way that suppliers' inventory and the associated costs were pushed back up the supply chain when just-in-time or efficient consumer response came into vogue.

Many companies use questionnaires to establish the green credentials of their suppliers. A survey based on that of Exel, the forerunner to DHL, included the following questions (Worsford, 2001):

1 Do you have a formal environmental policy statement?

2 Is your company aware of the environmental impacts of its business and does it make efforts to measure them?

3 Does your company have procedures in place to mitigate its environmental impact?

4 Does your company strive towards industry best practice (please provide details)?

5 Do you set and achieve multiple goals and what is your approach to continuous improvement?

6 Do you have a nominated staff member with responsibility for environmental practice?

7 What training have they undertaken?

8 Do you monitor the environmental and ethical practices of your suppliers?

9 Has your company been prosecuted for any breach of environmental regulations in the past five years?

'Carbon intensity' has become a major criterion in the selection of suppliers and logistics service providers and 'environmental stewardship' is influencing the outsourcing choices they will make when contracts come up for tender.

In addition to environmental compliance, companies must now ensure that their suppliers comply with legislation on ethical behaviour. In 2015 the UK Modern Slavery Act was passed, which requires that companies with revenues in excess of £36 million must prepare a 'slavery and human trafficking' statement. As well as this, the National Living Wage came into force. To meet the terms of its commitments, one UK logistics provider sent out a letter reminding its suppliers of their responsibilities: 'We expect all of the businesses in our supply base to uphold and maintain all legal, regulatory and legislative requirements in relation to their workforce.'

Humanitarian logistics

One example of what global logistics company, Agility, calls a 'social investment' is cross-industry collaboration in support of humanitarian logistics. The growth of 'charitable giving' on a global scale for major disasters such as famines, wars and earthquakes since the 1970s was not paralleled by the development of logistics capabilities for delivering aid to the affected areas. This was despite the huge growth in the world's freight transport capabilities. The Indian Ocean tsunami of 2004 highlighted the consequent chaos, with the UN's head of emergency relief complaining that, 'Relief efforts were stymied by infrastructure, logistical problems, lack of communications and too many organizations involved.'

Since then a number of the big players have developed formal partnerships to improve both provision and coordination. Under the aegis of the World Economic Forum at Davos, they created the Logistics and Transportation Corporate Citizenship Initiative. This was an attempt by TNT, DHL, UPS and others to work closely with the big NGOs and particularly the UN to improve logistics operations. Specifically this was aimed at extending activities such as the 'Airport emergency relief teams' that were created during the Indian Ocean tsunami and the Pakistani earthquakes. Such systems can prevent the sort of chaos seen in the early stages of these disasters by coordinating physical assets utilization and improving communication between different parts of the logistics network.

The big logistics providers are developing their existing charitable activities into a more coherent complex of services. TNT Group has used its long-standing relationship with the UN's World Food Programme as a basis for developing a more integrated response for both UN agencies and larger NGOs such as the Red Cross. DHL has a similar programme with the UN's Office for the Coordination of Humanitarian Affairs (OCHA) and the UN Development Programme (UNDP). The company has established a network of 'Disaster relief teams' across the world that can coordinate logistics resources quickly in the areas most vulnerable to natural disasters.

Agility, UPS and TNT work together in an initiative called Logistics Emergency Teams, or LETs. It capitalizes on each company's ongoing operations nearest to the site where humanitarian response is needed. By using these local resources such as warehouse management and transport capabilities, the response is quicker and more effective during crises. The LETs companies donate trucks and warehousing resources as well as logistics staff and coordination services. All staff deployed by the companies have augmented the World Foods Programme's response and are provided free of charge. Under the United Nations coordination mechanism for crisis response, WFP is the lead agency for logistics coordination for all humanitarian agencies, including interfacing with governments and military to maximize the effectiveness of assets during disaster response.

CASE STUDY   The Philippines typhoon

The catastrophic typhoon that hit the Philippines in 2013 crippled a large area of the country. With 9.8 million people affected, 660,000 displaced and local estimates of up to 10,000 deaths, the country struggled to cope, with its infrastructure badly damaged. However, there was a quick response from the 'disaster relief' segment of the international humanitarian logistics sector.

The United Nation's World Food Programme's dedicated logistics infrastructure was mobilized to respond to the crisis. As the organization's Country Director said:

> The main challenges right now are related to logistics. Roads are blocked, airports are destroyed. As the UN agency leading the humanitarian community's Logistics Cluster, WFP is working with the government to set up operational hubs and organize airlifts of essential supplies.

The WFP has what it calls the 'UN Humanitarian Response Depot', an emergency inventory location for the Asia-Pacific region in Malaysia with stocks of 'mobile storage units, pre-fabricated offices and generators'. Food, including 44 tonnes of high-energy biscuits and 300kg of IT equipment including digital radios was sent from a similar facility in Dubai. The initial access point was the airport at Cebu on Leyte.

To provide disaster relief, many other organizations utilized their own unique supply chains in which food, medicine, clothing and more were distributed to those in need. For example, MSF delivered 200 tonnes of medical and relief items such as vaccines, tents and hygiene kits into Cebu on chartered cargo planes from Dubai and Belgium.

After the initial disaster response, the efforts of aid agencies became increasingly long term. The bigger logistics operators were able to deliver the sorts of logistics resources required over a prolonged period of time. These capabilities included the positioning of materials handling and depot management resources for small local airports and harbours.

Summary

The CSR department plays an important role in facilitating the development of an ethical and environmental strategy as well as monitoring and achieving targets in sustainability. However, overall responsibility lies with senior management who create the vision and culture as well as with the company employees who not only put policies into action but who are best placed to develop their own initiatives. External certification of Environmental Management Systems is becoming increasingly important to validate progress towards objectives, and the role of third-party rating indices is growing. Logistics companies have a unique opportunity to aid global humanitarian crises through their worldwide distribution operations.

Key points

- Logistics and supply chain companies have to respond to pressure from a range of stakeholders to meet environmental and ethical standards of corporate behaviour.
- The CSR department is important in facilitating environmental initiatives but management and employees bear the main responsibility.
- Environmental Management Systems are becoming essential within a sustainability strategy to coordinate all activities, goals and resources.

- Customers and investors are looking for external certification of environmental progress in place of 'self-awarding' initiatives.

- Global logistics companies provide invaluable support to aid agencies in times of humanitarian disasters.

References

CDP (2014) *Why Companies Need Emissions Reduction Targets,* Carbon Disclosure Project, London

Confino, J (2012) Unilever's Paul Polman: challenging the corporate status quo, 24 April, https://www.theguardian.com/sustainable-business/paul-polman-unilever-sustainable-living-plan

DHL (2015) DHL Corporate Responsibility Report, http://cr-report2015.dpdhl.com/organization-strategy/external-recognition.html

EPA (2016) Guide to Developing an Environmental Management System – Plan, Environmental Protection Agency, https://www.epa.gov/ems/guide-developing-environmental-management-system-plan

McGrade, M (2016) Sustain in order to gain, FT Adviser, http://www.ftadviser.com/2016/08/10/investments/alternative-investments/sustain-in-order-to-gain-zueIaGgzhPPQ7yEhBdmQ4K/article.html

Worsford, F (2001) *The Green Logistics Company,* Croner, London

Sustainable warehousing and distribution

07

THIS CHAPTER WILL FAMILIARIZE THE READER WITH

- The factors that need to be taken into account when developing environmentally sustainable warehousing
- The certification schemes that exist to promote warehouse development best practice
- Sustainability strategies and how warehouse operations can be made less harmful
- Financial imperatives for investing in higher specification green warehouses and materials handling equipment
- Best practice as demonstrated by two leading distribution operations in the United Kingdom

There has been comparatively little research into the impact of warehousing upon the environment and local communities. This is surprising given that vast warehouse facilities, sometimes upwards of a million square feet, are being constructed at strategic locations throughout developed and developing markets. This trend has been driven not only by the desire to consolidate inventory holdings on a regional basis, but also by omni-channel, e-retail strategies of retailers and manufacturers.

In the context of the modern logistics industry, warehousing and warehousing activities include not only the full range of distribution facility operations but, increasingly, value-adding logistics services such as postponed manufacturing. This means that warehouses become units of major economic activity, sometimes employing more than 1,000 people. The consequence of this is that the environmental and societal impact of warehousing goes far beyond the four walls of the building. For example, there are obvious issues related to the movement of trucks to and from the facility, but for many local residents the real problems are caused by visual intrusion of the building; the movement of staff at the start and end of shifts; the consequential congestion and noise; water run-off from large staff car parks; and noxious odours emanating from the building. All of these issues will be discussed in detail in this chapter.

The activities that take place within the warehouse also have consequences in terms of greenhouse gas (GHG) emissions. These are

Table 7.1   Framework for assessing warehousing's impact on the environment

Macro level	
Land use	Brownfield or Greenfield
	Water management
	Use of recycled materials in construction
Environment	Visual intrusion
	Travel plans
	Green energy
Ecology	Landscaping
	Biodiversity
Micro level	
	Energy
	Light
	Heat
	Power
	Water
	Warehousing activities
	Materials handling
	Land and buildings
	Building regulations

known as 'operational carbon' and this (to some extent) is separate from the 'embodied carbon' or 'carbon footprint' of the physical warehouse itself. There is, of course, a large amount of interaction between the building fabric and the operations that take place in and round it. Lighting is one example. Latest best practice requires there to be more natural light allowed into the warehouse and this impacts on the design of the building. This is also the case with minimizing (or indeed in warm climates) maximizing air flow. Therefore the way the building is designed has an impact on energy usage and hence operational costs. Adapting work by Clive Marchant and Peter Baker in *Green Logistics* (McKinnon *et al*, 2012), warehousing's impact on the overall environment can be assessed using the framework shown in Table 7.1.

Land use

Although it is usually cheaper and quicker to build on greenfield sites, there are many environmental reasons why it is better to develop 'brownfield' sites (ie land previously used for industrial purposes). Not least of these reasons is that it offers an opportunity to clean up areas that are often contaminated. In addition they provide a source of regeneration and employment in already populated areas. Conversely, building on greenfield sites, especially in rural locations, can leave an occupier with the problem of recruiting staff (especially if there is full employment). This can lead to the influx of low-skilled, low-paid migrant labour to communities that lack the infrastructure (housing, social and transport) to cope. Locating warehouses on greenfield sites can also increase the carbon emissions of staff travelling to work, as in many cases there will be little provision of public transport.

Local authorities are more likely to support the development of brownfield sites especially when the developer commits to enhancing local infrastructure such as roads and drains. The use of brownfield sites can also provide opportunities to reuse or recycle building materials. This not only reduces the embodied carbon footprint of the building infrastructure but also reduces GHG emission generated by the movement of building materials to the site.

Certification of sustainability and government incentives

As green logistics becomes a top public policy issue around the world, governments have started to require or encourage the adoption of environmental standards for logistics property development. Best practice now includes:

- using solar panels and wind turbines;
- reducing waste in construction;
- using environmentally friendly, recyclable materials;
- reducing CO_2 emissions;
- reducing water usage and use of rainwater ('grey water');
- reducing pollutants;
- increasing biodiversity and enhancing local habitats;
- increasing energy and resource efficiency;
- storm water collection and use of permeable paving;
- energy efficient lighting;
- 'green' roofs.

To incentivize developers to work towards best environmental practice, industry and governments have established initiatives that can measure and accredit the sustainability of warehousing projects.

One of the world's largest property certifications is the United Kingdom-based Building Research Establishment's 'Building Research Establishment Environmental Assessment Method' (BREEAM). Since 1990 it has set environmental standards for a range of building types and, via a network of third-party examiners, audits every stage of a development. The certification process is not aimed specifically at warehousing, but it does cover the sector (along with others such as offices, data centres, hospitals, residential, etc). The assessment provides:

- market recognition for low environmental impact buildings;
- assurance that best environmental practice is incorporated into a building;
- a benchmark that is higher than regulation;

- a tool to help reduce running costs, improve working and living environments;

- a standard that demonstrates progress towards corporate and organizational environmental objectives.

CASE STUDY Prologis Park, Dunstable

Prologis Park in Dunstable is a new-build distribution facility that brought about the regeneration of an urban brownfield site and has been a source of new jobs in the area. The first stage of the development, DC1, was a 28,808m² building. As well as BREEAM certification, DC1 achieved an Energy Performance Certificate (EPC) rating of A and a reduction in emissions of 45 per cent compared to the 2011 UK Building Regulations. Features include:

- High levels of air tightness and insulation to improve thermal efficiency.

- Roof lights to 15 per cent of the warehouse roof area and narrow plan dual-aspect offices to maximize the availability of natural light.

- Brise Soleil to office elevations to reduce solar gain and improve thermal comfort.

- Energy efficient systems that contribute to the project's operational emissions reduction target, including energy-efficient lighting throughout with movement controls, daylight sensing and dimming to make use of natural light wherever possible.

- LED external lighting in yards and car parks.

- Office heating via air source heat pumps.

- A 12,000 litre rainwater harvesting system providing water for non-potable use and a mains water leak detection system.

- Mechanical ventilation with heat recovery.

In addition to building for light and heat efficiency, the warehouse was designed to incorporate low or zero carbon-emitting energy generation systems. These include rooftop photo-voltaic arrays and rooftop solar thermal systems that provide a renewable source of hot water.

Regarding the construction, the building achieved certification under the Considerate Constructors Scheme as well as full BREEAM credits for site management. As the site was brownfield there was considerable waste to dispose of, and 97 per cent of this was diverted from landfill for reuse or recycling. The ecology of the site was enhanced and the project exceeded BREEAM benchmarks.

The overall design and construction of the building was assessed and passed on all metrics including:

- management (including responsible construction practices);
- health and wellbeing (including safety and warmth);
- transport (access to public transport and cycling facilities);
- energy use and generation (including reduction of carbon emissions and energy efficiency);
- water (use minimization and waste water reduction);
- materials (including responsible sourcing of materials and insulation);
- pollution (including noise, impact of refrigerants and surface run-off);
- land use and ecology (including site selection and biodiversity);
- innovation.

Martin Cooper, Director Project Management at Prologis UK commented:

> We have achieved this [carbon emission reduction and energy savings] by following our established sustainability strategy, which is based on three key metrics – BREEAM certification, reduction of operational CO_2 emissions and embodied carbon mitigation.

The building not only brought benefits to the eventual occupant, but according to Prologis was designed and built with the local residents in mind:

- The layout of the park and use of screen bunding minimized noise pollution.
- The overall building height was minimized to mitigate visual intrusion.
- The building's roof and cladding were coloured sympathetically, again to minimize visual impact.

A similar scheme to BREEAM is Leadership in Energy and Environmental Design (LEED), which has been developed in the United States and Canada. LEED is a third-party verification organization that awards points for each property development based on levels of environmental compliance. Federal, state and local government can then make a decision to award tax credits, tax breaks, reduced fees, grants or loans based on the number of points achieved.

In terms of European legislation, the 2010 Energy Performance of Buildings Directive is the main regulation which, transcribed into national law, governs many aspects of property sustainability, including that of the distribution sector. It requires that:

- Energy performance certificates (EPCs) are included in all advertisements for the sale or rental of buildings.

- EU countries must establish inspection schemes for heating and air conditioning systems or put in place measures with equivalent effect.

- All new buildings must be nearly zero energy buildings by 31 December 2020 (public buildings by 31 December 2018).

- EU countries must set minimum energy performance requirements for new buildings, for the major renovation of buildings and for the replacement or retrofit of building elements (heating and cooling systems, roofs, walls, etc).

According to property developer Prologis, this Directive has meant that 'green' warehousing has now become best practice in the industry; in other words, a gold standard against which all warehousing is measured.

Of these points, perhaps the most important is the award of the EPCs. This allows companies to choose the most efficient buildings in terms of energy as well as helping them to minimize their carbon footprint. This is not straightforward as the different climates experienced across the region mean that different building styles are required. For example, UK warehouses are designed to optimize air tightness and insulation whereas those in Southern Europe require air circulation to prevent over-heating in summer months. For this reason, EPC certification is devolved to national level.

Improving sustainable operations in the warehouse

When looking at their overall response to improving their sustainability, logistics and supply chain companies typically focus on the following topics.

1 Lighting

Warehouse lighting is a very important part of overall energy usage, accounting for up to two-thirds of electricity costs. To reduce expenditure on this item, companies are increasingly installing more energy efficient lighting. Movement sensors allow lights to switch on only when areas are being accessed. Increased automation will lead to lower lighting requirements. In some cases, warehouse lighting costs have been reduced by 60 per cent, with new lighting infrastructure projects paying for themselves in just two years.

LED lighting is now seen as the most energy efficient system. Not only is it more efficient, but the bulbs last between five and seven times longer than traditional bulbs. LED's other benefits include:

- integration with enhanced sensing controls;
- maintenance savings;
- reduced electrical infrastructure;
- lower radiated heat;
- better light quality for employees;
- lead- and mercury-free fixtures.

2 Heating

Monitoring heating usage and ensuring that load-bay doors are closed when not required. Positioning heating units away from open bay doors is one such example of an easy fix.

3 Energy use reduction

'Strategic energy waste maps' can be developed to assess the energy usage of machinery within the warehouse environment. Those that are working inefficiently can be identified and addressed.

4 Energy generation

Solar panel (photovoltaic) installation has become popular, especially utilizing the large roof space that is characteristic of warehousing. The electricity generated from large projects can be fed back into the grid and thus some companies have encouraged investment from third parties, while benefiting from savings themselves.

5 Water usage reduction

Reuse of 'grey' water is an important part of any new warehouse constructed and managed to the latest environmental standards. Identifying leaks and vehicle wash management are also important.

6 Loading systems

Systems exist that allow for the optimal loading of trailers and containers through 3D visualization. Stacking pallets, where possible, increases the utilization of each vehicle.

7 Zero waste to landfill

Best practice in waste management now proscribes the use of land-fill sites. Warehouses generate large amounts of packaging waste that can be collected for recycling. Domestic waste (such as plastics, bottles and cans) can be sorted and, when recycling is not an option, sent for incineration in energy recovery schemes. Food waste can also be diverted from landfill to anaerobic digesters that produce electricity and fertilizers for agricultural use.

Packaging technologies reduce waste

Packaging materials are a major generator of waste, within the warehouse and in the home or office of the end-recipient. With the massive growth in e-retailing and related parcels deliveries, the problem has become worse. Inefficient dispatch systems can mean that multiple orders can result in multiple consignments without consolidation into the same box. In addition to this, the use of sub-optimal packaging size can mean that more air is shipped than product within a box.

To address this latter problem, new technology has been developed that customizes packaging for each individual order. Fully automated, each picked product is scanned and a flat carton is cut to precisely the right size. The product is then mechanically packed with order information automatically inserted alongside any other required marketing or customized instructions.

One of the major benefits of such a system (outside of the cost reductions resulting from using less labour) is the reduction of weight and size of the cartons. As well as the lower shipping costs, the reduced volume and weight means that fewer shipping containers are required, reducing carbon emissions.

One company that has implemented this packaging solution estimates that it will pay for itself in about two years. A summary of the benefits include:

- environmental impact in terms of packaging waste and lower carbon emissions;
- cost savings as no need to procure and store boxes of different sizes;
- less warehouse space required;
- no risk of correct size box being out of stock;
- reduction (or elimination) of the need for filler materials;
- increased packaging productivity and efficiency through automation;
- reduced material costs overall.

8 Warehouse layout

An inefficient layout of a warehouse (for example the location of fast and slow moving items) not only wastes time but also increases the fuel use of forklift trucks.

9 Paper reduction

Reducing the number of copies of proof of deliveries (PODs) required; double-sided printing or moving to a paperless environment completely.

10 Green roofs

Depending on the prevailing climate, roofs may need to be insulated to prevent heat loss or coated with reflective material to keep the warehouse cool ('cool roofs'). This also has an effect on the local environment as less sunlight is absorbed by roads and buildings, meaning that urban areas do not heat up as much.

Other schemes

As well as initiating specific projects or programmes to reduce logistics-related waste, there are many generic issues that sustainability strategies can involve. These include cycle-to-work, community out-reach and landscaping and habitat creation.

Return on investment of green projects

Designing and constructing a warehouse with sustainable features is more expensive than one built to lower standards. Although operating costs are likely to be lower, the occupier will be keen to establish what sort of return on investment will be delivered by the more sustainable facility. The shorter the lease the less likely it is that higher rental costs will be off-set by cheaper operating costs.

The potential cost savings created through sustainable building features are substantial. Prologis believes that can be between £230,000 and £335,000 a year in the United Kingdom for a large facility. To calculate the level of savings that can be achieved (and hence compare ROI), a baseline case must first be identified. This can be attained by using the minimum building regulations in place and comparing them with the energy efficiency of 'gold standard' building practices.

Prologis undertook an audit of its buildings and published the data in its 2010 Sustainability Report (Cox and Graham, 2010); see Table 7.2. This shows that, compared to national 'baseline' regulations and the efficiencies these create, there is a significant opportunity to reduce carbon emissions much further. For example, a 37,353 square metre Prologis warehouse located in Kettering emits 54 per cent fewer metric tonnes of CO_2 than the UK baseline or minimum standards for a newly constructed building; ie 298.82 metric tonnes of CO_2/annum compared with the UK baseline of 646.21 metric tonnes. This also means cost savings. The same warehouse consumes 47 per cent less energy than a warehouse constructed to minimum building standards: 22.62 kWh/m²/annum (ie, kilowatt hours per square metre per year) compared with the baseline of 43.08 kWh/m²/annum.

Table 7.2   Reductions in annual carbon emissions from EPC-rated distribution
facilities

Country	Buildings with EPC-Rating	Weighted Avg. Reductions in CO_2 Emissions (%)
Germany	34	41.7
Hungary	5	34.8
Poland	11	34.3
Slovakia	4	58.5
UK	17	39.5

Prologis-owned facilities; reductions in emissions, calculated based on country-specific baselines.

In 2010, when this research was published, Prologis believed that this translated into annual savings of between £70,000 and £100,000. In 2016, with energy prices approximately a third lower than 2010 (Energy Savings Trust, 2016) the savings would be less, although still very significant. This latter point is very important when looking at the ROI calculations used to justify purchasing/renting higher specification green warehousing. When energy costs are high, it makes much more sense from an economic perspective to invest more in better specification property. As discussed in detail throughout this book, cost implications are just one factor for companies when they take supply chain decisions, but when setting the savings against long-term investment costs, the balance is of course a very important one.

The ROI calculation is similarly critical for 'smart' materials handling equipment. For instance, expensive roller conveyors are a common feature of many warehouses, especially given the increase in the number of parcels being shipped in the e-retail sector. Rather than have motor-driven conveyors working all the time (perhaps 16 hours a day in the case of double-shift operations), more sophisticated options are now available, such as conveyors with sensors that work only when a package is present. However, more advanced materials handling equipment is more costly. In one example (Materials Handling & Logistics, 2016), a company made an initial investment of $315,000 in a smarter conveyor system against the cost of $280,000 for a traditional one (12.5 per cent more). Managers had worked out that the extra costs would be paid back by energy savings, which worked out at $16,344 a year. Over an estimated 10-year lifespan of a conveyor it can be seen that savings would be over $150,000. In addition to the direct costs, there were other advantages that would also have an indirect impact on the cost-benefit analysis. For example, the new conveyor was quieter than traditional types as it

---

Return on investment – 'Green and gold'

When environmental initiatives result in cost savings they are sometimes referred to as 'green and gold'. Below are three examples of where a focus on environmental impact can bring about benefits within a warehouse. They show the return on 'green' warehouse lighting initiatives:

Example 1. 20,000m² clothing warehouse (three stories of mezzanine racking) built in 2002 operating 12 hours per day, five days per week. Audit identified that implementation of lighting controls, lighting replacement and reduction of lighting levels could result in €30,000 saving with a payback period of three years.

Example 2. Ambient warehouse (1,000m²) operated 11 hours per day, Monday to Friday. Lighting cost savings identified of 37 per cent with a payback period of 2.4 years.

Example 3. Audit of 25,000m² warehouse, operating 24/7, found that 10 energy saving opportunities could save 51 per cent of costs with a one-year payback period.

Another way of looking at these initiatives is that for many businesses a 20 per cent cut in energy costs represents the same bottom-line benefit as a 5 per cent increase in sales.

Considerable challenges have also been identified. These can include:

- Lack of senior management commitment and staff engagement.
- The need to communicate policy clearly to staff at all levels.
- No defined responsibility for energy use or performance monitoring.
- Lack of technical knowledge potentially resulting in like-for-like replacement.
- Lack of expertise to build the business case.
- A financial structure that works against improvement.
- Maintenance or capital investment budget.

operated less of the time, so there was less impact on employees' hearing, mitigating the risk of law suits or pay-outs. Also as a result of the conveyor working only when necessary, there was a reduction in the risk of workplace accidents.

Green energy opportunities

There are opportunities not only to reduce the amount of energy usage within the warehouse, but also to use the building itself to generate energy to meet its own requirements and to feed back into the energy grid as a revenue-generating activity. This can be achieved, for instance, by using the large expanse of roof space to generate solar power or constructing a wind turbine within the footprint of the facility.

The 'solar footprint' of Prologis increased by 30 megawatts (MW) in 2015 to 149 MW spread over nine countries. Its target is to increase its footprint to more than 200 MW by 2020. To put this in perspective, this equates to powering 22,000 average homes each year with renewable energy (Prologis, 2015).

In addition, the large footprint that usually accompanies warehouses can be used for ground thermal exchange units (air and water can also be employed where appropriate). Another example of 'green energy' that results from utilizing the waste products generated by the warehousing activities includes the use of waste packaging for incineration.

Warehouse operations best practice case studies

CASE STUDY CEVA Logistics with Crown Paints

Paint manufacturer Crown Paints, in partnership with its logistics provider, CEVA Logistics, has embarked on a number of sustainable initiatives at its Hull distribution facility.

Electricity

The electricity consumption for the Hull site decreased by 10 per cent in 2015 compared to 2014. This has been achieved in a joint effort to improve energy saving behaviours such as turning off lights when not in use and using equipment efficiently.

Paper

Crown Paints Hull used 560 reams of paper in 2014 and reduced this by 7 per cent to 520 reams in 2015 – only recycled paper is purchased and all paper is recycled after use. One project reduced the number of copies of proof of delivery notes from three to one. Following the introduction of a printer that printed double-sided paper, the amount of A4 paper used was halved.

Waste

CEVA's Hull site is zero waste to landfill. A waste sorting centre was created to sort through two trailers of waste from Crown Paints every day and to segregate the waste streams – the segregated waste is passed to recycling partners.

Ongoing improvements

The heating system for the facility has been linked to the bay doors in the warehouse. Now when the bay door next to the heater is open the heater automatically turns off with no effect on heating the warehouse; previously heat was lost through the doors.

A pallet stacker innovation allowed the loading of 32 pallets on every single deck trailer rather than 26, reducing the number of journeys and the mileage/carbon footprint by 19 per cent through utilizing the capacity of the trailers more efficiently.

United Biscuits Logistics

United Biscuits, a leading manufacturer of biscuits in the United Kingdom, operates a 325,000 ft^2 central distribution centre in Leicestershire, employing 320 full-time staff. The site distributes 130 million cases per annum, which equates to 400 loads per day in and out of the facility using its own 50 tractor units and 250 trailers supplemented by a large haulier base.

The company developed its own environmental road map at the end of 2005, with the aim of eliminating waste, reducing energy consumption and driving down CO_2 emissions through a 'Fewer and friendlier miles' sustainability programme. As part of UB's CSR and sustainability agenda it also targeted additional reductions in packaging, water usage and sustainable and ethical sourcing.

Reduction in CO_2 emissions

Reducing CO_2 has become a key logistics strategy, with the result that emissions from transport in 2015 (for like-for-like volume) were 43.5 per cent lower than 2005.

The company has also initiated projects using alternative fuels. Waste vegetable oil is a by-product of UB's manufacturing processes and, in partnership with Biomotive Fuels (part of Convert2Green) it trialled a unique conversion system to operate 44 tonne trucks on used cooking oil as a direct fuel. Following these early trials, UB formed a consortium with the University of Leeds Energy Research Institute and Convert2Green, gaining funding from a government grant in 2013 for further trialling. The trial resulted in:

- 2,300 tonnes CO_2 saved;
- fuel substitution average rate of 85 per cent (23 months);
- 97 per cent carbon saving;
- overall 'well to wheel' benefit of 82.5 per cent carbon saving over fossil diesel;
- 40 per cent reduction in tail-pipe particulate emissions vs diesel;
- no increase in repair and maintenance spend and no mechanical issues;
- good driver feedback;
- fuel consumption performance in line with standard diesel.

Supplier management

A review of transport operators through an environmental risk-based approach is being initiated. This involves visiting high-risk hauliers (based on frequency of use and distance travelled) to:

- promote positive relationships;
- communicate the standards expected; and
- seek opportunities to benchmark in-house activities against similar operations.

The company believes that by installing customer account managers and having single-point staff contacts, vehicle fill rates will be improved, resulting in fewer vehicles on the road.

Water usage reduction

Although year-on-year water reduction is difficult for a site that does not utilize water in any manufacturing process and whose usage fluctuates according to staffing needs through welfare facilities, minor incremental improvements have been found through flush-saving devices and infra-red taps. Further improvements are being sought through the regular maintenance of grey-water harvesting, identifying water leaks and commensurate repairs, and better vehicle wash management programmes.

Waste packaging

The site has minimal waste generated through normal operations. However, a co-packing programme is in place to provide customer bespoke displays, producing quantities of cardboard waste which, although captured through a recycling programme, prevents the opportunity of waste reduction due to the nature of how the cardboard is printed, stamped and coded. The need to protect the product from damage through the manufacture, transport and storage of the product to the final shelf display can drive excessive packaging use. UB Logistics is looking to implement a 5 per cent reduction in waste to landfill year-on-year based on its 2014 baseline by:

- improving packaging design;
- maximizing recycled content;
- improving recyclability;
- delivering product protection to reduce food waste, while ensuring no increase in the carbon impact of packaging.

Energy consumption and waste

UB Logistics is targeting a 20 per cent reduction in machine energy waste through the development of high bay storage and automation. This will be achieved through the reduction of vehicles operating in the warehouse; the removal of non-essential and obsolete electrical fittings/furniture; improved lighting technology; and the ongoing investment in new high-speed, efficient machinery and optimal production layouts.

Site facilities management and on-site contractors are developing a strategic energy waste map so as to understand the equipment currently on site and to record key energy usage on a daily basis. This will help identify any significant power consumption on site and inefficient equipment.

Environmental culture

Employee environmental awareness is very important at the facility and is an important part of staff training programmes. Contractors and suppliers are encouraged to source suitable alternatives in accordance with the company's environmental ethos, utilizing available industry organizations such as the Energy Savings Trust.

Engagement is a key subject within the facility, driving 100 per cent involvement. There is a health and safety and environment review involving in some way all employees, contractors and suppliers.

Summary

Warehouses, and the operations that take place inside them, can have a major impact on the environment not only in terms of the land use, but also due to congestion, visual impact, odours, noise and water run-off. Consequently the establishment of a local environment plan as well as engagement with the local community is very important. Modern warehouses can be designed and built to extremely high standards reducing levels of 'embodied carbon' within the fabric of the building. This generally equates to lower running costs and 'operational carbon' as energy use is minimized. The potential to use large roofs for photovoltaic arrays also means that warehouses can produce a source of revenue.

Key points

- Green warehousing design and build is regarded as being the 'gold standard', delivering a range of environmental and potentially financial benefits.

- As warehouses increasingly become centres of economic activity it is important to recognize the impact on the local environment and community.

- Environmental initiatives related to warehouse operations have the potential to offer 'green and gold' benefits. Reducing light and heating bills, for example, also reduces carbon emissions.

- The balance between capital building costs and operational costs depends on the price of energy. When energy prices are low there is less incentive to buy/lease a higher specification warehouse.

- BREEAM certification ensures warehouse developers achieve the highest levels of specification, with environmental factors taken into account at every stage of the process.

References and further reading

Cox, S and Graham, L (2010) *Sustainability Measured: Gauging the energy efficiency of European warehouses,* Prologis, San Francisco, CA

Energy Savings Trust (2016) Our Calculations, http://www.energysavingtrust.org.uk/about-us/our-calculations

McKinnon, A C, Browne, M and Whiteing, A (2012) *Green Logistics: Improving the environmental sustainability of logistics,* Kogan Page, London

Materials Handling & Logistics (2016) www.mhlnews.com/green-warehouse-investments%20

Prologis (2015) *Built with Purpose: Corporate sustainability report 2015,* Prologis, San Francisco, CA

Sustainable packaging initiatives

08

**THIS CHAPTER WILL FAMILIARIZE
THE READER WITH**

- The importance of supply chain packaging initiatives in terms of environmental, societal and financial benefits
- The benefits to the environment of protecting products during transit and storage
- The concept of lifecycle assessment of packaging, demonstrating the difficulty in making informed 'green' choices
- Strategies for the reduction of packaging materials both in volume and weight
- The environmental costs of refillable and non-refillable packaging
- The need to protect perishable food products in emerging markets

Smarter packaging initiatives were identified in the Accenture/World Economic Forum research (WEF, 2015) as having the potential to deliver social, environmental and financial benefits within the supply chain.

The packaging industry has three goals (INCPEN, 2003), which align very closely with the concept of 'triple advantage' described in Chapter 1:

1 Meet consumer/business needs in terms of product protection, safety, handling and information.

2 Environment: save more resources than are used in the manufacture of packaging.

3 Economic: save costs in distribution and merchandising of goods.

Although packaging waste is regarded by many in the industry as a major problem, significant efforts have been made by the industry to increase its sustainability. According to the Industry Council for Packaging and the Environment (INCPEN), 60 per cent of all packaging from industry, commerce and households is recovered and recycled. Indeed, a certain amount of packaging is required for consumer goods under EU law. The Packaging (Essential Requirements) Regulations 2003 set out minimum weight and specifications for packaging, ensuring that it is fit for purpose and acceptable for safety and hygiene. The law requires packers and fillers of packaging, and importers, to ensure that packaging contains less than 100ppm in total of lead, cadmium, mercury or hexavalent chromium and that essential requirements are met regarding:

- minimizing packaging volume and weight in line with safety, hygiene and product/consumer acceptance;
- designing packaging to permit recovery or reuse and recovery;
- minimizing the impact of packaging waste on the environment;
- manufacturing packaging to minimize the presence of hazardous substances in emissions, ash or leachate when packaging waste is incinerated or landfilled.

The method by which the industry shows it is complying with European legislation on recycling is through the mechanism of buying Packaging Recovery Notes (PRNs). This is usually undertaken through compliance schemes.

Although at face value the goal of reducing packaging would seem to be sensible, it has to be done in a way that reduces the risk of unintended consequences. Packaging exists to protect the product it contains and without sufficient or appropriate packaging a greater level of waste can be generated. A study by the US Chamber of Commerce concluded that a 1 per cent increase in packaging resulted in a 1.6 per cent decrease in food waste. For fresh meat, fish and salads, 'controlled' or 'modified' atmosphere packaging has led to a significant reduction in wastage of fresh product in shops and homes.

If assessed as part of the whole life of the products they are designed to protect, reduced packaging does not necessarily equate to lower carbon emissions. Chips that are prepared in a microwave, for example, have much higher packaging requirements than oven-baked chips but the microwavable chips only generate a tenth of the emissions from cooking of those prepared in an oven. It is for this reason that an individual target of, for example, increasing the renewable component of packaging, is not regarded as the primary aim. Instead packaging's overall contribution to reducing carbon emissions should be measured; there is no single way of measuring sustainability. For instance, any of the following factors could be taken into account when developing a metric:

- renewable or non-renewable resource element;
- recyclable or not;
- biodegradable or inert;
- reusable or non-reusable;
- made from recycled or virgin material;
- lightweight or heavy duty.

However, the main point is whether the packaging results in lower whole-life emissions or not. That is not to say that efforts have not been made to increase the sustainability of individual elements of packaging, just that the bigger picture is more important. The example in Table 8.1 shows that, depending on the metric, either packaging type (a rigid tub or disposable plastic pouch) could be judged as more sustainable.

Table 8.1   Which packaging is greenest?

Stain remover	Tub	Plastic Pouch
Weight	78g	18g
Recyclability	Yes	No
Residual waste	26g	18g
Filling energy	80/min	16/min

SOURCE INCPEN/Reckitt Benckiser (2015)

Solutions for the reduction of packaging

The packaging material and design used in the storage and transportation of products is crucial to reducing logistics costs, carbon footprint and packing waste. Many US shippers were forced to look at more efficient packaging solutions in the mid-2000s when parcels companies introduced the principle of charging by dimensional weight (ie charging on the basis of the parcel's volume and not just its weight). This led to many companies reviewing how much air they were shipping in their supply chains. At the time Wal-Mart was believed to have reduced its packaging material volume by 3,425 tons, moving 727 fewer containers due to increased package density and saving $3.5 million in transport costs (Wal-Mart, 2006).

Apple managed to reduce the amount of plastic it used in the packaging of its 20-inch iMac by 66 per cent and the amount of paper it used by 42 per cent while reducing the space it took up by 41 per cent. The reduction in the size of its sixth generation iPod packaging allowed it to ship 140 more units per pallet than the fourth generation version (Jindel, 2008).

Packaging of goods for e-retail

The e-retail phenomenon has created an additional challenge for packaging companies. Whereas previously consumers would collect a product from the shops themselves, much of the retail sector is now characterized by the shipment of high volumes of small packages from distribution centres. This has increased the cost of packaging (many products are now individually wrapped in an inner and outer packaging case) and the cost of transport is inflated by the weight and volume of the packaging. There are environmental costs related to the production and recycling of the additional packaging. Too much packaging and the costs of the logistics (both in financial and carbon emissions terms) are incrementally too high; too little packaging and the product can be damaged in transit, which means that the entire amount of energy invested in design, production, storage, packaging and transport has been lost.

E-retailers can minimize packaging costs by looking at the following factors:

- Minimizing packaging layers. Whereas most e-retail packages contain inner and outer layers it may be possible to develop packaging that eliminates the second layer.

- Use of sustainable packaging materials from certifiable sources.

- Use of recyclable content where this uses less energy than virgin materials.

- Minimization of application of printing inks or adhesive labels where these compromise recyclability.

- Designing packaging to be reused (eg for returns).

To assess the sustainability of a packaging strategy it is advisable to measure the spend on packaging, pack weight per parcel and proportion of goods returned as damaged.

CASE STUDY Lakeland reduces packaging waste through automated packing solutions

UK home products retailer, Lakeland, has been using an automated packing solution for 70 per cent of the products it dispatches for its home shopping output for a number of years. The remaining output has been packed manually into 13 different box sizes, mainly smaller, oddly shaped and larger parcels. As the proportion of smaller orders and back orders was on the increase as a result of participation in a number of UK and international e-commerce marketplaces such as Amazon and eBay, it searched for an automated packing solution that could handle smaller orders.

The aim was to optimize the packaging process by eliminating the stock of different size boxes and its inventory management, improving efficiency, reducing the cost per box and avoiding any void-fillers. Lakeland also needed a solution that was scalable in order to cope with volumes of complete parcels fluctuating from regular daily output up to peak periods such as Christmas and Black Friday. The solution also needed to be able to combine marketing information enclosed within the carton.

There are several solutions on the market that cut cardboard to the right size for the items in the order but these still require manual parcel creation, packing, sealing and labelling. Lakeland chose to work with CMC Machinery packaging technologies to implement a fully automated packing solution for small orders, which resulted in improved efficiency, reduced cardboard cost and improved trailer fill.

The technology scans each individual order/product and produces a flat carton. The machine then packs the order with no void fill to the size of the products and inserts invoices and additional marketing material inside the carton based on the country of the order origin. A final dispatch label is then added to the carton. This is completed at a rate of 1,000 parcels per hour. Lakeland took the opportunity to integrate the solution with catalogue/marketing media and dispatch-note inserters to further reduce the need for any manual intervention during the packing process.

Based on anticipated volumes over the first few years, the cost of the machine and the reduced labour requirement, the project will provide a return on investment within less than 2 years. Lakeland has also been able to reduce volumetrics in both weight and size of the cartons, which means there is no longer the need to fill empty space in the box with void-fill products. The impact on producing cartons the actual size of the product means a greener footprint for the company due to being able to dispatch the same number of parcels in fewer shipping containers.

Lakeland has also experienced the knock-on effect of savings in inventory as it no longer needs to stock numerous different sized boxes; it now only has to stock pallets of fan-fold cardboard, from which it can produce any size box, personalized and robust. The cardboard is also totally recyclable. Lakeland sees the packing solution as an important investment to support its growth and to enhance its service proposition for years to come.

Refillable packaging – pros and cons

It is often suggested that refillable packaging is the most sustainable way of reducing or eliminating waste. The returnable glass milk bottle, recovered daily by a milkman, is held up as the waste-free model that could or should be replicated. Other models in the past included the now defunct collection of glass bottles that had a returnable deposit. Of course these types of models are few and far between due to changing consumer behaviour, the dominance of grocery multiples and the lack of a robust economic model to support them. It is even disputed that, in terms of lifecycle assessments of the greenhouse gas emissions of products, refillable packaging is more sustainable than single-trip packaging, as will be discussed.

Successful refillable packaging business models depend on a number of factors:

- The supply chain being controlled by the producer with few other parties involved. The producer controls the circulation of the packaging, which ensures 'high capture rates' of used packaging.

- Parts of the product or packaging having a certain value to the producer or consumer, which makes recovery, reuse or refilling economically worthwhile.

- The contents are valuable or worth protecting with more expensive packaging.

- Transport costs involved in the refill are low, ie the proximity of filling to consumption is important.

- Refilling can be outsourced to the consumer.

- Producers and consumers want to demonstrate green credentials and the positioning of the brand (and the additional product value/price) generates enough value in the supply chain to support otherwise uneconomic refilling.

Loughborough University, undertaking research for the UK's DEFRA, categorized 16 refillable solutions (Lofthouse and Bhamra, 2006); see Table 8.2. Of these different models, it is obvious that many are extremely niche and would, even if adopted in full by retailers, manufacturers and consumers, have a negligible impact on the market.

These models can be broadly categorized into three different systems, as classified by the Industry Council for Packaging and the Environment (INCPEN) and Centre for Remanufacturing and Reuse (CRR): *(continues on p 152)*

Table 8.2   Refillable solutions

Type	Description	Possible applications
1. Lightweight self-contained refill delivered through dispenser	Customers buy a self-contained refill which they take home and put into their durable dispenser. Design of products with lower energy requirements	Wipes, razors, face creams, fabric conditioner and air fresheners, etc
2. Lighter weight refill through part reuse	Customers buy a new bottle of product and reuse the spray pump	Cleaning products
3. Empty packaging refilled in shop	Customers take the original packaging back to the store for it to be refilled with the same product	Shampoo, conditioner, shower gel, bath products and fabric conditioner
4. Self-dispense	Customers take re-usable container back to the store where they refill it with the same product	Dry goods, personal care products and cosmetics
5. Original packaging swapped for new product	Customers return empty packaging to a unit where they leave it and pick up a new product. The old packaging is refilled for future use by someone else	Toner cartridges, single use cameras and Calor gas
6. Door-to-door delivery, packaging replaced	On demand the customers receive full packaging and leave empty packaging for supplier to collect, when they are finished. Returned packaging is refilled for other customers	Milk bottles and vegetable box system
7. Deposit system	Customers return empty packaging to supplier for a financial incentive	Soft drinks and beer bottles
8. Top up card	Customers pay for a service that is delivered on the production of the payment card	Downloadable music and payment systems for services such as mobile phones

(Continued)

Table 8.2 *(Continued)*

Type	Description	Possible applications
9. Creation	Customers buy the constituent parts to make the product themselves. They buy refills to allow them to repeat the process	Soft drink makers and orange juicers
10. Door-to-door delivery, packaging refilled	Customers dispense quantity required from a delivery van, using special containers and only paying for the quantity taken	Detergent products
11. Refilled with different product	Once original packaging has been used it is refilled with a different product	Toys filled with sweets or durable packaging used to store other products
12. Dispensed concentrate	Customers buy a dispensing unit. They also purchase refills containing concentrated product that are delivered through the dispenser	Coffee machines
13. Dispensed product	Customers buy a dispensing unit. They also purchase refills that are delivered through the dispenser	Personal care products in showers
14. Concentrate mixed in original packaging	Customers buy a concentrated refill that they dilute with water and mix using the old packaging	Laundry products
15. Fill your own packaging	Customers fill their own packaging with product in shop	Bags for life
16. Bulk purchase	Customers buy in bulk and refill a sampler package at home	Cooking ingredients (such as oil, vinegar, peppercorns) and household cleaning products

1 In-plant refilling: packaging such as bottles are returned to the manufacturer where they are refilled and dispatched once again to the consumer; eg milk round.

2 Home refilling: including detergents and cooking ingredients.

3 In-store refilling: a variant of the first classification where consumers return to the store to replenish their product.

In Point 1 the manufacturer retains ownership of the primary packaging whereas in Points 2 and 3 the primary packaging belongs to the consumer. Therefore the model depends to a large degree on the willingness of the consumer to either 'buy in' to the ethos of sustainability or for the economic case to be compelling.

Reusable packaging schemes

Business to consumer

In the United Kingdom, reusable packaging schemes still enjoy some traction. Milk rounds for example, which operate an 'open-return' refillable system, are still very popular in some communities despite the overwhelming dominance of supply to the general market through grocery retailers (which offer only single-trip packaging). The bottles remain the property of the dairy, collected regularly in return for full ones. Organic vegetable boxes operate on the same basis – the delivery driver picks up the empty box and leaves the full one in its place.

Whereas both these examples rely on markets which, in the case of home delivered milk specifically, are dwindling due to retail competition, the gas cylinder sector has demonstrated much more resilience. The consumer enters into an agreement with the gas company (usually through a distributor or retailer) and pays a deposit for the canister, although title to the cylinder legally remains with the gas company. When replenishment is required the customer simply swaps the canister for a new one and pays for additional gas. The cylinder is returned to a central refilling station by the retailer. This model relies on the market concentration of a few gas companies that are able to determine the basis on which they engage with their customers. The robustness required by the packaging of a hazardous product such as gas means that it would be uneconomic to operate a 'single-trip' system.

There are other examples that result in a 'high capture rate' of empty packaging. For example, some brewers, such as Samuel Smith, have sold beers, ciders and soft drinks in refilled bottles. They have been able to do this as the sales take place on their owned premises, which means they can ensure that there is a 'closed loop'. However, the fact that many more people are drinking beers off-site has meant that many companies have been forced to abandon the refillable model in favour of one-way bottles and cans.

More usual is the example of the brewer Scottish and Newcastle. For many years its 'Newcastle Brown Ale' was sold in refillable bottles largely through pubs and other on-trade sites, which made it possible to collect used bottles efficiently. However, as off-licence sales increased, capture rates of used bottles fell substantially and management took the decision to change the bottle design to one with less glass. Although this made refilling impossible, there were significant savings in weight and transport costs, as well as of course associated greenhouse gas emissions. Bottle weight fell from 430g to 320g, a decrease of over 25 per cent (Lofthouse *et al*, 2008).

Increasing complexity in the brewing downstream supply chain also played a role in the dwindling of refillable bottles. As with Scottish and Newcastle, many found that off-licence sales were becoming an increasingly important part of their distribution channels. To meet this demand with lighter, more economic bottles, many turned to contract packers rather than investing heavily in their own bottling lines. This introduced another party into the supply chain and made the task of returning bottles for refilling even more complex and uneconomic.

UK Government legislation also played an unwitting role in the demise of the refillable bottle. In 1989 laws were passed that forced many brewers to divest large parts of their estates. Large pub chains came into existence, sourcing beverages from a variety of suppliers, many internationally based. The vertical integration that had been so important for brewers to maintain high capture rates of refillable bottles was lost as supply chains became fragmented and far more complex.

Another challenge within the United Kingdom (and elsewhere) is the centralization of manufacturing and distribution. Samuel Smith is an example where a local brewer has a regional distribution network to its own outlets. This is now the exception rather than the norm. Most distribution networks are extended over the whole country, highly fragmented and complex, factors that do not favour reuse and refill models. Other problems militating against refilling include:

- Manufacturers (especially those in the beverage sector) use bottles as a means of product differentiation and marketing. The reduction in generic packaging means that refilling would be even more difficult.

- Damage to packaging. 'Scuffing' of bottles in the cleaning process – once acceptable – is widely seen as off-putting to modern consumers.

- Consumer markets are increasingly supplied from foreign markets, for instance in the European wine sector. This means that the distance to return bottles and packaging makes the exercise uneconomic.

- European law. Some refilling schemes may run counter to European regulations on competition as they could be seen to favour local suppliers over competitors from other EU nations.

The United Kingdom is not alone in this trend away from refillables. The United States, New Zealand and Australia have all witnessed similar changes in consumer behaviour, although in Germany, Denmark, South Africa and Mexico the market is still strong. In the latter two countries, the high cost of glass is a major factor, giving refillable schemes a competitive advantage over one-use alternatives. In Germany and Denmark cultural and regulatory factors are more important. In most developed countries economies of scale exist (through established infrastructure networks) to produce, distribute and sell single-use packaging that makes refilling uneconomic. The only way this situation could be changed would be through government legislation which, due to the additional cost burden placed upon manufacturers, retailers and consumers, would inevitably be unpopular.

Reusable packaging doesn't just relate to refilling cartons. UK retailer B&Q in conjunction with CEVA logistics and WRAP conducted a trial on the reuse of transit packaging for kitchen components (WRAP, 2010). The trial found that a reusable packaging solution could be reused an average of 22 times, delivering thousands of products to customers, with no reported damage.

CASE STUDY B&Q and CEVA trial reusable transit packaging

Over a two-year period between 2008 and 2010 UK DIY retailer B&Q and global logistics company CEVA ran a trial to assess the feasibility of introducing multi-trip packaging for the movement of kitchen components. The trial related to the transport of 'long' items such as plinths, pelmets and cornices, which were traditionally vulnerable to damage.

The packaging used by B&Q previously had been a single-trip box made of corrugated board wrap designed to protect the product as it was transported to customers' homes from B&Q's fulfilment centre in Branston. This involved:

- 290,000 cardboard long boxes;
- £300,000 overall cost;
- assembly time involving two operators per shift;
- packaging left at customers' houses for their disposal (high probability it would end up in landfill);
- 400 tonnes of waste per year.

To address some of the problems the single-trip packaging caused, while at the same time minimizing risk of damage to the 'longs', B&Q and CEVA developed a multi-trip alternative. This was constructed robustly of woven and corrugated plastic, designed to protect the product while at the same time be light. To be economic, each packaging solution had to achieve at least 20 uses.

Development was not straightforward. Having successfully trialled 48 'Longspac', as they were called, an additional 400 were ordered. Unfortunately due to design and manufacture issues most of these failed. A further 100 were ordered addressing the problems and these successfully achieved 22 reuses.

By the end of the trial, the new packaging had managed to eliminate 3,200kg of waste while at the same time successfully moving the product damage-free.

Rolled out to the entire operation, B&Q and CEVA believe that as well as reducing the amount of packaging used by 400 tonnes per year, if each 'Longspac' is reused 20 times over £150,000 would be saved annually. They calculated that the reduction in packaging would equate to a saving of 327,000kg of carbon dioxide equivalents. However, the calculations of commercial viability are not straightforward. The companies had to take into account the following:

- Relative purchase cost of single-trip packaging (corrugated cardboard and tape) compared to the Longspac.
- Number of reuses that could be achieved.
- Loss rate of Longspac per delivery cycle.
- Difference in product damage rates between single-trip packaging and Longspac.
- Time and resources required for packaging and handling using single-trip packaging versus Longspacs.
- Cost of operating a closed-loop system to track, inspect and clean Longspacs.
- Length of time taken for the Longspac to complete each distribution and return cycle.
- Seasonal variation in deliveries and the impact this has on the pool of reusable packaging required.

Business to business

Within the B2B sector far more reuse and refilling takes place due to the potential to create more 'closed loops' within upstream supply chains. Packaging often tends to be more robust due to its industrial environment and therefore there is a higher value placed on it by supply chain partners. The bulk movement of goods (a characteristic of upstream logistics) requires sturdier packaging, also impacting on the value. Obvious examples include the use of kegs for the transport of beer to pubs and licensed premises; the principle also applies to the movement of hazardous goods or even furniture and kitchen worktops from manufacturer to retailer.

Lifecycle assessment

Lifecycle assessment (LCA) has been defined as 'a quantitative evaluation of the environmental performance of a product system across its lifecycle' (UNEP, 2013). Although of course there are many conclusions that could be drawn by an LCA from an economic and social perspective, there has been much focus on packaging and the impact this has on the environmental performance of a product across its entire life. In some respects the development of the concept of LCAs as a rigorous methodological exercise has been a response by manufacturers, retailers and packaging companies to convince regulators and policy makers that a nuanced approach is required to the problem of packaging waste.

As discussed earlier, although it may seem sensible to introduce schemes to reduce packaging waste from the perspective of mitigating CO_2 emissions, unless full product LCAs are undertaken, there is a risk that decisions based on narrow metrics may be counterproductive. An LCA approach encourages supply chain partners – and politicians and regulators – to avoid making decisions that shift environmental burdens from one part of the product lifecycle to another. This means that it is rarely straightforward to make an assessment of the most sustainable approach to packaging and generalizations are unhelpful. As a report by UNEP (2013) asserts, 'The optimal packaging design from an environmental performance standpoint will vary according to packaging system characteristics such as raw materials chosen for use, the specific product being packaged, and the corresponding supply chain.'

In reality packaging decisions are based on a number of trade-offs between 'least bad' options. For instance, when analysing the implementation of an EU packaging directive, one study concluded that no type of packaging was always better or worse for the environment, irrespective of all assumptions made (Ecolas-Pira, 2005). An example of this is the refillable bottle sector. Studies have shown that when the capture rate is high (as in a closed-loop supply chain) and distances involved are low (as in the Samuel Smith brewery example cited earlier), refillables do have a lower carbon footprint. However, this is not conclusive when capture rates are low even when transport distances are local. Certainly over longer distances single-trip packaging generates lower greenhouse gas emissions. The main reason for this is that the packaging needs to be stronger and heavier if it is going to be reused, therefore adding to transport costs and CO_2 emissions. If, the packaging is designed for multi-use, but is only used once by the consumer before it is disposed of, then it may well be worse for the environment. If a lighter, single-trip package is used, it may generate a smaller carbon footprint especially if the consumer then recycles the packaging rather than sending it to landfill.

LCAs can be limited to the packaging itself or be extended to a wider product system to understand how it impacts on the product in overall terms. If limited to the packaging, an LCA will evaluate:

- The materials used in the primary packaging (that which immediately protects the product) such as plastic granulate or cardboard. These materials could be virgin (either renewable or non-renewable) or recycled.

- The secondary or tertiary packaging (such as totes, corrugated cardboard packaging or pallets). These may be reused, recycled or disposed of. In some cases they may have to be cleaned. If for instance bulk transport is used, tankers would need to be cleaned, probably with chemicals, which would add to the environmental impact of the product.

- The subsequent reuse, recycling or disposal of the primary packaging material by the consumer once the product has been used or consumed.

Generally, it is true that when one packaging is compared to another of similar weight and of the same material, the lighter the packaging the better. This is called in the industry 'lightweighting'. However, this only works if the product is protected to the same degree by the lighter packaging with no diminution of its life. A further factor, of course, is that the packaging needs to be kept in a state that is not harmful to the consumer – a primary and fundamental function of packaging. In the real world, scenarios such as this rarely exist. To be lightweight and retain resilience, it may be necessary to use other raw materials, which could have a completely different set of environmental dis-benefits and trade-offs. As the report by UNEP concludes:

> Conducting cross-material comparisons that emphasize minimizing solid waste can potentially lead to packaging designs that are associated with minimal waste, but when evaluated using LCA lead to increased energy demand from raw material production or other lifecycle stages.

Even recycling rates are not a clear indicator of the overall impact of packaging on the environment and, as with packaging weight, should only be used as one of a number of factors in decision making. This is because ensuring that a type of packaging is recyclable can result in a higher raw material burden. A study by packaging manufacturer Tetrapak found that 1 litre cartons produced using certain materials could environmentally outperform a functionally equivalent carton using alternative materials despite lower levels of recycling of the former (UNEP, 2013).

As mentioned above, a holistic approach includes the impact of the packaging on the product. For example, a cucumber bought shrink-wrapped lasts three times as long as one bought 'loose' without packaging. If the shrink wrap results in a significant reduction in food waste, then there will be a considerable saving in the amount of energy, water and greenhouse gases emitted. As Miller and Aldridge (2012) point out, an unwrapped cucumber loses 3.5 per cent of its weight in three days due to evaporation of water content. This contrasts with the shrink-wrapped version, which loses just 1.5 per cent of its moisture content over two weeks. Keeping product fresher for longer means less food waste and consequently:

- less fertilizer used to grow the product;
- less energy used in greenhouses and poly-tunnels;
- less water required to grow the product;
- lower levels of pesticide and herbicide used in growing replacement products for those that spoil in fridges;
- lower CO_2 emissions generated by the transport of ultimately wasted products;
- less methane produced by products rotting in waste landfill sites.

Finally, it is not always the case that renewables necessarily have less of an environmental impact than petrochemicals, however counter-intuitive this may sound. Much depends on the carbon intensity of the process required to collect and process used packaging.

How packaging can reduce food waste in emerging markets

It is estimated that in the developing world between a third and a half of food is lost post-harvest, between farmer and consumer. This occurs through poor handling or biodeterioration by micro-organisms, insects, rodents or birds. Livestock products, fish, fruit and vegetables are most at risk due to poor standards of refrigeration. Most fresh produce is transported in an unpackaged form and is often sold at markets where handling dramatically reduces its shelf life.

One of the core reasons behind the wastage is the extreme level of fragmentation of production and indeed food supply chains as a whole. The industry in developing markets is dominated by micro-farmers who own less than one hectare. They have access to very limited resources in terms of temperature control and for that matter very little understanding of how to sympathetically handle produce. Marketing channels are disorganized and complex involving traders, middlemen and wholesalers, which leads to enormous inefficiencies. On top of this, transport systems and operations are expensive and undeveloped.

Warehousing and storage facilities throughout the food supply chain in developing countries are often weak or non-existent. This includes at the farm premises themselves and at each supply chain node as far as the market or port. Temperature-controlled facilities are often in short supply and sanitation is poor. In addition, there is a lack of training and awareness related to temperature requirements and on ethylene restrictions for mixed loading. For example, ripening climacteric fruit (bananas, avocados and tomatoes) should not be transported with leafy or succulent vegetables which will be harmed by ethylene emissions. This latter point can be addressed by improved packaging, better training as well as research and dissemination of best practice.

There is an acute lack of packaging technology in developing countries, including labelling. Packaging is important not only to protect the products in transit, but also once they have been purchased by the consumer. In many countries, such as India, most vegetables are transported loose.

The problem is most acute in the perishable fruit and vegetable sector. Considerable research has been undertaken showing that use of (very cheap) low density polyethylene film, combined with temperature controlled storage (13–14 degrees Celsius) can extend the shelf life of bananas, for example, from five to seven days up to 45 days. Even at a very basic level, the use of corrugated fibre board (CFB) and moulded trays or partitions, instead of timber, significantly reduces bruising. The use of CFB boxes would be a first step towards unitization of shipments on pallets, and the introduction of forklift trucks would be a major step in reducing product damage.

In terms of labelling, there is a lack of regulatory systems that provide supply chain partners and consumers with essential data about the product. This can be addressed by governmental initiatives and regional coordination.

Whereas in developed countries there is much debate about how packaging can be reduced, it would seem that the opposite is true in emerging markets. By introducing the latest packaging technologies, very real social and economic benefits can be delivered. The trick will be to achieve this while at the same time mitigating the impact of packaging waste on the environment.

Summary

The role of packaging in the supply chain is gaining importance, not least due to the increasing volumes of e-commerce shipments. It is fair to say that packaging has become the target of much negative publicity in recent years as people, and consequently governments, have viewed it as a source of waste. This is unfair. Without proper packaging, products can be damaged or may perish, which is far more wasteful in terms of resources and carbon emissions than the extra packaging needed to keep them safe. There are many initiatives that can reduce the unnecessary use of packaging and in doing so reduce the amount of 'air' shipped around the world. Making decisions about the right sort of packaging is difficult, as illustrated by the pros and cons of lighter but 'single-trip' bottles compared with heavier, reusable ones.

Key points

- The relative merits of packaging should be measured on a lifecycle assessment basis.
- Modern, complex supply chains limit the instances when reusable packaging can be economic.
- Reusable packaging is not necessarily better than 'single-trip' packaging in terms of environmental benefit – it depends on the supply chain.
- Too little packaging and the product can be damaged in transit with all the energy invested in design, production, storage, packaging and transport lost.
- More packaging, not less, is required in emerging markets to reduce post-harvest food losses.

References

Ecolas-Pira (2005) *Study on the Implementation of Directive 94/62/EC on Packaging and Packaging Waste and Options to Strengthen Prevention and Reuse of Packaging, Final Report 03/07884,* European Commission, Brussels

INCPEN (2003) *Packaging Reduction: Doing more with less,* Industry Council for Packaging and the Environment, London

INCPEN/Reckitt Benckiser (2015) Responsible packaging for resource-efficient sustainable supply chains, http://www.incpen.org/resource/data/incpen1/docs/BCMPA%20January%202015.pdf

Jindel, S (2008) How the iPod is killing air freight, *Traffic World,* 13 October

Lofthouse, V and Bhamra, T (2006) *An Investigation into Consumer Perceptions of Refills and Refillable Packaging,* Loughborough University, Loughborough

Lofthouse, V, Bhamra, T, Trimingham, R, Lee, P, Vaughan, P and Bartlett, C (2008) *Refillable Glass Beverage Container Systems in the UK*, WRAP, London

Miller, L and Aldridge, S (2012) *Why Shrink-wrap a Cucumber? The complete guide to environmental packaging*, Laurence King, London

UNEP (2013) *An Analysis of Lifecycle Assessment in Packaging for Food and Beverage Applications*, United Nations Environment Programme, Geneva

Wal-Mart (2006) Wal-Mart launches 5-year plan to reduce packaging, http://corporate.walmart.com/_news_/news-archive/2006/09/22/wal-mart-launches-5-year-plan-to-reduce-packaging

WEF (2015) *Beyond Supply Chains: Empowering responsible value chains*, World Economic Forum/Accenture, Geneva

WRAP (2010) *Reusable Packaging for Delivery of Kitchen Components at B&Q*, WRAP, London

Global or local?   09
The ethical debate

**THIS CHAPTER WILL FAMILIARIZE
THE READER WITH**

- Why 'globalization' has become an increasingly divisive term
- The political arguments over the ethics of globalization
- The reasons behind a new wave of local and regional supply chains and their benefits
- The controversy over free trade agreements including a detailed examination of TTIP
- The arguments over 'food miles' and whether they have any ethical or environmental validity

Over the past few decades the world's economy has become ever more integrated, allowing manufacturers to unbundle and outsource production processes to remote suppliers. Globalization, it was assumed, would be an unstoppable juggernaut as manufacturers and retailers looked for ever-cheaper sources of labour with which to produce goods for markets in the West, exploiting the comparative advantage some countries have developed in certain sectors and processes. In some cases this advantage lies in the level of value add they can contribute, in others, in lower costs, especially those related to labour.

However, 'globalization' has become an increasingly divisive term that has inflamed political opinion with many people holding it responsible for a range of social ills. Multinational manufacturers, retailers and logistics companies have come under sustained criticism from many quarters for undertaking practices that would seem unethical or environmentally harmful in their home markets. They have also come under attack, as will be discussed below, from politicians who blame globalization for the loss of jobs in Europe and North America, as these are exported to cheap labour markets in Asia or Mexico. It could be argued that the vote by the British electorate in June 2016 to leave the European Union was just part of a global trend to roll back many decades of the movement towards free trade in goods and services, but also, crucially, the free movement of people. Despite this, it is important to remember that globalization has been fundamental to lifting many millions of people out of poverty and has been a major factor in the industrialization of developing countries.

One of the first major challenges to globalization occurred in the economic crisis of 2008–9. Since then, governments around the world have enacted over 1,500 'beggar-thy-neighbour' measures to protect their domestic markets. Of these the majority remain in place today, despite efforts to roll back such legislation. Protectionism can be seen as a response by governments to dampen growing anger in some quarters about the displacement of jobs from developed markets to those primarily in Asia. Even the WTO's Bali agreement was eventually undone by one country, India, seeking to protect its domestic agricultural industry. It had been estimated that if the trade-facilitation measures agreed in Bali had been enacted, the cost of shipping goods would have been cut by more than 10 per cent. This would have raised global output by over $400 billion a year, primarily benefiting poorer countries.

A short survey conducted in September 2014 for research organization, Transport Intelligence, asked industry executives about their views on the future of globalization. The survey consisted of an electronic questionnaire circulated to senior supply chain and logistics executives located around the world. Over 150 people took part. The findings showed that there was a considerable divergence in respondents' views (see Figure 9.1): 42 per cent believed that supply chains would become more global, while 40 per cent thought that they would become intra-regional. The only other significant result was the response more 'inter-continental', which attracted 14 per cent of respondents.

Figure 9.1   In the future, do you believe that supply chain and logistics businesses will become more...?

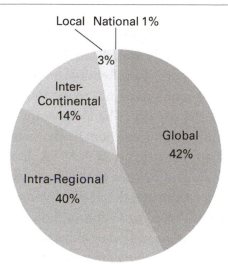

SOURCE Transport Intelligence (2014)

What does this tell us? Already it seems that there is a shift away from the belief that the future is going to be more global. A large constituency thinks that intra-regional trade will characterize the supply chain of the future. However, very few people believe that supply chains will go full circle towards localization.

Globalization is, first and foremost, an economic force based on accessing cheaper labour as well as (probably less important) other countries' comparative advantage in goods and services. However, it is clear that to analyse its impacts without reference to the political situation would be to ignore a vital dimension in its long-term development.

Re-shoring: the political dimension

It was once rare for politicians to talk about supply chain management. However, with globalization at the top of the political agenda in Europe and the United States, the subject has become increasingly common, although not necessarily in a positive way. Re-shoring of jobs has become a mantra for some, harking back to a time when developed economies were characterized by manufacturing rather than the services sector.

Politicians on the Left and Right of the divide have sought to make globalization and consequently global supply chains an ethical issue. For example, Donald Trump, when Republican presidential nominee, promised to 'bring back' millions of jobs to the United States which he sees as lost to China and Mexico. The Democratic contender Bernie Saunders attacked Hillary Clinton whom he characterized as being an 'outsourcer-in-chief' for her support of NAFTA. In the United States the issue has become contentious due to the numbers of jobs involved. Factory jobs have fallen from a peak in 1979 by some 7 million. Most of these have been transferred to China (although many have been lost as a result of automation and other efficiency gains).

Apple has had to defend its manufacturing strategy against robust criticism. In an article published in *Wired,* journalist Edwards Humes considered the lengthy supply chain involved in producing the iPhone. Some parts, he said, 'go on a hopscotching world tour from one country to the next and back again as one piece is joined to another to create an assembly, which is then moved elsewhere in the world for another part to be inserted or attached' (Humes, 2016). Almost all Apple's products are manufactured outside of the United States. When President Obama quizzed Steve Jobs on what it would take to produce the iPhone in the United States he was met with a resilient and profit-driven response: 'Those jobs aren't coming back.' In other words, cost savings and flexibility offered by producing across Asia outweighed any benefits of a US company creating US jobs.

Comparison is often made between the numbers employed by Apple in the United States and the large US automotive manufacturers at their peak. Apple's staff numbers in the United States amount to 43,000, just over a tenth of the employees working at General Motors in the 1950s. However, Apple employs an estimated 700,000 staff through sub-contractors, mostly working in Asia. The reasons behind the strategy are clear. Asian factories have access to large pools of semi-skilled labour that can fulfil the level of flexibility required to meet the high-tech sector product lifecycle needs. High-tech supply chains must be really agile and this means that sub-contractors have to be able to add new shifts, with 24-hour working when required. This is just not possible in the United States. In addition to this, the requisite industry 'eco-systems' no longer exist – intricately woven networks of suppliers providing every conceivable high-tech component.

The impact of outsourcing seems to have fallen disproportionately on middle class employees. Growth in the service sector has been sufficient to offset the loss of low-skilled, 'blue collar' manufacturing positions, but lower and middle management staff have struggled. A study concludes that:

> Contrary to conventional wisdom, the more offshorable occupations are not low-end jobs, whether measured by wages or by education. Roles still exist for highly skilled staff in whatever the industry. At the same time, top employees are the main beneficiaries of the success of the companies undertaking the outsourcing. (Blinder, 2009)

Although statistics on the impact of outsourcing and offshoring of jobs are sparse, it has been estimated that this trend accounted for perhaps 3 per cent of net job loss (gross job gains minus gross job losses) in the United States in the early 2000s (Blinder and Krueger, 2009). It has been blamed by analysts for the 'jobless recovery' following the dot-com bubble recession: although there was economic growth, the benefits of this were not seen in terms of employment in the United States; rather job-creation occurred elsewhere, largely in Asia. One report suggested that in 2000 just under 10 per cent of US employment was susceptible to offshoring. Other studies suggest as much as a quarter of jobs in the United States could be at risk (Levine, 2012).

According to figures from the Reshoring Institute, this trend does seem to have slowed or even reversed. In 2014 and 2015, it appears that the number of jobs brought back to the United States was roughly equal to the number that was outsourced. This was largely due to economic considerations – the rise in wages in China has made the economy less competitive on the world stage – rather than any political measures. This has boosted employment in previously depressed regions.

Of course, while many (from the Right and Left of the political spectrum) see globalization as a deleterious phenomenon that destroys jobs and rewards only senior management, there are counter-arguments. For example, if manufacturers did not outsource parts of their production overseas, their businesses would rapidly become uncompetitive and employment would be lost in any case. In addition, it allows consumers to benefit from lower-cost products that are at least designed in the West.

The speech at the World Economic Forum meeting in Davos in 2014 by David Cameron, then the British Prime Minister, concerning what he described as 'the practice of offshoring where companies move production facilities to low cost countries' ran counter to the usual arguments. Although it was designed to tap into the fashion to talk about the effects of outsourcing some production activity to China and the consequent loss of lower skilled jobs in many Western economies, the speech was far more nuanced. Cameron claimed that there was an opportunity for some jobs previously outsourced to come back to Britain. He cited as evidence a survey of SMEs that found that more than 1 in 10 companies had brought some production back to Britain in the previous year – more than double the proportion sending production in the opposite direction. This included computer company Raspberry Pi and fan engineer Vent-Axia, which were repatriating production operations out of China and back into Britain. The reasons behind this trend were, according to Mr Cameron:

> rising costs in the emerging markets, a natural consequence of these economies developing and their people becoming wealthier. Senior pay in China now matches or exceeds pay in America and Europe while rising oil prices and complex supply chains are increasing transport costs too.

This last point is questionable, with shipping lines increasing fuel efficiency through very large container vessels and both sea and air freight rates so low that parts of the transport sector are barely economic. However, he was on firmer ground when he asserted that, 'By shortening their supply chains, they can develop new products and react more quickly to changing consumer demand. More customization. More personalization. Better and faster customer service.' Importantly he also cited energy costs, with the effect of shale-gas in the United States in particular driving for 'reshoring'.

What Cameron was trying to articulate was that rather than returning to older, less efficient production processes, the increasing unit labour costs in China offer Britain and other advanced economies the opportunity to pick certain types of operations for inclusion in high productivity manufacturing operations while lower adding-value processes remain outsourced to either China or other emerging economies. This is probably a fairly accurate portrayal of the changes taking place in the global economy.

It should be noted that most politicians have not undertaken such an analytical approach to the issue. As mentioned above, politicians to the Left and Right have promised to roll back globalization as part of their populist manifestos. However, when in power, this may be more difficult than they would like to make out.

Local sourcing: the supply chain trend of the future

Globalization strategies over the past 30 years have meant that most global brands have sourced products from low-cost labour markets located in developing regions. Now, however, due to the development of consumer markets in Asia, Africa and Latin America, many products manufactured locally will stay within the local market. This will occur due to the development of a 'middle' or 'consuming' class. By 2020, 1.8 billion people in emerging markets will enter the 'consuming class', spending $30 trillion, up from $12 trillion today. Emerging markets constituted just under half of world GDP in 2012, up from about a third in 2000. In the next decade this shift will continue (albeit at a much slower speed) (McKinsey, 2012).

Manufacturer Unilever believes that by 2020 there will be far more people that 'have lots' in developing markets than there are 'have nots'. The consumer packaged goods sector is in fact a very good example. Emerging markets are very important to these manufacturers because their goods are quite low value and within reach of populations that are just starting to increase their living standards. High demand for every day, high-volume, low-price products will be driven by increasing migration of 'have nots' to 'haves'.

Unilever has stolen a march on some of its competitors, such as Procter & Gamble, and forecasts that in a few years' time around two-thirds of its sales will be generated in emerging markets. Already 57 per cent of its revenues come from these regions. What is important is that Unilever's production strategy involves local production for local markets. Unilever, followed by its peers, has invested heavily in local and regional facilities; for example it has invested $500 million in production and distribution facilities in Mexico as well as $75 million in a factory in Colombia.

Another factor in the 'localization' of supply chains in emerging markets will be the development of 'mega-cities' – usually defined as cities of over 10 million people. The top 10 fastest growing mega-cities in the world are all in emerging markets – four in China and three on the Indian sub-continent. At a smaller level, Boston Consulting estimates that the number of cities in emerging markets with populations of more than 50,000 will be four times the number in the developed world by 2030. This demonstrates the level of urbanization that is occurring (BCG, 2010). Another illustration is that, in 2005, retailers and consumer goods manufacturers had to develop distribution channels in 60 cities in China to reach 80 per cent of the country's population. In 2020, these companies will need to be present in 212 cities to reach the same market.

The consequence of this is that logistics will increasingly be focused on cities rather than countries. Mega-cities will create their own economies of scale, supplied by local/regional production facilities and consumer goods will be customized to local tastes. Each city will develop its own unique eco-system, which takes into account the movement of people, data, finance, energy, waste, goods and services. Transport demands will be specific to each city's needs and capabilities: poor planning and infrastructure will result in high logistics costs. Fulfilment, packaging, miniaturization and reverse logistics will require increased intensity of logistics provision. Although there may be some homogeneity in logistics and supply chain terms, it will be very dangerous for business to take this for granted. There will be far more customization and specialization in terms of product delivery.

Benefits of local sourcing

The emergence of markets for goods produced locally presents manufacturers with the opportunity to increase sales and brand awareness. By developing a local sourcing strategy, integrating numerous micro-enterprises, there are benefits in securing supplies as well as improving quality. Producing and supplying goods in the same market (or in the same trading bloc/region) also reduces tariffs and duties, making products more competitive.

Gaining credibility (the 'Social licence to operate') in the local market with suppliers, consumers, non-governmental organizations (NGOs) and governments is not straightforward and requires time and commitment. However, achieving this level of trust facilitates business and mitigates regulation and bureaucracy as well as potentially providing a source of subsidies. On a global scale it improves the company's reputation, especially among consumers who increasingly regard ethical practices as critical to their buying behaviour.

There are also environmental benefits to the development of local economies and societies. Producing and supplying markets locally reduces the transportation element of the supply chain and hence carbon emissions. There are obvious advantages to the suppliers as well, not only the additional revenues that accrue to them. For example, if they become part of high-value supply chains they benefit from access to new technologies and are able to improve the quality of their products and processes. Longer-term contracts mean that employees gain training and will be incentivized to stay with the supplier. An increase in wages means that more value is created in the economy, leading to greater tax receipts and more investment in infrastructure, which leads to a virtuous circle of value generation.

CASE STUDY Unilever's inclusive business programme

It is in the long-term interests of global manufacturer, Unilever, to help with the development of emerging markets around the world. As consumers generate additional disposable income they are likely to spend it on the low-cost products that consumer packaged goods companies such as Unilever produce, stepping up from the products previously sourced from local markets. As Unilever (2013) itself says, 'An inclusive approach makes sense for our business. It helps to secure essential supplies. It expands the markets for our products, and increases the resilience of our business model.'

To help micro-enterprises and smallholder farmers (SHFs) with whom Unilever has an indirect relationship through its larger suppliers, the manufacturer has developed a 'Partner to win' programme. It estimates that in total its supply chain supports 1.5 million SHFs who in turn employ 7 million people. Unilever describes its approach as supporting:

- Provision of equitable and reliable market access by making its value chains transparent and establishing long-term partnerships with its key suppliers.
- Development of interventions that help smallholder farmers and their communities improve agricultural practices, business capabilities and life skills.
- Strengthening of women's economic standing and changing farm dynamics to facilitate improvements in their position and wellbeing.
- Promotion of young agricultural entrepreneurs to make rural value chains more attractive for the generations to come.

The company says that since 2006 it has enabled 600,000 SHFs and 1.8 million small retailers to improve their agricultural practices and increase their sales. It aims, by 2020, to have had a positive impact on 5.5 million people. Specifically it has run projects in Kenya with smallholder tea farmers through the Kenya Tea Development Agency; in Madagascar with vanilla producers; and in Indonesia with black soy bean growers.

As an example of one of its initiatives, Unilever asserts that by promoting the role of women in farming, yields could be increased by 20–30 per cent. This would have an important impact in terms of raising many of their families out of poverty. Research suggests that women reinvest 90 per cent of income into their families, compared with just 30–40 per cent amongst men. Empowering women is important to Unilever as, in addition to the ethical imperative, the company benefits directly from the fact that 70 per cent of its consumer base is made up of women.

TTIP: the ethical dimension

Currently being negotiated, two free trade agreements, the Trans-Atlantic Trade and Investment Partnership (TTIP) and the not dissimilar Trans-Pacific Partnership (TPP), have attracted much criticism from many activists not only for their aims and content, but also for the secretive and allegedly undemocratic process in which they have been negotiated. As regards TTIP, to counter these concerns, the EU has made a concerted effort to increase transparency through its 'Trade for All' initiative, which has opened up far more of the proceedings to public scrutiny than previously. This is unlikely to satisfy many critics who oppose the free trade deal on principle. The TTIP negotiations have three 'pillars' or streams: tariffs and market access; regulatory cooperation; and trade rules.

It may seem strange that free trade agreements that have the potential to create economic growth and hence prosperity should be so widely pilloried. Frank Appel, CEO of Deutsche Post-DHL, speaking in New York in 2013, commented that he thought that an Atlantic free-trade agreement offered, 'at the very least one additional per cent of growth in both regions [United States and Europe] respectively and generates innovative momentum in many industries and sectors'. This was echoed by Michael L Ducker, chief operating officer and president, international, of FedEx:

> An ambitious, high-standard TTIP covering such a large proportion
> of global economic output will break down trade barriers and create
> alignment between the US and EU on 21st century trade issues. The US
> and EU must seize this moment to capitalize to the fullest on this global
> leadership opportunity, as the rewards will be enormous.

The opposition to the deal has been generated not so much because it simply facilitates the movement of goods between the two regions but because it will move the two regions towards a single market with potential implications for labour conditions, consumer standards and public services. In addition to the economic impact, this could have environmental and social consequences for the EU and United States.

TTIP and the labour market

According to an independent study published by the EC (2016), TTIP will have a range of economic and social benefits and disadvantages in terms of the labour market:

- Overall, wages in the EU for high-skilled and low-skilled workers are expected to rise between 0.3 and 0.5 per cent depending on the economic scenario. Wages in the United States are also expected to rise between 0.2 and 0.4 per cent.

- Some sectors would be more affected than others. For example the EU's electrical machinery sector could see a drop in employment of 7.5 per cent if all tariffs are eliminated and 25 per cent of non-tariff barriers (NTBs) are removed (the 'ambitious' scenario).

- In the United States, the automotive sector would be hardest hit, with employment falling by 2.9 per cent under the same conditions.

- Agriculture is expected to see much higher gains in the United States than in the EU.

- The textile sector in the EU is expected to be the largest beneficiary, with gains in employment of 2.3 per cent.

TTIP and the economy

For consumers there are also implications. The same independent study suggests that the price of imported goods and services from the United States will fall by 4.1 per cent for EU consumers. The biggest falls will be in agricultural goods where the removal of tariffs could result in foods becoming 20–30 per cent cheaper.

Overall modelling by Ecorys for the European Commission estimated that there could be a 0.38 per cent increase in household income, taking into account the impact on jobs, wages and retail prices, if the 'ambitious' scenario were achieved. However, the study acknowledged that there would be many differences depending on a number of variables including whether a person is employed in the city or countryside, is employed or self-employed, unemployed or inactive/retired. In addition the study expected that people at the top of the socio-economic classification would benefit more than those at the bottom.

TTIP and human rights

It may surprise many that human rights have been an important part of the TTIP negotiations. In response to increased concern about the direction of the negotiations, EU Trade Commissioner Cecilia Malmström stated in 2015 that:

> It is clear Europeans want trade to deliver real economic results for consumers, workers and small companies. However, they also believe open markets do not require us to compromise on core principles, like human rights and sustainable development around the world or high quality safety and environmental regulation and public services at home.

Many NGOs have criticized the process, which they believe has downgraded provisions related to health, education and welfare and fundamental human rights, trade barriers and tradable commodities, which can then be negotiated away. To meet these concerns, elements exist in the EU proposal relating to:

- safeguarding labour standards and environmental protection;
- promotion of fair and ethical trade;
- the role of corporate and social responsibility;
- support for the initiatives of the International Labour Organization (ILO);
- elimination of child labour and modern slavery;
- health and safety at work provisions.

Looking at these individual rights in more detail, TTIP is not believed to create more wage inequality between rich and poor, although the rich are thought to become marginally better off ('Right to an adequate standard of living'). The less ambitious the scenario achieved, the fewer benefits for the lower paid (or unemployed or retired) due to income gains being smaller.

The increased economic activity created by TTIP is expected, however, to have a negative impact on the environment ('Right to a clean environment'). Demand for coal and other 'dirty fuels' is expected to rise and some energy-intensive sectors, such as textiles, are expected to see the highest growth in output. This will also potentially mean increased levels of pollutants.

The 'Human right to culture' (the provision to respect and promote the diversity of cultures) is also being taken into account in the negotiations. For example, audio-visual services and broadcasting has been left out of the TTIP remit and the European Commission has retained the right to allow subsidies of cultural activities. This is similar to provisions in the NAFTA treaty that were inserted to protect Mexican and Canadian cultural identities.

'Human right to education' is another area which EC negotiators have now promised to protect. This means that governments will retain the right to run monopolies in educational services and award exclusive rights to certain educational providers. Obviously this would run counter to free market provisions that apply to 'commercial' sectors. However, these rights are maintained on an EU Member State basis, and as such have nothing to do with TTIP negotiations.

TTIP and the environment

In the draft interim technical report undertaken to audit the impact of TTIP on the environment, the analysis was divided into five sections:

1 Climate change

2 Air pollution

3 Land use, ecosystems and biodiversity

4 Material and energy use

5 Water and waste

Most of the expected impact on the environment comes from the restructuring of the European and US economies following the implementation of TTIP. Hence, a reduction in the output of engineering and metals sectors will reduce their impact on the environment in Europe. With greater economic development, levels of greenhouse gases, pollutants, materials and energy use as well as water use and increases in waste are expected. These are all indirectly related to TTIP and it could be argued would occur anyway due to any number of economic or financial stimuli to the European or US economies. However, there are a number of more directly related consequences of the trade deal. For example, additional trade in environmentally-friendly goods and services could result and this would actually have a positive impact on the environment.

Perhaps more important, there are also potential gains to be achieved through increased regulatory coherence, which is also being discussed within the TTIP negotiations. These technical barriers to trade relate to regulations (such as health, safety, consumer protection or environmental) that may be more stringent in one jurisdiction than another. This acts as an effective barrier to trade as, for example, consumer electrical goods manufactured in the United States are not able to be exported to the EU if they do not meet the required environmental standard. In fact for goods such as refrigerators or freezers, the US standards often permit much less efficient operating levels and would not be allowed in to the EU.

Obviously there are two options for negotiators: to lower EU standards to come into line with those of the United States, or to insist on higher standards. The stated aim of TTIP is to 'reduce unnecessarily burdensome, duplicative or divergent regulatory requirements affecting trade or investment... without restricting the right of each party to maintain, adopt and apply timely measures to achieve the (overall) legitimate public policy objectives'. This fundamental economic aim of TTIP brings it into conflict with those who believe that environmental standards could be relaxed in order to broker a deal. This is why so many lobby groups are keeping the pressure on regulators and why to them transparency in negotiations is so important. Those opposed to the deal assert that it will be overwhelmingly bad for the environment. Green groups believe that it will:

- Lock the EU into the import of fossil fuels from the United States and intensify the use of greenhouse gas-emitting resources.

- Prohibit the use of subsidies to support renewable energy projects (by eliminating buy-local provisions).

- Create more carbon emissions in the United States due to less stringent environmental standards.

- Prohibit US states from pursuing environmentally-friendly policies due to the EU's desire to prevent buy-local policies in the United States.

TTIP and food quality

There have been a number of accusations levelled at TTIP and its growing influence on European law. Due to the aim for increased regulatory coherence across the EU and US jurisdictions, many believe that legislation that could derail the talks has been dropped. The Green Party, for instance, has highlighted that a Fuel Quality Directive has been shelved and food safety provisions, such as a resolution against the treatment of meat with lactic acid, have also been dropped after lobbying. It is also suggested that regulations on labelling for meat from cloned animals have been diluted and the use of previously banned chemicals in poultry preparation allowed.

The thrust of these accusations is that TTIP is already having an impact on European consumer health as the European Commission negotiators prepare the ground for the agreement. Lobbyists believe (rightly or wrongly) that measures that US negotiators would never agree to (due to corporate pressure in their home market) are being taken off the legislative agenda.

Dispute resolution

Another criticism aimed at TTIP by NGOs has been the proposal for an Investor-State Dispute Settlement (ISDS). This is described as an international law instrument that would provide an arbitration system for new rules and regulations to be challenged by companies that feel they discriminate against their investments. According to critics this would reduce or eliminate Member States' ability to introduce environmental regulation as there would always be a threat that it would be challenged by the new court. Further, the judges in the court would be unelected and unaccountable to the populations to which their decisions applied. According to some, the ISDS would be anti-democratic. Keith Taylor, MEP, stated:

> This measure would allow corporations to sue governments via secret tribunals (made up of corporate lawyers) if a government takes action that a corporation can prove limits their profits. If included, we'd be one step closer towards corporations writing our laws instead of governments.

Following representations from Member States and the European Parliament, the ISDS was amended by the European Commission to what it called the Investment Court System (ICS). The ICS differed in that its decisions were subject to appeal. The European Commission hoped that this would provide confidence that Member States would still retain the right to regulate within their own jurisdictions on all matters including, of course, environmental and social.

TTIP and Brexit

As the deal was being negotiated between the EU and the US governments, it is unclear whether the UK, post 'Brexit' will be included. This will no doubt depend on the relationship the EU and UK negotiate in the coming years. If the UK attempts to negotiate its own TTIP agreement with the United States, all the contentious issues highlighted above would become major political considerations. However, as there are fewer vested interests, it may be that the UK has a better chance of securing a deal than the 27-member EU.

Trade-off in environmental and ethical decision making

Is the 'food mile' metric unethical?

Globalization has significantly increased the transportation element of supply chains with a corresponding increase in the amount of greenhouse gas emissions. The multiple grocery retailers in particular have been attacked for the centralization of distribution networks that sees their suppliers transport goods long distances, often across borders, to regional or national distribution centres. In many cases these products are then transported further long distances to the retail outlets, which ironically could be close to where the products originated or the gateway through which they were imported. Campaigners would like to see the number of 'food miles', as they have been dubbed, reduced by a return to local companies supplying local markets.

The campaign to minimize food miles on environmental grounds has been gathering pace. Politicians in developed markets are increasingly calling on consumers to shun produce that has been transported long distances, especially by air freight. However, such a course of action would have a detrimental impact on farmers in emerging countries who are dependent on getting their goods to developed markets.

Much attention is being focused on how vegetables and flowers imported by air from Africa cause greenhouse gas emissions that contribute to climate change. Cutting this trade could have an overall negative impact on African development: export horticulture is one of the few genuine opportunities to bring direct and indirect benefits to the rural poor in developing countries. Air freight is currently the only possible mode of transport from most of Africa for highly perishable produce, with more than 1 million people in sub-Saharan Africa depending on this trade for their livelihoods.

It has also been pointed out that climate change is likely to significantly affect the poor in Africa. If there is a link between greenhouse gas emissions and increasing global temperatures, it could be argued that people in developing countries should not be made to pay the cost of the mistakes made by industrialized economies.

While focusing on air freight (which generates a tiny proportion of total emissions) is an easy target for environmental campaigners, this approach conceals far worse problems. These include the clearance of Amazonian rain forest to grow soy to feed livestock in Europe or the United States, which can then be described as 'home grown'. It is also forgotten that much of the produce exported from Africa is carried in the belly-holds of scheduled flights, filling spare capacity on passenger airplanes that would have flown anyway.

Local versus global sourcing

Although the debate over the merits of local or global sourcing is defined largely as a binary judgement, in fact the argument is far more nuanced. Rather than looking narrowly at the transportation of a product to identify its carbon footprint, a full lifecycle analysis (LCA) needs to be carried out before judgement can be made. Factors within this LCA include:

- seasonality of produce;
- efficiency (and energy use) of manufacturing processes;
- use of herbicides, pesticides and chemical fertilizers;
- use of temperature-controlled storage and transportation;
- distances involved in upstream and downstream supply chains;
- the fuel efficiency of upstream and downstream transportation;
- the type of transportation mode employed;
- water use;
- land use efficiency and biodiversity;
- visual impact of agriculture/horticulture methods;
- labour – eg migrant labour (both working conditions and impact of migratory populations on local communities and services);
- quality of produce (eg flavour).

From the number and complexity of these factors it is evident that it is not possible or desirable to generalize about the ethics of moving products over long distances. An additional layer of complexity can be added to the argument by including the benefits (and in some cases negative impacts) of facilitating the growth of export markets in developing markets.

Seasonality of produce

There are three main strategies that have been adopted by the food industry to supply markets with fresh produce, even when items are out of season:

1 Cultivation in an artificial and protected environment (such as glasshouses and poly-tunnels).

2 Controlled storage of produce.

3 Import of produce from overseas markets (where they are in season).

Many research projects have been undertaken on various produce to identify the relative merits of which approach to adopt from a greenhouse gas limiting perspective.

Apples are a good example of the perils of making generalizations about globalized supply chains. During the summer and autumn months in the northern hemisphere, it makes sense (from a carbon perspective) to source apples locally. However, when they are out of season (winter and spring) apples are stored in refrigerated cold stores in controlled conditions. This means that it makes more sense to import apples from the southern hemisphere as throughout their lifecycle overall carbon emissions are lower.

Lettuces are grown in open fields in the United Kingdom from May to October. During the rest of the year, most lettuces are imported from Spain, although some are grown in glasshouses. A study found that the Spanish farms used higher levels of fertilizer, pesticides and water than their British equivalents. Fertilizer is particularly important as it is a major generator of GHGs due to its manufacturing process. Although in Spanish glasshouses heating is not required in the summer season, high levels of electricity consumption were recorded in order to keep product cool post-harvest. In summary the report found that:

- The Global Warming Potential (GWP) of UK glasshouse production was greater in the winter than in open fields in Spain due to the energy required to heat the glasshouses.

- This was the case even though lettuces from Spain were transported by road over 2,600km – road freight emissions were lower than emissions from heated glasshouses.

- Road emissions accounted for between 40–50 per cent of primary non-renewable energy use (PEU) for Spanish lettuces due to the distance transported.

- Lettuces grown in summer in open fields in the United Kingdom also had higher GWP than Spanish equivalents even taking into account the transport by road. This was due to the higher levels of mechanization in the United Kingdom and higher yields in Spanish farms.

On this basis it would seem rational for an environmentally-conscious consumer to buy Spanish lettuces all year round rather than field-grown British ones (Hospido *et al*, 2009). However, GHG emissions are just one part of a multidimensional matrix for decision making. For instance, the report also found that in terms of land use, Spanish farms based on indoor cultivation resulted in high levels of heavily transformed environment with large scale use of concrete for buildings and roads, for example. This would have significant impact on biodiversity, especially when compared to cultivation in open fields.

Water use differs widely by type of cultivation and by season. By far the greatest water use was recorded in Spain for lettuces planted in August and September to supply the United Kingdom in the winter months. In addition to this, due to the source of the water in Spain (groundwater rather than grid or river water), more electricity is used to pump the water into irrigation systems.

It can be concluded from the study that making the 'right' or even 'best' decision on whether to buy local or global is highly challenging. Even making an informed decision based on GWP could be seen as ethically flawed if issues such as water, land usage and social impacts are not taken into account. In the case of lettuce and other salads, perhaps the biggest ethical issue is the volume of food waste post-consumer. Although this falls outside the remit of this book, it is worth noting that according to WRAP, 23 per cent of all fresh vegetables and salads are thrown away. WRAP estimates that 61,000 tonnes of waste were generated from lettuces alone. Rather than concentrating efforts on the sustainability of production and supply, it would seem sensible to address this core problem (WRAP, 2009).

Summary

Globalization has been a key trend in the past few decades as manufacturers and retailers have sourced increasing volumes of goods from low-cost providers located in remote parts of the world. Although this has largely been beneficial to developing economies, with many large manufacturers such as Unilever now focusing the development of their supply chains on local markets, many have criticized the impact it has had on employment in Europe and North America. Politicians in the West are now being faced with opposition to free trade deals such as TTIP, which although they have considerable economic merit, may have implications in terms of societal and environmental impact. This chapter also looked at whether the 'food miles' movement had any validity in terms of ethical and environmental credentials and found that it was impossible to make any generalized conclusions.

Key points

- There has been a reaction to the globalization of supply chains, with many politicians calling for the repatriation of manufacturing jobs, however unrealistic this may be.

- TTIP and other free trade deals have the potential to deliver increased economic prosperity to many parts of society.

- However, there will be losers and people fear that there would also be societal and environmental dis-benefits.

- Manufacturers are increasingly investing in local markets in the developing world as consumers there become wealthier. This will lead to a virtuous cycle of economic growth.

- The arguments over food miles are complex and depend on type of product, the conditions in which it is grown, how and how far it is transported, water requirements and whether or not it is in season. In many cases there is no single right answer as there will also be a range of societal factors to take into account.

References

Blinder, A (2009) How many US jobs might be offshorable? *World Economics*, **10** (2) p 69

Blinder, A and Krueger, A (2009) *Alternative Measures of Offshorability: A survey approach*, National Bureau of Economic Research, Working Paper 15287, Cambridge, MA

Boston Consulting Group (BCG) (2010) *Winning in Emerging-Market Cities*, BCG, Boston, MA

Duhigg, C and Bradsherjan, K (2012) How the US lost out on iPhone work, *New York Times,* 21 January, www.nytimes.com/2012/01/22/business/apple-america-and-a-squeezed-middle-class.html

European Commission (2015) *Trade For All: Towards a more responsible trade and investment policy,* European Commission, Brussels

European Commission (2016) *Trade SIA on the Transatlantic Trade and Investment Partnership (TTIP) between the EU and the USA,* Ecorys, Brussels

Fleming, S (2016) Reshoring and FDI boost US manufacturing jobs, *Financial Times,* 29 March

Hospido, A, Milà i Canals, L, McLaren, S, Truninger, M, Edwards-Jones, G and Clift, R (2009) The role of seasonality in lettuce consumption: A case study of environmental and social aspects, *The International Journal of Life Cycle Assessment,* July

Humes, E (2016) Your iPhone's 500,000 miles journey to your pocket, *Wired,* https://www.wired.com/2016/04/iphones-500000-mile-journey-pocket/

Levine, L (2012) *Offshoring (or Offshore Outsourcing) and Job Loss among US Workers,* Congressional Research Service, Washington, DC

McKinsey & Co (2012) Winning the $30 trillion decathlon: going for gold in emerging markets, http://www.mckinsey.com/business-functions/strategy-and-corporate-finance/our-insights/winning-the-30-trillion-decathlon-going-for-gold-in-emerging-markets

Unilever (2013) The Sustainable Living Plan, https://www.unilever.com/sustainable-living/the-sustainable-living-plan/enhancing-livelihoods/inclusive-business/

WRAP (2009) *Household Food and Drink Waste in the UK,* WRAP, London

PART III
Ethical Issues
in the Supply Chain

Societal and environmental supply chain responsibility

THIS CHAPTER WILL FAMILIARIZE THE READER WITH

- The approach to selecting and monitoring suppliers to ensure they meet sustainability standards
- The impact of resource extraction and water use on the environment in upstream supply chains
- How major multinationals are having to adapt their approach to environmental and societal disclosure to meet increasing consumer demands for ethical standards
- The legal requirements for manufacturers and retailers related to the disposal, recycling or reuse of end-of-life products
- The challenge of dealing with illegal waste
- How manufacturers are complying with legislation on conflict minerals and what this means for their supply chains

Setting the standard for suppliers

Manufacturers and retailers are coming under increasing pressure to ensure that the way their products are sourced, made and then disposed of is sustainable from an ethical and environmental perspective. This 'whole life' approach has placed additional burdens on the supply chain, but it also provides an opportunity to achieve far higher levels of supply chain visibility.

In most sectors of industry outsourcing has now become the norm, which means it is absolutely critical for companies to maintain the highest levels of management control over suppliers. As will be outlined below, considerable risk accrues to the economic owner of the supply chain unless it identifies potential threats, including of course ethical and environmental, within each part of the process. Consequently best practice involves ensuring that suppliers are selected and monitored on a range of sustainability metrics. The process for supplier *selection* should include:

- questionnaire and self-information;
- external audit;
- insistence on an Environmental Management System (EMS);
- provision of necessary permits and licences; and
- formal contracts specifying acceptable standards.

The next stage, *monitoring*, is fundamental to ensuring that the standards that have been agreed are complied with. Sustainability reporting is the practice of measuring, disclosing and being accountable to internal and external stakeholders for organizational performance towards the goal of sustainable development. Some companies, such as Japanese consumer electronics manufacturer Sony, use surveys to understand the environmental practices of its suppliers (Srai *et al*, 2013).

Another issue identified is the lack of consistent key performance indicators (KPIs) against which to measure performance of suppliers (Pimenta and Ball, 2015). Some of the metrics include:

- material intensity;
- resource use;

- water quality and consumption;
- energy use;
- hazardous substances use;
- wastewater disposal;
- waste disposal, reuse, recycle and reduction;
- carbon emissions;
- packaging waste;
- soil degradation;
- noise.

In addition to these environmental items, it is necessary to add societal metrics such as:

- factory building conditions;
- working time/overtime practices;
- modern slavery compliance.

Although the economic owner of the supply chain has the ultimate vested interest in ensuring that sustainability underpins the entire supply chain, there are alternative management methods that can be employed to make this happen. For instance, the customer can impose a system of environmental and ethical processes and standards upon its first-tier supplier base. This occurred when, due to the pressure applied by global brands such as Uniqlo and Marks & Spencer, Zhejiang Qingmao Textile, Printing and Dyeing Co Ltd in China undertook a series of upgrades to its wastewater treatment facilities. This led directly to a reduction in the number of complaints by local residents and an improvement in the immediate environment and ecology (CITI, 2015).

Unless the economic owner is very powerful, it may not be able to have the same influence on Tier 2 or Tier 3 suppliers. As the UN Global Compact asserts, 'Industry collaboration and multi-stakeholder partnerships are important tools for advancing your company's supply chain sustainability objectives, particularly for issues that are too challenging and complex to tackle alone' (UNGC, 2010). So, in most cases it will be necessary to work in partnership with suppliers. As described by Pimenta and Ball (2015), collaboration includes direct engagement between the various levels of the supply chain, in which the focal company (the economic owner) commits itself to the improvement of its suppliers' environmental performance.

A hybrid approach can be successful. Automotive manufacturer Hyundai required all its first-tier suppliers to implement a certified EMS in 2003 and to facilitate this it provided suppliers with training. By 2008 nearly all its suppliers were certified, up from just a third five years earlier. Other support can include technical assistance, workshops and an exchange of information including best practice. The latter facilitates the development of supply chain structures that have sustainability at their core.

Sustainability throughout the supply chain

When looking at supply chains it is possible to identify three distinct sectors:

1 Upstream (including mining and extraction of raw materials).

2 Downstream (manufacturing and assembly).

3 Reverse logistics (recycling and disposal).

1 Upstream environmental impact

The impact of resource extraction

Upstream, many of the materials used in products such as consumer electronics start life being mined in Latin America, Africa or Asia. Just as companies have recently been required to take responsibility for sourcing non-conflict minerals (see below), many environmental lobby groups are campaigning for original equipment manufacturers (OEMs) to ensure that materials used in their products are sourced in a sustainable manner.

Resource extraction, including mining, has the potential to result in a devastating impact on the surrounding environment, not only due to the physical disruption but also to the chemicals utilized in processing raw materials. The influx of immigrant workers can also have a negative impact on indigenous peoples and destabilize local communities. Some of the key issues include:

- use of child/forced labour;
- conflict minerals;
- environmental impact (deforestation, etc);
- chemicals used in process;
- impact of migrants upon indigenous communities.

To provide companies and ultimately consumers with some level of confidence in the sustainability of minerals extracted in developing countries, assurance labels such as the 'Fairmined Initiative' have been created. These certify that the small-scale and artisanal mines from where the gold originated meet certain standards. According to Fairmined, its third-party certification process 'transforms mining into an active force for good, ensuring social development and environmental protection.' They are able to guarantee:

- a 'fair' price for the minerals;
- a market incentive to cover the costs of responsible mining;
- investment in social development and environmental protection.

In return for having to pay higher prices, companies involved in the gold industry are able to mitigate the risk to their brands from bad publicity in a growing market of ethical consumers.

As with conflict minerals, to reduce reputational risk some global manufacturers may be tempted to exit from markets in some emerging countries, especially where the mining industry is informal and small scale. Many of the problems highlighted above may seem insuperable. The aim of organizations such as the Alliance for Responsible Mining is to encourage companies to remain in these markets since to leave would have major impacts on livelihoods and economies. However, staying requires a higher level of engagement and cooperation with local people to ensure that acceptable environmental and societal standards are met.

A problem endemic in small-scale mining is the uncontrolled use of chemicals in the extraction process. Mercury is widely used in gold recovery, for example, and this has major implications not only for the environment but also the health of miners and their communities. To address this major issue, ARM (2016) recommends supply chain partners and NGOs work together in a collaborative partnership to:

- Determine where toxic chemicals are used and take measures to educate the miners and the communities about their impacts and best practices.

- Mitigate the risk of contamination to people and ecosystems.

- Incorporate alternative technologies that can be easily and efficiently adopted by artisanal miners.

- Create financial and credit systems that will allow miners to access funding for technological advances.

- Facilitate access to new markets to create incentives for formalization and the progressive elimination of chemical use.

The challenges continue in the processing of minerals further downstream. The diamond industry, for example, has been beset by problems due to a lack of commercial transparency and working conditions in cutting and polishing factories as well as jewellery manufacturing. To try to address the issue, diamond company De Beers, launched the Best Practice Principles (BPP) Assurance Programme in 2005 and made compliance compulsory for all its suppliers. De Beers' prominence and position in the market allowed it to force through the initiative, which includes provisions for human rights, anti-corruption and anti-money laundering, health and safety, labour standards and the environment.

The role of water use in supply chains

Especially in emerging markets, little or no financial value is placed on water and its use is generally uncontrolled. This has led to the creation of highly inefficient production processes. Data from the IFAD, laid out in Table 10.1, shows the high level of water required in the production of a number of everyday products.

Table 10.1   Water volumes required in food production

Product	Water required (litres)
1 Tomato	13
1 Apple	70
1 Glass of wine	120
1 Bag of crisps	184
1 Hamburger	2,400
1kg of rice	1,000–3,000
1kg of beef	13,000–15,000

SOURCE The International Fund for Agricultural Development (IFAD, 2016)

Due to population growth and changing patterns of food consumption, water use and management is becoming more critical. For example, increased standards of living in China have meant that consumption of animal products such as pork and beef have increased significantly. This not only has had the more publicized impact on the level of farming methane emissions, but has also resulted in the increased use of irrigation water to grow animal feed and provide water to the animals themselves, not to mention the water used in processing meat.

According to the World Resources Institute, a billion people live in water-scarce regions. By 2025 it is forecast that this figure will rise to 3.5 billion, with water demand rising by 40 per cent in the next two decades (WRI, 2016). Much of this demand comes from industry and agriculture in Taiwan: to increase water supply to manufacturing, a river was dammed and water diverted from agricultural use. This raises issues of: 1) the impact of such a move on local environments, and 2) the impact on food production.

An increasing number of manufacturers and retailers are recognizing the issue of water use in their supply chains. Global brewer SABMiller first started to calculate its 'waterprint' in the late 2000s. It found that 90 per cent of the water it used was in the growing of the ingredients rather than in the manufacturing process itself. It achieved a target of a 20 per cent reduction in water use by 2015 and is reducing use again in the next five years. It believes it can cut water use from 3.5 litres per litre of beer to 3.0 litres per litre of beer by 2020.

UK retailer Tesco has recognized that it has a responsibility for the environmental impact of the factories from which it sources fashion items, not least in the effect it has on water supplies and waste water. Textile washing, dyeing and finishing use large amounts of water, energy and chemicals. The retailer has invested $200,000 in the Partnership for Cleaner Textiles Programme in Bangladesh, run by the International Finance Corporation (IFC) with the goal of establishing a world-class water, energy and chemical management practice. Four of Tesco's mills are in the process of completion and another seven have joined the programme. So far the four mills have saved 128,942 cubic metres of water and 3,904 tonnes of carbon GHG annually. This is an average reduction of 22 per cent water per mill (Tesco, 2016). Tesco has commissioned a project with Cranfield University to identify ways in which its supply chain water usage could be made more resilient. The company says that 30 times more water is used in its supply chain to grow, process and manufacture the products it sells than it uses in the operation of its retail outlets.

Water is of course not only used in production but as a way of disposing of waste from the manufacturing process. This means that waste water can contain pollutants such as organic solvents, heavy metals, acid/alkalines and Volatile Organic Compounds. In many parts of the world there are still few controls over the disposal of polluted wastewater and China often comes in for heavy criticism. In the 2015 Corporate Information Transparency Index report, the authors stated:

> Results of investigations by environmental groups have clearly demonstrated that wastewater discharged from many industrial pollution treatment plants does not meet standards, and these plants have instead become centralized 'pollution sources'. (CITI, 2015)

Perhaps the most long-lasting impact on global supply chains would occur if water were priced in the same way as energy or other inputs into the manufacturing process. Presently one of the key reasons for outsourcing manufacturing to remote locations is the low level of cost, both labour and production. If water were no longer regarded as a free or at least cheap resource, but instead as a tradable commodity, the additional costs might become a new factor in the decision on where to locate production facilities or source goods. Figures from Trucost, suggest that profits would be hit hardest in the food and beverage sector should water be priced at its 'real' value. Schemes for water pricing already exist in California and the Murray-Darling Basin in Australia, although it is more difficult to see them being introduced in emerging markets such as Bangladesh. Governments would undoubtedly be wary of putting off new investment (Bernick, 2013).

2 Downstream environmental and societal impact

Pollution can be a problem in all manufacturing sectors, not just those that have adopted outsourcing, such as fashion and consumer electronics. A potential challenge to the outsourcing model is that it reduces control and visibility, meaning that economic owners have to work harder to identify breaches of environmental compliance. If they do not proactively undertake environmental audits, for instance, they can be held responsible by lobby groups (and hence consumers) for washing their hands of their environmental obligations.

In the past many global brands have been wary of publishing lists of their suppliers. This may be for good commercial reasons, but unfortunately it has been perceived as a convenient method of creating obfuscation in the supply chain. Global manufacturers in China have been some of the worst culprits, although this situation is now changing. Still, according to CITI (2015), only nine major brands out of 49 revealed a full list of their suppliers. Those that have adopted this 'best practice' include: Apple, Adidas, H&M, Levi's, Nike, HP, Puma, Dell and Timberland. For companies that use a large number of suppliers, the job of screening them and reporting regularly on violations is extensive, time-consuming and costly. Nevertheless, most of the global brands have decided it is better to buy in to this task than face opprobrium in the media.

Although many companies have attempted to undertake the role of auditing their supplier base from an international head office, this has proved to be difficult and ineffective. Locally based monitoring units can far more easily compile violation records and place pressure on suppliers to put in place corrective action plans. Third-party independent agencies often produce records of environmental breaches.

CASE STUDY Apple's supply chain under fire

Environmental practices

Apple has come under intense criticism for the behaviour of some of its suppliers:

- Pegatron (iPad mini) accused of improper disposal of waste (Kaiser, 2013).
- Foxconn (iPhones and iPads) and UniMicron (PCBs) also said to have dumped heavy-metal waste water (Mozur, 2013).
- Catcher (iPads) accused of dumping hazardous waste unsafely (Miller, 2014).
- In response to the criticism, Apple put forward a robust defence, including building a comprehensive sustainability programme designed to deflect further criticism and mitigate damage to its brand. 'We do not tolerate environmental violations of any kind and regularly audit our suppliers to make sure they are in compliance,' said a spokeswoman for Apple. Initiatives have included:
- Replacing outdated or inefficient heating, cooling and lighting systems, repairing compressed air leaks, and recovering and redirecting waste heat. In the first year of its energy efficiency programme, improvements at 13 sites resulted in a reduction of over 13,800 tonnes of carbon emissions.
- In 2015 Apple launched its Clean Energy Programme to reduce carbon emissions across its supply chain, which makes up nearly three-quarters of Apple's total carbon footprint. In China, Apple worked with suppliers to install more than 2 gigawatts of clean energy. Foxconn, its first partner, will create 400 megawatts of solar energy by 2018.
- In 2015 Apple launched a waste diversion programme at 22 factories, including all final assembly facilities, to help suppliers reduce, reuse or recycle. To date, efforts have diverted 73,773 tonnes of waste from landfill. Foxconn Guanlan became the first supplier to recycle or responsibly dispose of all its production waste without using landfill.
- In 2013 Apple started the Clean Water Programme to reduce the use of freshwater in its suppliers' processes: 73 of its suppliers' facilities accounted for 70 per cent of the top 200 suppliers' known total water use. Through baseline assessments, performance evaluations, technical support and supplier training, Apple helped them save more than 14.4 million cubic metres of freshwater.

- Apple undertook an initiative to identify and prohibit the use of toxic chemicals in the manufacturing process. In 2015 all final assembly facilities were free of proscribed chemicals. The company is now working towards eliminating their use at other assembly facilities.

Apple has invested heavily in turning around the public's perception and enhancing its brand, seemingly successfully. Beijing-based Institute of Public & Environmental Affairs rated Apple number 1 in the IT industry sector of its Corporate Information Transparency Index (CITI), a system for evaluating brands' green supply chain practices. The report commented: 'Apple not only solves environmental problems from its factories, but also works with these factories to set up robust interactive communication with surrounding communities to resolve environmental disputes between such communities and suppliers.'

Employee conditions

A *New York Times* article also criticized the company for labour practices at its major supplier, Foxconn, following a series of events that raised questions about the working conditions at the factories in China (Duhigg and Barboza, 2012). The article described poor working conditions within Foxconn facilities, which prompted Apple CEO Tim Cook to state: 'We care about every worker in our worldwide supply chain. Any suggestion that we don't care is patently false and offensive to us' (Musil, 2012). Apple declined to comment in the article.

As a result, Apple entered a partnership with the Fair Labor Association (FLA), the first technology company to join the association as a participating company. In doing so, the company agreed to uphold the FLA's workplace code of conduct throughout its entire supply chain. The FLA spent 3,000 staff hours investigating three of Apple's factories and surveying more than 35,000 workers. Apple and its supplier Foxconn agreed to its recommendations, and the FLA plans to verify progress and report publicly. Three Foxconn factories were scrutinized by the FLA: Guanlan, Longua and Chengdu (the factory at the centre of the *New York Times* exposé) (Duhigg and Barboza, 2012).

While Apple was the focus of the controversy, the changes made at Foxconn will occur throughout the industry. This will mean that the improved working conditions will also affect factories that manufacture electronics for companies such as Microsoft, Amazon and Dell. Apple and its main supplier Foxconn have agreed to share the cost of improvements to be made at the factories that manufacture iPads and iPhones.

3 Recycling and disposal

The end-of-life supply chain is problematic for manufacturers and governments alike. Whereas once the disposal of goods such as electronics equipment and cars was seen as the responsibility solely of the consumer, legislation in Europe and North America has tended towards pushing this responsibility onto the producer.

Global companies are now also expected to report annually on several key sustainability metrics within Corporate and Social Responsibility reports. For instance, Intel states that it is able to recycle 75 per cent of its waste, most of which comes from construction of its production facilities. It also recycles 75 per cent of its chemical waste. It has goals to reduce waste over a period of time and to eventually achieve 0 per cent landfill (it stood at 7 per cent of chemical waste in 2012).

Even the most basic of household objects can be major pollution hazards. For instance, a cathode ray tube television screen contains 2–4kg of lead, barium and phosphorus and more modern flat screens contain mercury. Lead solder is usually used to connect semiconductors to mother boards and integrated chip units. Not only does this have potential detrimental impact on the health of workers, but waste products need to be disposed of in a responsible fashion.

Many manufacturers were involved in recovering product prior to legislation, not least because it is financially beneficial to be able to refurbish or repair faulty products and reintroduce them back into the supply chain. However, the legislation has gone further, enshrining in law the moral responsibility of the producer to ensure the safe disposal of the product at the end of its life. In Europe the main legislation covering the electrical sector is the EU Directive on Waste Electrical and Electronic Equipment (WEEE). Any equipment that connects to the normal electrical power supply or normal industry standard of a three-phase supply is covered by the regulations. This includes:

- large household appliances;
- small household appliances;
- IT and telecommunications equipment;
- consumer equipment;

- lighting equipment (with the exception of household luminaries and filament light bulbs);
- electrical and electronic tools (with the exception of large-scale stationary industrial tools);
- toys, leisure and sports equipment;
- medical devices (with the exception of all implanted and infected products);
- monitoring and control instruments;
- automatic dispensers.

The regulations apply to importers, manufacturers who make goods under their own name as well as those who brand goods from suppliers under their own name. They must either arrange for the collection, treatment, recycling and environmentally-sound disposal of WEEE, or pay a Producer Compliance Scheme (PCS) to do this on their behalf.

The law has been tightened further following a vote in the European Parliament in 2011. From 2016, Member States of the EU will be expected to collect 85 per cent of e-waste which has been produced, with a 50–75 per cent recycling target. The legislation has meant that, by law, manufacturers have had to extend their supply chain to include reverse logistics, whether or not there was a commercial imperative for so doing. This issue is now seen as an essential part of their CSR policies.

Disposal is not always straightforward. Although many technology manufacturers in the developing world use licensed waste treatment companies to remove their toxic waste, some unscrupulous companies have been found to sub-contract the movement to illegal operators that then dump it indiscriminately.

Illegal trade in waste

Where there is regulation that carries a cost burden, grey or black markets will develop. This has been the case in the disposal of end-of-life product. It is estimated that 12 million tonnes of e-waste is generated in the EU, and presently two-thirds of this is unaccounted for, despite the WEEE regulations. It is believed that this waste either ends up in landfill, treated at sub-standard facilities or exported illegally.

The illegal export of waste from developed countries to the emerging world is now a major industry which, despite efforts by authorities, only seems to be getting worse. The United Kingdom is the biggest exporter in Europe for second-hand electronic equipment, followed by France and Germany. Germany and Belgium are the most important in terms of the export of second-hand cars. Italy is important in the export of refrigerators.

As more regulations are imposed on the disposal of products in the Western world (for instance, Land Fill Tax), the incentives to export the problem to countries with lower standards of regulation become ever greater. The problem was addressed in 1989 by an international treaty to which over 150 countries signed up – the Basel Convention. Many campaigners thought that this agreement did not go far enough, and in fact legitimized the dumping of hazardous waste exports. It was amended in 1995 to cover all forms of hazardous waste exported from the OECD group of countries to the rest of the world. It is clear that this law is being flouted, although this is unrecognized in many countries of export and also those of import. For instance, India has no record of any illegal import of waste as it doesn't track this problem as a crime. China banned the import of e-waste in 2000 but there is evidence that it is still going on, especially in Guangdong Province, the centre of waste recycling in the country.

One report by the Basel Action Network and Silicon Valley Toxics Coalition estimated that 50–58 per cent of e-waste that was collected for recycling in the United States found its way illegally to Asia. Recycling and processing facilities in Asia, Africa and elsewhere are often unregulated, putting at risk the workers, local communities and the wider environment (BAN, 2002).

Computers and electronic equipment can contain lead and mercury and the uncontrolled burning of cabling can result in the emission of dioxins that can travel long distances and find their way into the food chain. In Kenya alone it is estimated that the amount of waste annually includes:

- 11,400 tonnes of refrigerators;
- 2,800 tonnes of televisions;

- 2,500 tonnes of personal computers;
- 500 tonnes of printers;
- 150 tonnes of mobile phones.

The UK Environment Agency says that it takes illegal export of e-waste very seriously, working in conjunction with the Interpol Global e-waste Crime Group. One problem the regulator faces is that companies are allowed to export functional items that can be reused in developing markets, and it is sometimes difficult to assess what is working and what is not (for example, second-hand television monitors would have to be plugged in to be tested) and the vast volume of exports makes it impractical for authorities to regulate effectively.

In one investigation (Milmo, 2009), GPS tracking devices were placed in TV monitors that had been disabled. From a UK recycling centre, the monitors were then tracked to a recycling facility in Ghana. According to Greenpeace, inspections at European seaports in 2005 found that almost half of all waste was being exported illegally. Criminal gangs see this as a relatively low risk method of making large sums of money as illegal waste export does not attract the same levels of attention from police authorities or penalties from judicial authorities. The Belgian customs authorities believe that 90 per cent of illegal waste is exported by co-loading into used cars that are being moved legally.

The problem is deeply intractable, as to ban the export of second-hand equipment would impact severely on many economies in the developing world, especially markets in Africa. The trade supplies low and middle income families with information and communications technology equipment they would not otherwise be able to afford. This access provides them with significant opportunities for economic advancement, which authorities should be encouraging.

There is evidence that manufacturers are more accepting of the need to take responsibility for the disposal of their products – especially those in the consumer electronics sector. A forum in 2012 brought together a range of private sector companies, including Dell, HP, Nokia and Philips with government and intergovernmental organizations under the auspices of the United Nations Environment Programme (UNEP) and the Secretariat of the Basel Convention to discuss the issue of increasing e-waste in Africa (see box below). Instead of looking at e-waste as solely a problem, it is now being seen as a potential opportunity. One tonne of obsolete mobile phones contains more gold than one tonne of ore, and the same can be said for other precious substances. Recycling of this equipment will provide manufacturers with a much cheaper source of the 'rare earth minerals' essential to their production, and at the same time provide business for African economies. It will also reduce the pressure on exploiting natural resources as well as carbon dioxide emissions.

The African e-waste initiative

The African e-waste initiative is a partnership between four OEMs: HP, Dell, Nokia and Philips, and a specialist recycling company, Reclaimed Appliances Ltd and the United Nations Industrial Development Organization (UNIDO).

Developed to address the fast growing e-waste crisis in Africa, the initiative seeks to build on some of the strengths of the recycling industry. For instance, a compelling business model has meant that collection of waste in Africa can be highly effective. In Ghana, 95 per cent of waste is collected as 'refurbishers' and scrap metal businesses are willing to pay a good price for obsolete equipment. The price scrap metal can fetch on the international market supports this model. The vision of the e-waste initiative is that all waste can be collected and properly treated to international standards as part of a profitable business model, and as a result protect health and the environment.

At present the companies work together in four countries: Ghana, Nigeria, Kenya and South Africa. In Kenya the project was initially set up by HP, which was the second recycler working to international standards. It has since developed as a hub for the entire region, with 20 per cent of materials coming from the informal sector. Its goal is to becoming self-sustaining. The centre's customers include the International Committee of the Red Cross which chose it because it offered 'a formal, accessible channel for the safe, environmentally responsible dismantling and recycling of e-waste, allowing us to meet our environmental credentials in the region'.

> The initiative depends on viewing e-waste as a resource, and consequently an opportunity. It believes that the work that has been undertaken will act as an encouragement to major global recyclers to come to the continent. Although additional investment will be required to scale up operations, if governments and other stakeholders can be involved there is no reason why regional solutions cannot be developed. Although producers accept responsibility for their part of the market, the extensive second-hand and counterfeit element means that they do not have full control. Therefore government will have an important role in the development of recycling projects, not least with the enforcement of recycling legislation.

It has been suggested that OEMs adopt the same Extended Producer Responsibility (EPR) for their end-of-life supply chains that is undertaken in developed countries. This would only work, however, if more flexibility is given to manufacturers over how they deal with obsolete equipment, combined with the introduction of world class recycling centres in various emerging markets. Governments have a role to play in this, as well as ensuring that administrative processes are fast, efficient and corruption free.

One example of an early recycling initiative is Nokia's partnership in Kenya with Safaricom, which involves a network of collection points for mobile phones. This is likely to be just the start, with EPR proposals likely to be formally adopted in legislation across the region. Projects are likely to include:

- the establishment of collection centres;
- establishment of take-back schemes by producers and Producer Responsibility Organizations (PROs);
- treatment facilities;
- disposal mechanisms.

However, it will not be straightforward to implement these schemes in the developing world. One of the reasons is the large amount of counterfeit products in the market, which nobody wants to take responsibility for. Also, in many markets there is already a large amount of second-hand equipment in circulation, imported from the developed world. It is not clear whether EPR commitments would cover this equipment if it has already been refurbished by a third-party operator. Given that much of this equipment has only a short life span, this only adds to the problem. Another factor is that government commitment to this problem is not as robust as it could be, with the subject generally low priority and with there being inadequate facilities to deal with the waste.

It is significant that there have been calls to relax the control of e-waste exports to certain locations in the developing world. Some markets are now becoming expert in the processing of waste, and see the opportunities that building a strong recycling competence can create. For instance, one market in East Africa is looking at creating a 'virtual mines' model from recovering the precious metals in imported e-waste.

'Conflict-free' minerals

The interest regulators and administrators are paying to manufacturers' supply chains does not end with labour practices and environmental behaviour. Increasingly companies are being asked to verify that materials used in the production of finished goods are ethically sourced in other ways. This is most apparent in the mining of minerals in parts of Africa, which has been tainted by corruption and human rights abuses in regions of armed conflict.

For example, in West Africa cassiterite, wolframite, coltan, tantalum, tin, tungsten and gold – all used extensively in high-tech manufacturing – are extracted (sometimes illegally) and then passed through multiple intermediaries (both legitimate and criminal) before entering the supply chains of global electronics manufacturers. In some cases the profits from these minerals directly fund armed groups that are involved in waging civil wars in countries throughout the region, especially in the Democratic Republic of Congo (DRC).

In 2010, the issue was addressed in a piece of US legislation that has prompted many manufacturers to take an active interest in the upstream provenance of their materials. The issue was included in the Dodd-Frank Wall Street Reform and Consumer Protection Act and decreed that all publicly listed companies reporting to the SEC must disclose any exposure they have to conflict minerals in this region. They must describe materials as 'DRC Conflict Free', 'Not DRC Conflict Free' or 'DRC Conflict Free Undeterminable'. 'Conflict free' is defined as those minerals that do not finance or benefit armed groups in the DRC or adjoining countries.

One unforeseen consequence of regulation and legislation was that it acted to drive manufacturers away from the region entirely – a de facto embargo – causing widespread hardship to the local populations. In the case of tungsten specifically, the DRC is not a major supplier of the mineral (less than 3 per cent of the world's supply) and consequently there was little incentive for manufacturers to source from a market that presented an administrative headache or cost burden. It is slightly different for tin and tantalum: both minerals are found in large quantities in the country and with the potential for additional reserves, the DRC could become strategically important. According to a report undertaken by Estelle Levin Ltd:

> As a result of the requirements [of the Dodd-Frank Act], from April 2011 many downstream companies took a precautionary approach and decided to stop sourcing from DRC and the region altogether, since the potential legal and reputational risks and the costs involved in due diligence activities made it easier and more cost-effective for them to source minerals from elsewhere. (Jorns and Chishugi, 2015)

The problems were exacerbated in the DRC by a presidential mining ban in 2010/11 that had the unintended consequence of increasing smuggling and illegal mining – completely contrary to the original aims. Due to the economic hardship that this was causing to the miners and local economies, many NGOs changed their core message. Instead of avoidance, they wanted consumer electronics manufacturers to engage with the mines and their communities.

Hewlett Packard, along with Apple, Motorola and Intel, have been at the forefront of developing an alternative solution to this problem that will provide conflict-free minerals while ensuring that investment in the region continues. As with other forms of supply chain risk, increasing visibility to Tier 2/3 suppliers is at the heart of their efforts. The auditing and tracing comes at a cost. The US Securities and Exchange Commission estimated that the cost of compliance would be $3–4 billion to start up and with annual costs of between $206 and $609 million. For the aerospace industry alone it could cost anywhere between $100 million and $2 billion.

The 'Enough project' – an organization campaigning against the use of conflict minerals – measure manufacturers on three key metrics:

1 *Tracing.* Most consumer electronics manufacturers, starting with Apple, have undertaken mapping of their supply chains to identify the smelters from which they source goods.

2 *Auditing.* Following on from identifying where their goods are sourced from, the next stage is to audit the smelters for use of non-conflict minerals – the so-called Conflict-Free Smelters (CFS) programme. In 2010, the Electronics Industry Citizenship Coalition (EICC) and Global e-Sustainability Initiative (GeSI) Extractives Work Group launched the first Conflict-Free Smelter (CFS) Programme. This independently audits smelters and refiners to determine if they are sourcing DRC conflict-free minerals. There is the hope that consumer electronics manufacturers will instruct their suppliers to only use materials sourced from these smelters.

3 *Certification.* In DRC and surrounding areas a certification system has been set up with the aid of the US Government, NGOs and consumer electronics companies, called the Public-Private Alliance for Responsible Minerals Trade (PPA). Mines certified as 'clean' by a regional government body can provide minerals to smelters involved in the CFS programme. Manufacturers such as Intel, Motorola and HP were behind this initiative.

In the past, Congolese tin may have been smuggled across the border and passed off as Rwandan; now, with new controls in place this is proving much harder for the armed groups involved. This has led, by one estimate, to armed groups' revenues from conflict minerals dropping by 65 per cent in two years.

Not all manufacturers are making progress. The 'Enough project' has identified Nintendo as lagging far behind the rest of the industry in auditing its supply chain, along with Sharp, HTC, Nikon, and

Canon (Dranginis, 2016). The minerals of course are not only used by the consumer electronics industry: they are sourced extensively for the automotive, industrial machinery, mining and jewellery sectors, all of which are considerably less developed in their response to this problem.

'Mass balance' model

There are two main models to ensure that the minerals entering the supply chain are 'conflict-free': 'product segregation' or 'mass balance'. The former ensures that all the way along the supply chain 'conflict-free' verified minerals do not mix with other minerals from any other source, so-called 'closed loop' or 'closed pipe'. This means that the supply chain is fully traceable from the mine to the smelter and beyond, and it would usually contain a number of predetermined players, ie a single mine, a single exporter, a single trader, etc, all pre-validated and with direct relations to one another.

For some other sectors, for example where fair trade programmes exist in certain lines of food products such as bananas, this is achievable. In long and complex supply chains where materials undergo processing and transformation, this is far more difficult to achieve on an economically sustainable basis. Consequently, the 'mass balance' programme was developed. In this model minerals from certified mines can be 'blended' with other non-certified sources to create scale volume. The benefit of this is that the process is much cheaper and economically viable, while giving the certified mineral sources a much bigger market. This is a practical approach to ensuring that good mines are able to market their resources more effectively than through a closed loop of limited buyers. For buyers, there is a consistent flow and quality of product. On the downside, it is not possible to trace back the product to individual mines.

The 'Enough project' hopes that in the coming years all smelters will be audited. Many of the costs of auditing are covered by companies such as HP in their efforts to make all minerals used in their supply chains traceable. However, it will take efforts by companies in other sectors that presently are not displaying the same level of concern to encourage smelters to participate in such programmes. In the automotive sector, Ford and GM have signed up to the PPA initiative and

Hewlett Packard's approach to conflict-free minerals

In understanding its supply chain, Hewlett Packard scrutinizes both its first-tier suppliers and the smelters identified by those suppliers that process mineral ores into metals. HP requires its first-tier suppliers to provide information about the smelters they use, adopt a DRC conflict mineral-free policy, and set the same requirements for their own suppliers.

HP has also been working to mitigate an embargo of minerals from the DRC and is committed to using metals produced from 'closed pipe' projects if they are available. These metals, which directly benefit local communities, are available through programmes such as the Solutions for Hope Project and the Conflict-Free Tin Initiative. To establish a complete conflict mineral-free supply chain, a mineral must be certified at the source and during the chain-of-custody process in the DRC. Creating a validated supply of minerals to smelters from the mines poses significant challenges. Because there is no way to distinguish minerals from different mines, a form of secure traceability at all stages from mine to smelter is needed.

In addition to the operational work outlined above:

- HP publishes the identity of its 195 3TG smelters and refiners that it has confirmed to be in the supply chain.

- HP has been a member of the CFS Programme audit review committee since its inception. HP also helped to develop the Conflict Minerals Reporting Template to facilitate the common exchange of information between suppliers and the smelters used in their supply chains.

- HP believes that the deep-rooted problems in the DRC require coordinated action by the business, government and NGO community. HP has committed resources to education, administration and the development of tools to validate mineral sources.

The key to achieving its goals is growing the number of CFS-compliant smelters. When a critical mass of these smelters is attained, HP plans to require its suppliers to source only from them. HP states that the journey toward conflict-free minerals for itself and all companies sourcing these minerals will take time.

in aerospace, Boeing, Northrop Grumman, United Technologies and Lockheed Martin have started pilot projects.

Table 10.2 OECD five-step process

Step	OECD Recommendation	Ford action
1	Establish strong corporate management systems	Assigned accountability and cross-functional team; revised policy and supplier guides to address conflict mineral issues
2	Identify and assess risk in the supply chain	Requiring supplier material content reporting and assigning prioritization of suppliers based on declared content
3	Design and implement a strategy to respond to identified risks	Balanced strategy of Ford and industry action to ensure robust sourcing policies, practices and reporting
4	Third-party audit of smelters'/refiners' due diligence practices	Participation in the conflict-free sourcing program through the Automotive Industry Action Group
5	Report annually on supply chain due diligence and outcomes	Public disclosure in this Sustainability Report and planned SEC filing for 2013 calendar year

The OECD has been at the forefront of the campaign against the use of conflict minerals (OECD, 2015) and has developed a Due Diligence Process framework (see Table 10.2) which companies such as Ford (2014) have followed:

Starting in May 2014, Ford will be required to report annually to the SEC whether our products that contain Conflict Minerals are 'conflict free'. All suppliers globally that provide parts contained in Ford vehicles, service parts, or other parts sold by Ford are required to support this effort. Specifically, suppliers will be required to respond to an annual survey to identify whether products they manufacture or contract to manufacture for Ford contain any Conflict Minerals necessary to the functionality or production of their products. If any Conflict Minerals are contained in the affected product supplied to Ford, the supplier will be required to determine the country of origin of these materials and whether the Conflict Minerals can be identified as 'conflict free', and to report this information to Ford.

Preliminary results of Ford's research show that about one-third of its suppliers use conflict minerals in its products, involving thousands of parts. Tracing these parts back to their countries of origin and deciding on whether they are conflict-free or not is an immense task and will take several years (plus a large amount of money).

If a part is determined to be non-conflict free, then Ford has committed to work with the supplier to find alternative sources that do not involve raw material processors that support, directly or indirectly, armed conflict. The company is also looking at developing certified conflict-free smelter capacity and eventually, when enough exists, to insist that its suppliers use these resources.

As part of its efforts, Ford (as well as other automotive manufacturers) is looking at extending the International Material Data System (IMDS) to include conflict minerals. The IMDS was established in 1997 by a number of the world's largest manufacturers to establish the content of all the components used in vehicles. This was brought about due to legislation by various authorities on end-of-life disposal of vehicles, creating the need to be able to identify and trace substances and materials of concern (such as chemicals) before they are scrapped. Although the database identifies all the materials involved in the production of a car, it does not identify the countries where they are extracted or processed. This is a key element of the extension of the IMDS.

Ford also uses its Global Material Integration and Reporting portal, which enables it to communicate with its suppliers and holds information such as suppliers' certification status. In 2012 it carried out a survey through this portal to identify which of its suppliers were affected by the conflict minerals legislation and then assist with compliance.

Although compliance is costly, some commentators believe that it will provide benefits to the companies involved in the long run. For the first time it will allow them to map out their supply chains, giving them deep visibility. This will provide them with all sorts of advantages in terms of risk mitigation strategies, far beyond the conflict-free dimension. An example of this is Intel. To achieve its goal of making its microprocessors totally conflict-free (they are at present conflict-free of tantalum), it has already mapped 90 per cent of its supply chain.

CASE STUDY   Fairphone

The challenges facing the consumer electronics industry are so great in terms of the ethical deficit within the supply chain, that one innovative manufacturer has established a business model based on its 'clean' credentials. The Dutch smart phone manufacturer, Fairphone, is a start-up that seeks to use only 'conflict free' components as well as adhering to ethical practices in the treatment of its suppliers' staff at its facilities in Singapore. The company also provides a breakdown of the cost of the phone to show full visibility of its business (Fairphone, 2013); see Table 10.3. The Fairphone seeks to address many of the elements of sustainable manufacturing and logistics discussed in this book:

● Cyclical economy. The phone is designed on a modular basis, which allows parts of it to be updated without the need to buy a completely new phone. The founder says he wants to sell fewer rather than more phones.

● The manufacturer has sourced many components from conflict-free sources in DRC and has developed its own fair trade gold supplier in Peru.

● Treatment of its suppliers' staff. Fairphone employs a representative to ensure that staff are humanely treated and work no more than 60 hours a week.

The manufacturer started its quest to source only conflict-free minerals by working with programmes such as the Conflict Free Tin Initiative (CFTI) and Solutions for Hope to source tin and tantalum from validated conflict-free mines in South Kivu and Katanga, DRC. The tin was used for solder and the tantalum was used in capacitors on printed circuit boards.

Table 10.3   The economics of a 'Fairphone'

Consumer price	€325
Taxes and re-seller	€67.50
Ethical Investments	€22
Product	€185
Of which	
Inbound logistics	€2
Packaging	€1
Operations	€45
Net result	€5.50

SOURCE Fairphone

Figure 10.1 Fairphone's ethical supply chain

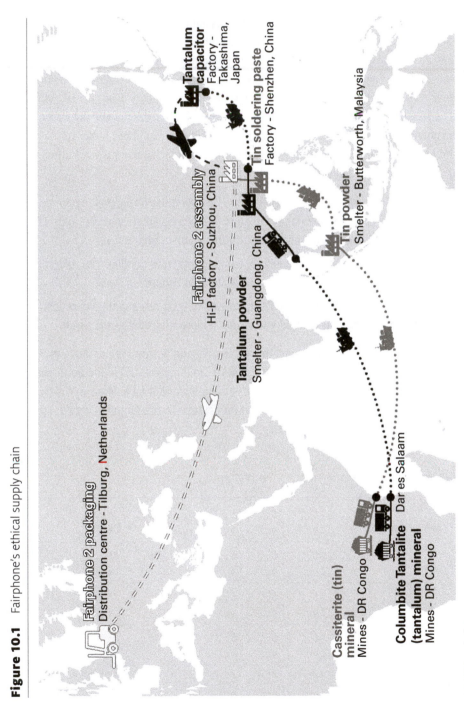

Fairphone 2 packaging
Distribution centre - Tilburg, Netherlands

Fairphone 2 assembly
Hi-P factory - Suzhou, China

Tantalum powder
Smelter - Guangdong, China

Tantalum capacitor
Factory - Takashima, Japan

Tin soldering paste
Factory - Shenzhen, China

Tin powder
Smelter - Butterworth, Malaysia

Cassiterite (tin) mineral
Mines - DR Congo

Columbite Tantalite (tantalum) mineral
Mines - DR Congo

Dar es Salaam

SOURCE Fairphone

The challenge to find conflict-free tungsten took longer and the company worked with Austrian tungsten smelter Wolfram Bergbau und Hütten AG (WBH) and Rwandan mine New Bugarama Mining Company. The mine employs 700–1,200 local miners and is an important part of the local economy.

Once Fairphone has complied with all the necessary regulations to prove that the tungsten was not destined for military or nuclear use, it is exported to Austria for smelting. At this point it is combined with recycled tungsten and from there shipped to China where it is processed for use in the phone. Its management commented:

> Instead of turning away from conflict and high-risk areas like the Democratic Republic of the Congo (DRC) and the surrounding countries, we wanted to find a way to source traceable, conflict-free minerals directly from this region to support the economies of the communities most affected by conflict.
>
> Fairphone works with its partners to take back and recycle old phones as part of its aim to 'urban mine' materials. In Ghana, it has collected over three tons of phones and recycled them in Europe. It collects phones and initiates activities locally for repair, refurbishment and separation or pre-processing.
>
> One of the unique aspects of Fairphone is that its ambition is to design a supply chain that can be copied and implemented by much bigger rivals. Therefore the suppliers it uses must be capable of scaling up to meet large volumes on an economically sustainable basis.

Summary

With the large amount of outsourcing in most supply chains, it is increasingly difficult for 'economic owners' (the major brands) to ensure high levels of environmental and ethical behaviour upstream, downstream and in their reverse logistics operations. Despite this, demands from government (and increasingly consumers) mean that manufacturers and retailers must invest more time and money in achieving visibility than ever before. A range of ethical and environmental considerations must now be taken into account when using suppliers. How do they treat their workforce? What is their water usage policy? How do they dispose of pollutants and waste products? Do they use conflict minerals? In the modern supply chain industry, turning a blind eye to malpractice or failing to investigate is no longer an option.

Key points

- Manufacturers and retailers must put in place detailed processes to select and monitor their suppliers.

- Best practice suggests that a collaborative approach is most effective in ensuring that suppliers comply with sustainable business policies.

- Responsibility for environmental and ethical practices of suppliers reaches from the point when minerals are extracted (or products harvested) all the way to when they are disposed of.

- E-waste is a growing problem, although there have been innovative public-private partnerships to deal with it.

- Although implementing strategies to deal with conflict minerals is expensive, there are ultimately benefits to supply chains in terms of visibility.

- Overly burdensome regulations can lead to manufacturers and retailers withdrawing from challenging markets, with consequent negative impacts on local economies and societies.

References

ARM (2016) Alliance for Responsible Mines, http://www.responsiblemines.org/en/resources/arm-publications

BAN (2002) *Exporting Harm: The high-tech trashing of Asia,* The Basel Action Network, Seattle, WA

Bernick, L (2013) The true cost of water, Greenbiz, www.greenbiz.com/blog/2013/04/29/true-cost-water

CITI (2015) *Greening the Global Supply Chain,* Institute of Public and Environmental Affairs and the Natural Resources Defense Council, Beijing

Dranginis, H (2016) *Point of Origin: Status report on the impact of Dodd-Frank 1502 in Congo,* Enough Project, Washington, DC

Duhigg, C and Barboza, D (2012) In China, human costs are built into an iPad, *New York Times,* www.nytimes.com/2012/01/26/business/ieconomy-apples-ipad-and-the-human-costs-for-workers-in-china.html?_r=0

Fairphone (2013) Cost breakdown of the first Fairphone, https://fairphone. com/wp-content/uploads/2013/09/FAIRPHONE_CostBreakdown_ 150dpi_130913.jpg

Ford (2014) Ford sustainability report, http://corporate.ford.com/ microsites/sustainability-report-2013-14/default.html

Hidrón, C and Koepke, R (2014) *Addressing Forced Labor in Artisanal and Small-scale Mining (ASM),* Alliance for Responsible Mining, Colombia

IFAD (2016) The International Fund for Agricultural Development, www.ifad.org/topic/facts_figures/overview

Jorns, A and Chishugi, A (2015) *Assessment of Impacts of Closed-pipe Supply Chains in DRC,* Estelle Levin, London

Kaiser, T (2013) Apple's Chinese suppliers in trouble for environmental pollution, DailyTech, http://www.dailytech.com/Apples+Chinese+ Suppliers+in+Trouble+for+Environmental+Pollution/article33103.htm

Miller, J (2014) Apple and Dell supplier in China 'neglects staff safety', BBC, http://www.bbc.co.uk/news/technology-29062514

Milmo, C (2009) Dumped in Africa: Britain's toxic waste, *The Independent,* http://www.independent.co.uk/news/world/africa/dumped-in-africa-britain8217s-toxic-waste-1624869.html

Mozur, P (2013) China scrutinizes two Apple suppliers in pollution probe, *Wall Street Journal,* http://www.wsj.com/articles/SB1000142412788732 3420604578648002283373528

Musil, S (2012) Tim Cook: Apple cares about 'every worker' in its supply chain, CNET, https://www.cnet.com/uk/news/tim-cook-apple-cares-about-every-worker-in-its-supply-chain/

OECD (2015) Due diligence guidance: towards conflict-free mineral supply chains, http://www.oecd.org/daf/inv/mne/EasytoUseGuide_English.pdf

Pimenta, H and Ball, P (2015) Analysis of environmental sustainability practices across upstream supply chain management, *Procedia CIRP,* **26,** pp 677–82

Srai, J S, Alinaghian, L S and Kirkwood, D A (2013) Understanding sustainable supply network capabilities of multinationals: A capability maturity model approach, *Proc. Inst. Mech. Eng. Part B, Journal of Eng. Manuf.,* **227,** pp 595–615

Tesco (2016) www.tescoplc.com/tesco-and-society/sourcing-great-products/ working-in-collaboration/saving-water-in-garment-industry-bangladesh/

UNGC (2010) *Supply Chain Sustainability,* UN Global Compact Office and Business for Social Responsibility, Geneva

WRI (2016) World Resources Institute, www.wri.org/our-work/topics/water

Ethics in the supply chain: societal impact

11

THIS CHAPTER WILL FAMILIARIZE THE READER WITH

- The extent to which complex supply chains conceal unethical labour practices
- Modern slavery legislation and why it was considered necessary to introduce it
- The problems associated with auditing of suppliers' operations
- Problems experienced in the fashion and high-tech sectors
- The consequences of supply chain best practice for supplier employees
- Mitigation strategies and what this means for supply chain risk

One of the defining features of the next decade in terms of the supply chain strategies of global retailers and manufacturers may be the pressure they will come under to justify their sourcing decisions from a corporate and social responsibility (CSR) perspective.

There has been growing pressure on companies to demonstrate that they implement ethical policies when it comes to the conditions in which their suppliers' employees work, not least their wages and their environmental practices. No longer is it morally acceptable for manufacturers to outsource production or for retailers to purchase goods from suppliers without having full visibility of these issues. The CSR dimension is critical to supply chains. With globalization of industry predicated on the trade-off between cheap labour, production and transport costs on the one hand, and more expensive inventory holdings on the other, a shift in the cost dynamics of any one of these factors is highly important.

One of the consequences of the unbundling and outsourcing of manufacturing processes has been the fragmentation and increased complexity of supplier networks. This is especially pronounced when outsourcing to production locations in emerging markets, as remoteness and lack of familiarity with the market can be make it difficult for manufacturers or retailers to operate effectively.

Even if there is a willingness to increase visibility of working practices and conditions in lower tiers of suppliers, the task is often challenging and made more difficult by an unwillingness of Tier 1 suppliers to cooperate. A study by the Ethical Trade Institute found that whereas respondents to a survey thought that it was 'very likely' that 10 per cent of Tier 1 suppliers could be undertaking modern slavery practices, this increased to 15 per cent in Tier 2 and 35 per cent in Tier 3 suppliers. Almost three-quarters of respondents believed that some modern slavery existed at the Tier 3 level (ETI, 2015).

The more vertical integration that a global company has, the less likely it is that worker abuse will occur. However, this can be a more expensive option in terms of supply chain costs – although this is not necessarily the case if reputational damage (and other risks) are factored in. In fact the impact of a disaster such as Rana Plaza (see below) on a brand is now recognized as being a major driver of change. The Ethical Trade Initiative report on modern slavery asserted, 'Most companies [in the study] felt that mitigating risks to workers [in their supply chains] was ultimately mitigating risk to the business.' This is backed up by the results of the survey in Chapter 4.

These days, the idea that global brands such as Gap or Tesco would own their own supply chain is unimaginable. Virtual supply networks are the norm, with thousands of suppliers being used, especially in sectors where the goods are largely commoditized (such as fashion and textiles). The problem is that the longer the supply chain, the less visibility there is of working practices. One of the strategies being employed by some of the biggest buyers of products is to consolidate their purchases around a smaller number of suppliers. Not only does this mean that they have more buying power, but they have more leverage with which to implement sustainable and ethical practices. This not only applies to Tier 1 but also (in theory) to Tier 2 and Tier 3 suppliers. This could be referred to as a more activist approach that can deliver all-round benefits. One of the downsides of consolidating production in a smaller number of locations is that risk from events such as natural disasters, fires or industrial action is greater. A balance needs to be struck between the commercial needs of the company, a range of supply chain threats and sustainable and ethical considerations.

Ethical initiatives that involve the collaboration of multiple Western manufacturers or retailers have been shown to be very effective. One of the problems many companies have faced when trying to change working conditions is their lack of leverage higher up the supply chain. Even very large international buyers may only represent a small proportion of a supplier's output so exerting enough pressure relies on a significant number of buyers grouping together to insist on improvements in employee conditions. This problem is possibly getting worse rather than better. For example, when sourcing goods from China, international buyers are dwarfed in importance by local retailers and manufacturers. Getting suppliers to improve their behaviour towards employees is consequently far harder. Many Western buyers are much smaller in size than the suppliers they are buying from, and consequently have no leverage over their behaviour.

Attitudes to competition, specifically competition law, may also stand in the way of effective cooperative efforts to develop ethical supply chains. Many companies are unwilling to talk to their rivals, either because the supply chain is seen as a competitive advantage and there is no desire to share information, or because they are fearful that competition regulators may take action against them. As highlighted below, this has led to independent third-party organizations being established to ensure that communication can exist between companies in a certain market within the bounds of legislation. Non-governmental organizations (NGOs) can play a role in this, such as the 'Stronger together' initiative.

Supply chain audits

Audits of ethical behaviour within the supply chain have become commonplace as manufacturers and retailers attempt to show that they are taking an active interest in the labour (and environmental) practices of their suppliers. Although this level of due diligence is a welcome step, employing an audit approach to supplier validation is seen as flawed due to failings highlighted in recent scandals (such as Rana Plaza). Despite audits of supplier premises being undertaken and the requisite boxes being ticked, there has been plenty of evidence that unscrupulous business owners have been able to deceive inspectors. Unless there is a culture of engagement and a real desire by the global brand to ensure its suppliers comply with its standards, unethical and potentially criminal activity will be allowed to continue.

To this end the audit is now being seen by many companies as a 'starting' rather than 'end' point in their discussions with suppliers. It should highlight areas of major risk and act as a road map for an action plan that addresses these risks. For many companies the problem is the lack of expertise and experience of employees 'on the ground'. Larger buyers are able to commit resources to visiting and inspecting suppliers thoroughly, as well as building relationships with them. Smaller companies do not have this option and therefore rely on third parties to undertake this for them – with sometimes unreliable results.

Best practice in ensuring ethical compliance

- Where possible, keep factory inspections in-house.
- Develop deeper, more open relationships with suppliers.
- Build trust – allow the supplier to admit to mistakes without fear of losing business.
- Make awards that reward best practice.
- Develop a 'toolkit' approach for suppliers, allowing them to audit their own businesses.

- Have regular (eg, quarterly) meetings with suppliers to discuss issues and best practice.

- Develop solutions to problems collaboratively.

- Implement 'supplier exchanges', allowing suppliers to develop solutions amongst themselves.

- Hold conferences where suppliers can showcase solutions to the challenges they face.

In fact many (if not most) global manufacturers and retailers are now at pains to show their CSR credentials due to high levels of internal and external scrutiny. Their businesses are continually reviewed internally by:

- *Supply chain:* what is the risk to the business from disruption that may occur due to supplier problems?

- *Financial:* what would the impact on the share price be if the company's reputation was tarnished?

- *Legal:* is the company likely to be prosecuted under national or international law?

Externally, multinationals are continually being monitored by:

- NGOs;
- governments and regulators;
- the media; and
- trade unions.

In addition to the concerns about the negative risks of poor employee conditions and practices, many of the leading multinational brands have adopted a positive response more in line with the 'triple advantage' strategy outlined in Chapter 1. This involves a holistic approach where merchandise buyers, for instance, fully understand that they should only deal with well-intentioned suppliers, where KPIs and training are aligned with these corporate goals and where accountability of management (at all levels) is fundamental. The ethical commitment has to run through the 'corporate DNA', not exist within a single CSR department. The direct benefit of this approach is that employees of suppliers who are well treated will produce better goods more efficiently, in the same way as if they were employees of the global brand.

By looking at the overall impact of the supplier on the supply chain, companies can avoid taking decisions which, despite looking attractive from a short-term commercial perspective, would have longer-term negative impacts on the business. In this a three-part process is often followed:

1 Does the supplier provide the goods at an appropriate price?

2 If yes, are the goods of a suitable quality?

3 If yes, does the supplier adhere to social and environmental policies?

Only if the company passes all three tests can it be added to the roster of accredited suppliers. Failure to reach the necessary standard should not necessarily be the end of the dialogue with the supplier. If the gap between practice and expectation is not too great, the multinational can work with a supplier to help it improve and eventually gain recognition. Not adopting a constructive approach can often be counterproductive, even with existing suppliers. If a supplier believes it will lose a contract every time it reports an issue to its customer, there is a greater temptation to cover up shortcomings. If there is a more open and productive dialogue to address an issue, both parties are more likely to benefit.

In summary, best practice in ethical supplier sourcing suggests that a multinational requires the following structures in place:

Management
- accountability of decision making right to the top;
- culture and ethos 'to do it right';
- instilling vision and values of staff;
- business strategy that fully understands risk;
- openness to collaboration with competitors;
- communication with customers, suppliers and investors.

Framework
- clear policies and procedures;
- realistic timescale – no cutting corners;

- non-competing sales, cost and ethical priorities;
- legal and compliance procedures.

Operations

- experienced staff 'on the ground';
- dedicated human resources and ethics departments;
- engaged legal and buying teams;
- fully costed supply chain decision making;
- communications, internal and external;
- technology to provide visibility.

China has seen a lot of publicity, not least due to the massive labour forces employed by consumer electronics companies, such as Foxconn, supplying major Western brands. Companies right across the industry spectrum are involved, with fashion being one of the biggest sectors. Asda-Walmart, for example, is the largest buyer of clothing from Bangladesh, with labour costs there half what they are in China.

Working conditions refer to basic labour principles and standards in the manufacturing of goods and services. They include such issues as:

- child labour;
- wages and benefits;
- working hours;
- forced labour;
- freedom of association;
- health and safety;
- harassment and discrimination.

Modern slavery legislation

Several international and national organizations and governments have published guidelines and legislation that companies sourcing goods from around the world are either encouraged or compelled to comply with:

- UN Guiding Principles on Business and Human Rights
- California Transparency in Supply Chains Act 2010

- European Convention on Human Rights
- European Union Directive (2014/95/EU)
- UK Modern Slavery Act, 2015
- OECD Guidelines for Multinational Enterprises

According to the International Labour Organization (2012) there are 21 million people in forced labour throughout the world, some of whom inevitably will be working in supply chains that reach into developed markets (see Table 11.1). Most of those in slavery are based in Asia, although the issue also exists in developed countries, such as the United Kingdom, where it is estimated 10–12,000 people could be considered in slavery. In fact the survey undertaken by the Ethical Trade Initiative (2015) found that 71 per cent of companies believed that there was a likelihood of modern slavery existing in their supply chains. A recent report by the lobby organization Knowthechain (2016) estimates that forced labour generates $150 billion in illegal profits each year.

In 2015 the UK Government passed the Modern Slavery Act, which sought to address the problem of 'slavery, servitude and forced or compulsory labour' in the global supply chains of UK companies. It placed a responsibility on companies over a certain threshold in size (£36 million in turnover) to publish a statement on their slavery and human trafficking policies and what they were doing to ensure that modern slavery was not occurring in their supply chains. As Theresa May, the Home Secretary at the time, commented:

Table 11.1   Forced labour worldwide

Asia	11,700,000
Africa	3,700,000
Middle East	600,000
Latin America	1,800,000
CIS, Central and South East Europe	1,600,000
Europe/North America	1,500,000

SOURCE International Labour Organization (2012)

> It is simply not acceptable for any organization to say, in the twenty-first century, that they did not know [about modern slavery in their supply chains]. It is not acceptable for organizations to ignore the issue because it is difficult or complex. And it is certainly not acceptable for an organization to put profit above the welfare and wellbeing of its employees and those working on its behalf. (Home Office, 2015)

Guidance related to the Act advises that companies should carry out an audit of their suppliers to ensure that they do not undertake unethical practices. It then sets out procedures for how companies should deal with issues that are uncovered, including contacting local NGOs, trade unions or the national government. Although there are no mechanisms for forcing UK companies to stop buying goods or services from a supplier that does not comply, the Government clearly believes that they will feel pressurized by the unwelcome publicity which would otherwise be generated.

The UK Government is quick to point out that there are benefits to companies that will accrue from compliance with the new law, which first came into effect for companies with a financial year ending on 31 March 2016. These include:

- protecting and enhancing an organization's reputation and brand;
- protecting and growing the organization's customer base as more consumers seek out businesses with higher ethical standards;
- improved investor confidence;
- greater staff retention and loyalty based on values and respect; and
- developing more responsive, stable and innovative supply chains.

One of the problems with the legislation is the difficulty in identifying when 'modern slavery' is actually taking place. As the Government itself admits, there is a spectrum of abuse, and poor labour conditions and practices do not themselves constitute a contravention of the law unless a level of coercion exists. Regulations are not enough to ensure employee protection in global supply chains – companies still retain a moral as well as regulatory responsibility for their suppliers' practices.

Some of the questions that an organization may want to consider when drawing up a modern slavery policy are:

- What minimum labour standards are expected of the business, its subsidiaries and suppliers, and how do these align to industry standards?

- Who in the business is responsible for: a) ensuring efforts are made to investigate and remediate the risk of modern slavery in the business and/ or supply chains, and b) ensuring that basic labour standards are met, and how are such behaviours financially incentivized and resourced to do so?

- How does the business factor legal and fair full labour costs into production and sourcing costs to avoid the need for seemingly cheaper slave or bonded labour in operations or the supply chain?

- What is the company's policy where a supplier is found to have been involved in modern slavery?

- When entering into a contract with a new supplier or renewing contracts with existing suppliers what checks, assurances and investigations will the company conduct or accept?

- What support or guidance is available to business operations or suppliers willing to remediate situations of slavery or forced labour found?

- What due diligence will the company commit to conducting regarding its supply chains?

- What is the company policy to support whistle-blowing? What procedures are in place to facilitate reporting, including reporting by workers through helplines?

- What is the company's policy and approach to remediation for workers if and where cases of modern slavery and forced labour are found; and what measures are taken to protect them from further victimization or vulnerability?

SOURCE Home Office (2015)

In addition to definition, another problem is that of visibility. When multiple tiers of outsourced suppliers are used, retailers or manufacturers based in Western countries often find it very difficult to see beyond the top or second tier of suppliers. According to Simon Platts, Sourcing Director at online retailer ASOS, as near-sourcing becomes more prevalent, pressure will increase on suppliers to meet rising demand. This will encourage suppliers to use outsourced providers themselves and mapping these lower levels of manufacturing will become even more difficult.

Employee conditions in the fashion industry

A spotlight was shone on labour practices in the fashion industry following the Rana Plaza, Bangladesh disaster (see below). The trend towards 'fast fashion' in the major Western consumer markets has reinforced retailers' need for cheap and, from the consumers' perspective, disposable fashion items. This was consolidated by the global economic recession, resulting in retailers attempting to provide their customers with ever cheaper products – Tesco's £3 pair of jeans, for example. In the United Kingdom the fast fashion industry is led by specialist stores Primark, Matalan, TK Maxx and ASOS, and by supermarket retailers, Tesco and Asda. Marks & Spencer has also been forced to focus its products around the offering of its rivals to avoid being out-competed.

These demand trends have influenced the sourcing strategies of the major fashion retailers, leading them to seek out ever cheaper sources of production. As labour costs are an important cost element, markets with large and cheap workforces have become popular. This has resulted in what some labour rights activists have called a 'race to the bottom', and they insist that legislation is required to provide for a 'living wage'.

It is not just the cost of labour that has upset activists. The just-in-time nature of 'fast fashion' has resulted in a move from long product runs to shorter production schedules, manufacturing much smaller quantities of goods. The consequence of this is that whereas previously the workforce would be able to rely on longer-term employment, terms are now much more temporary. This favours the employment of informal workers, even on daily terms. The short lead times also result in increased overtime requirements, meaning night shifts, weekend working and a greater level of flexibility in order to fulfil the contract.

The unpredictable nature and short-termism of a contract award has also led to an increased probability of an outsourced supplier sub-contracting to a third party. The Western manufacturer or retailer has even less visibility of the terms and conditions under which its products are being made and temporary labour is likely to be used to fulfil these ad hoc contracts. In Bangladesh and Guangdong, China, one campaign group claims that less than half of workers have a permanent contract.

The hyper-competition of high streets in the developed consumer economies has resulted in much lower prices. This has obviously had major benefits for customers, but it has only been made possible by retailers driving down costs with predictable consequences to the labour force in emerging markets. To compete effectively, global retailers have hundreds of suppliers around the world. Their buying power makes it possible to force down costs, but also to switch supplier quickly to remain responsive to the needs of the market. Retailers also like to exert a large degree of power over suppliers, preferring those that do not work for competitors.

Bangladesh factory disaster

The fire at a factory in Bangladesh demonstrated the reputational risks to Western manufacturers and retailers of sourcing from suppliers in the region. In April 2013, a clothing factory in Rana Plaza, Dhaka, collapsed killing 1,129 workers. The disaster was blamed on poor construction practices with the owner directly responsible (BBC, 2015). It transpired that UK retailers Primark, Matalan and Bonmarché were among a number of Western stores sourcing goods from the factory, and their reputation took a severe knock. Critics suggested that the cut-price clothing business model was based on sourcing unsustainably from low cost suppliers that would exploit workers in terms of pay and, in the case of the Rana Plaza factory, the structural integrity of its buildings.

As a result of the disaster, a range of retailers (including Marks & Spencer and H&M) have signed up to a new compact that will mean rigorous factory inspections and the introduction of fire measures. Of course these will come at a cost.

Although NGOs have been quick to criticize the conditions of many workers in Bangladesh, they perhaps recognize the problems faced by the country. If costs are driven up, either by minimum wages or by regulatory burdens, retailers and manufacturers may leave the market completely. Whereas Primark claims that it has done more than most for the workers of Rana Plaza, compensating families for example, there are many other companies that sourced products from the factory that have not come forward. It is these, which make up the majority of the market, who would be happy to source goods first and worry about the conditions in which they were manufactured later.

Following the fire at Rana Plaza, a multi-stakeholder Accord on Fire and Building Safety was developed in conjunction with retailers, unions and the United Nations. Tesco, although it did not source any goods from the Rana Plaza factory, has gone further, and has conducted structural surveys at all its suppliers' locations (it does not source from shared-use factories).

The importance of an ethical sourcing policy to reputation has not been lost on retailers. In its CSR report, Tesco highlighted that in May 2012 it launched a pilot project in Bangladesh which has:

- Increased pay for suppliers' workers by 19 per cent.
- Reduced working hours by 16 per cent.
- Decreased staff turnover by 45 per cent and absenteeism by 25 per cent.
- Increased efficiency by 20 per cent.

The company says that it hopes to roll out this programme to 100 factories, positively affecting over 250,000 fashion and textile workers. Tesco is committed to the Bangladesh market and says that while some commentators are calling for retailers to pull out, especially in the light of the Rana Plaza tragedy, it should remain. Western companies have the opportunity to provide a positive influence on working conditions. Tesco presently employs 54 people in Dhaka whose roles involve improving standards at its 100 suppliers' factories. To address the issue of temporary contracts, which has proved so problematic in terms of taking on and laying off staff, it offers the suppliers meeting its standards a two year permanent contract. It has also published a list of its suppliers in order to improve visibility.

CASE STUDY ASOS

UK online retailer ASOS has put ethical supply chains at the core of its business. The retailer sources garments from remote markets around the world, which include China, Eastern Europe, India, Turkey as well as from the United Kingdom. It has 182 suppliers using 476 factories located in 30 countries. This demonstrates the challenge ASOS has in ensuring that each of these facilities complies with the standards it has set itself.

To show its commitment to ethical trade at the highest level, ASOS has appointed a team that meets six times a year. It comprises:

- Retail Director
- General Counsel
- Sourcing Director
- People Director
- Head of Corporate Responsibility
- Sustainable Sourcing Manager
- Senior Ethical and Sourcing Manager

Its management states:

> We believe the workers in our supply chain should be safe at work, financially secure and respected by their employers. We are committed to being a responsible retailer, where every worker in our supply chain is protected. Achieving that requires us to set and uphold high standards ourselves, and to work together with suppliers to make sure they uphold these standards too.

To achieve this aim the company has established a Sourcing and Ethical Trade Department, which has the responsibility to develop a commercial strategy within a 'sustainable and ethical framework'. The department works across the company with buyers, merchandisers and technology teams to help them make ethical strategic choices.

Management believes that ethical trade is fundamental to the long-term success of its business as well as those of its suppliers. It stresses that only through partnerships with its suppliers can it improve labour standards.

To help develop its ethical trade programme, ASOS worked with a specialist consultancy, Impactt, which in 2014 undertook an independent review of its practices and strategy. Practical results of this review have been:

- Training of buyers and merchandisers to embed the issue of ethics within sourcing decisions.

- Factory visits for members of the buyers' team. These were designed to increase knowledge of production processes and timings (to understand the practical consequences of buying decisions).

- Involving buyers in the ethical risk rating of their suppliers and increasing buyers' awareness of the supplier and factory base.

The point of these initiatives has been to increase the level of engagement of ASOS's management, especially within the buying department, and to humanize decisions that could otherwise be made solely on the basis of commercial, short-term factors.

In terms of selecting and using the right suppliers, ASOS employs a range of tools:

- Supplier scorecards with which suppliers can be rated and compared against an ethical framework of indicators.

- Education for factory managers on health and safety.

- Factory audits undertaken by ASOS staff members.

- Improvement plans resulting in factory audits.

ASOS is clear that 'blacklisting' a supplier that fails its audits can be counterproductive. It states:

> Automatically de-listing a factory or supplier as a result of a breach often only displaces the issue, rather than fixes it, at the same time as potentially making things worse for the workers in those factories; instead, we genuinely try to make things better on the ground.

In 2015 ASOS joined a group of 14 retailers in the 'Action, Collaboration and Transformation' partnership, which as well as working with suppliers also engages with the global trade union, Industriall. Its goal is to address 'living wages' by reviewing purchasing practices, productivity and skills, freedom of association, and lobbying governments.

ASOS's supply chain strategy is ultimately to focus its sourcing on a smaller number of suppliers. This will give it greater influence and more leverage in terms of the ethical policies it is able to insist upon. By reducing Tier 1 suppliers, there will be an inevitable increase in Tier 2 producers, and consequently a lot more of the responsibility for ethical labour practices (as well as environmental compliance) will fall on Tier 1. This will no doubt increase the challenge for ASOS management and only through its commitment to longer, deeper relationships with its Tier 1 suppliers will it be certain that it can achieve its targets.

Labour issues in the high-tech sector

The consumer electronics industry has been the focus of attention for groups campaigning to improve the working conditions in factories throughout the world. Assembling electronic goods is a highly labour-intensive activity, which is one of the reasons why manufacturers have located this function in regions where labour is plentiful and low cost – such as China. The ease of access to global markets through ports and airports has facilitated this trend.

The electronics sector has also been at the forefront of the 'unbundling and outsourcing' phenomenon that has resulted in the creation of virtual manufacturing networks. This has meant that brands such as Cisco, Dell and a vast array of other household names, have focused their attention on design and marketing, leaving the production of goods to electronic component manufacturers (ECMs) such as Flextronics or Foxconn. It is estimated that three-quarters of manufacturing is outsourced.

One of the risks of this approach is that brands become tarnished if the outsourced providers do not live up to the expectations of consumers by failing to adhere to stringent working practices usual in the West. Migrant workers are often employed to meet the peaks and troughs of demand and their lack of representation often makes them vulnerable to exploitation. Pay is obviously at the forefront of concerns, not just the level but also the structure. Wages are designed to be flexible enough to meet production demands. This often equates to a low basic wage, augmented by:

- overtime – typically 150/200/300 per cent depending on weekday, weekend and statutory holiday working requirements;
- food subsidies;
- skills bonuses depending on grades;
- attendance bonuses.

While Foxconn has in place minimum wage protection in the season of low production, many others do not. Some companies do not allow their staff to resign in the peak season so as to maintain production levels; those that do sacrifice back wages. Shifts range from 8 hours a day in low season to 12 hours in peak season. During periods of high demand, workers can be expected to put in 60–100 hours overtime and work through the night if necessary.

The consumer electronics sector is characterized by heavy use of temporary labour. It is estimated that around 60 per cent of all employees are contracted on a temporary basis; in Mexico some companies utilize up to 90 per cent. Although temporary workers have rights written into European law, in many countries (especially in the developing world) the same level of protection does not exist.

The benefits of employing a temporary workforce, as in the fashion industry, are self-evident. Consumer electronics products have very short lifecycles and hence delivery schedules to support product releases are very tight. This means that companies such as Apple or Samsung need their suppliers to have access to a large pool of labour that can be brought on quickly to fulfil a contract. Flexibility is essential to be able to ramp production up and down as required, so employees are asked to work overtime to meet demand.

The use of agencies to employ temporary labour makes it even more difficult for global companies to ensure that basic standards of protection are in place. Some companies now have policies that prohibit their suppliers from using agency labour. For example, HP's Supply Chain Foreign Migrant Worker Standard says that 'foreign migrant workers shall be signed directly with the supplier, not with a recruitment agent.'

The concerns are not just about pay and conditions. Examples have been cited which include health and safety issues, for example exposure to toxic chemicals and lack of ventilation causing respiratory problems and skin allergies. Other health issues include:

- back problems from standing for long periods of time;
- noise pollution;
- stress;
- eye irritation (for example due to inspecting circuit boards).

A common complaint is the level of discipline regarding quality control – an issue given very high priority due to supply chain management strategies that aim to keep inventory to a minimum. Getting things wrong can result in a deduction from wages.

As with many modern industry sectors, supply chains are highly complex and multi-tiered. This means that it is often difficult for global manufacturers to identify abuses of workers in their supply chains, even if they have good intentions. According to the benchmark report by Knowthechain (2016), only three out of the 20 global brands it surveyed had conducted risk assessments on forced labour in their supply chains. This is despite 16 out of 20 having in place processes to reveal conflict minerals.

One notable example, also identified in this report, relates to Microsoft's auditing process. Microsoft states that during its factory review process, 'auditors examine documentation; visit production lines, dorms, canteens, and waste storage facilities; and conduct face-to-face interviews of workers and factory management'. Microsoft also audits suppliers below the first tier: 'Third-party auditors audit conformance with our Tier 1 suppliers annually and our Tier 2 suppliers based on their risk level.' Microsoft's team supplements these third-party audits with regular onsite assessments of Tier 1 factories and high- and medium-risk Tier 2 component suppliers.

International retail supply chains in fruit and vegetables

Retailers are now more able than ever to provide a wide range of exotic products to their customers, often sourced from emerging markets with much lower standards of production procedures and working practices than in the developed world. This includes the fresh fruit, vegetables (FFV) and fish sectors. This has meant that there is considerable reputational risk to international retailers if they are shown to be sourcing goods from farms where workers are being exploited. Some of the key issues include:

- *Temporary labour.* One of the major problems for FFV supply chains is seasonality. Products may be harvested over a short time-scale – perhaps weeks – which means that a high volume of labour is required to work intensively throughout this period. The work is often temporary, providing for an unstable labour force.

- *Child labour* is often employed in many parts of the world. Although it may be characteristic of many markets, and often an important source of family income, it is unacceptable for Western retailers to be seen as exploiting this form of labour.

- *Illegal workers.* Migrant workers, some illegal, are often employed on farms and, due to their lack of legal status, can be exploited by employers.

- *Wages.* Due to the manual nature of the work these are low, often below the legal minimum wage.

- *Exposure to chemicals.* In undeveloped markets good practice in the application of chemical fertilizers is often not adhered to. This can result in health and safety issues for the workforce.

The fact that these problems exist in the markets from which international retailers source their goods is not the fault of the retailer, of course. They bring welcome foreign exchange and the market they provide for farmers creates employment with all the associated trickle-down benefits to the local economy. However, this does not mean that they do not have a duty of care to the workers of the farms from which they source – a fact that the majority recognize.

In 2011, a report by the Centre for Research on Multinational Corporations (CRMC) (Vander Stichele *et al*, 2011), an organization part-funded by the European Union, highlighted the Peruvian mango supply chain as being of particular concern and named Dutch supermarket giant Ahold as being implicated. Peru exports about 300,000 tonnes of mangos a year, most of which are fresh. Most workers are hired for just three to five months a year due to the seasonal nature of the product. The mangos are shipped by sea to export markets. In the case of Ahold's mangos, they were exported by a large Peruvian agri-business, Camposol, to Rotterdam, bought on behalf of Ahold by Bakker Barendrecht, the retailer's exclusive fresh fruit and vegetable trading company.

Research by CRMC found that wages paid by Camposol were below the legal minimum and working hours were excessive, often 11 hours a day for six or seven days a week. Sanitary conditions were poor and drinking water was lacking. Health and safety conditions were sub-standard. This was despite both companies, Ahold and

Camposol, being signed up to the UN Global Compact, which seeks to protect workers' rights, and the fact that Camposol had signed Ahold's Business Social Compliance Initiative (BSCI). In fact, Ahold has in the past been commended for its commitment to improving the conditions of suppliers' workers. In this instance its due diligence processes were found to be wanting, with the resultant bad publicity and impact on its brand equity. In response to the allegations, Ahold made the following statement:

> In January [2011], Ahold representatives visited Camposol to review the situation. During this visit, several meetings took place with both top and middle management in charge of the fields, as well as with HR representatives. The Ahold representatives found Camposol to be willing to take responsibility for their business and for treating their employees fairly and respectfully. Camposol had already been informed that the BSCI process is now a requirement to do business with Ahold and they have started the process which begins with a self-assessment. An independent audit will be scheduled, and will lead to the identification of any areas for improvement. Because of the findings of our visit and Camposol's willingness to commit to the BSCI process we have not suspended them as a supplier which would be likely to have an adverse impact on their workers and have instead chosen to support them in the social compliance process.

This example highlights a number of key points:

- Retailers have accepted that they have a moral responsibility to the workers who help in the production of goods supplied to their stores.
- Consumers have a level of trust in retailers that the products they buy have been produced ethically.
- Campaign groups can have an immediate impact on the working conditions at international retailers' suppliers.
- Even major retailers that have a generally good track record of social commitment are susceptible to bad publicity if their CSR processes are not comprehensive.
- It is generally recognized that retailers are a source for good in terms of the influence they can have on conditions of employment in developing markets.

Mitigating risk through 'compliance'

Retailers and manufacturers have started to address the concerns raised by pressure groups over environmental and labour-related issues in a range of different ways. One of the key ways in which they have attempted to show their commitment to sustainability is through the publication of 'codes of conduct' which are then audited by external compliance consultancies. Auditing often involves site visits by these consultancies, which may use a tick-box approach.

These compliance efforts are not always effective (see the Rana Plaza case study above). According to one charity, suppliers can be informed in advance of a visit and can cover up illegal practices or brief employees on what they should be saying. Suppliers often feel that they have no option but to try and conceal actual working practices – they are squeezed between increasing cost pressures, including the cost of compliance, and the low prices they are being offered by their customers.

One common complaint, relating specifically to the supply chain strategies employed by the major retailers, is the effect of short lead times on overtime. Excessive overtime has been proscribed by many companies that have adopted codes of conduct. However, in order to deliver against tight schedules, companies often are forced to adopt practices that break the regulations to which they have committed.

CASE STUDY   Intel – mitigating supply chain risk through CSR

Intel, the world's largest manufacturer of microprocessors, recognizes that the practices of the suppliers in its supply chain are also its responsibility. In its 2012 CSR report the company states:

> We hold the many suppliers with whom we do business accountable for operating with the same high standards that we expect of ourselves. We communicate our expectations clearly, work to identify and address issues at the system level, and share our findings and best practices across the industry. Through accountability and transparency, we are raising the social and environmental performance bar for companies around the globe and building the supply chain of the future.

Intel's position with the supply chain is highly important. Admittedly it manufactures a larger proportion of its products in its own factories than other companies in the electronics sector, but it still does business with 16,000 suppliers in over 100 countries, and of course its own products are used extensively in the assembly operations of many OEMs. Its suppliers include Flextronics and Foxconn. Inevitably the number of its Tier 2 and Tier 3 suppliers will run into tens of thousands and therefore allocating responsibility for supplier ethics is critical to ensuring the integrity of Intel's supply chain.

Intel was a founder of the Electronic Industry Citizenship Coalition (EICC) and in 2004 adopted the Electronic Industry Code of Conduct which it expects all its suppliers to comply with. To help with compliance Intel offers its suppliers training and runs education programmes across all the key ethics categories. These include:

- child labour;
- forced labour and human trafficking;
- freedom of association and collective bargaining;
- diversity and non-discrimination;
- working hours and minimum wages;
- ethical practices; and
- worker health and safety.

Intel's approach to supplier selection embodies its CSR policy. Request-for-proposal documents, the first stage in the tendering process, include corporate responsibility metrics and questions. Its supplier audits take place on a quarterly basis and if a CSR issue is not, in its opinion, properly addressed, then steps are taken to 'exit' a supplier. As part of its Supplier Continuous Quality Improvement (SCQI) programme, Intel tracks the performance of its suppliers against a range of CSR metrics. The company stated that in 2012, 82 per cent of its suppliers met these standards.

It is perhaps of significance that in Intel's 2012 CSR report it highlights its relations with Taiwanese electronics supplier, Foxconn. The company had attracted a considerable amount of bad publicity over the previous years, mostly related to working and environmental practices in factories manufacturing goods for Apple. Intel is keen to highlight how it audited Foxconn's operations and identified significant CSR issues. In 2012, it re-audited Foxconn's locations and found that there were still outstanding issues related to working hours, labour conditions, safety and management systems. As a result Intel lent two members of senior management to help address the problems and share best practice. According to Intel this resulted in Foxconn's practices and processes improving to an acceptable level.

Conclusion

The issue of ethical labour practices in the supply chain, whether or not they conform to a definition of 'modern slavery', is now high on the corporate agenda. Businesses are driven by a combination of a desire to 'do things right' but at the same time by the fear of reputational damage and the impact that would have on sales, brand and share price. There is no doubt that a company with a clear policy on ethical sourcing is likely to benefit from a strong management, engaged workforce and a clear strategic vision. New legislation is proving a major catalyst for change as well, as this provides a clear directive for companies to address issues which, for commercial reasons, may have been ignored.

Customer response is also a major driver for change. Many companies believe that among the younger generations particularly there is an increasing desire for information on the conditions in which a product was manufactured, both in terms of its green credentials and labour conditions. This may not manifest itself overtly (although there is a niche customer segment for whom this is the overriding concern), more in an implicit trust that the retailer or manufacturer will employ ethical policies. If it is shown that the trust has been misplaced, the consequences will be severe. Customers still want cheap products, but at the same time goods that have been produced in an ethical way.

Standing in the way of the implementation of ethical labour policies are many challenges. It would be imagined that very few Western retailers or manufacturers would deliberately turn a blind eye to the issue (although that cannot be said for all companies in other parts of the world where the desire for short-term profit dominates). However, resistance can come indirectly due to a combination of:

- competing commercial priorities;
- lack of resources;

- historic buyer practices;
- lack of supply chain visibility;
- supply chain complexity;
- competition regulations that limit collaboration;
- weak management and lack of employee engagement.

In some cases of course they may be the victim of criminal activity by the suppliers themselves, which is a result of the weak governance that may exist in a developing country. This issue can only be addressed by a combination of corporate pressure by an alliance of Western manufacturers and retailers; international pressure from other governments and also work by NGOs. For instance, organizations such as the World Economic Forum have initiated programmes on supply chain ethics as well as corruption, actively encouraging engagement by the governments of emerging markets by demonstrating the benefits of complying with global best practice.

Summary

The unbundling and outsourcing of manufacturing processes and the sourcing of cheap goods from foreign markets by retailers has led to the development of complex and sophisticated supply chains. However, the lack of visibility characterized by multiple tiers of suppliers, combined with the lack of governance in many emerging markets, has created the environment in which unethical labour practices can develop. Pressure from the media and NGOs, however, as well as the increased interest shown in the provenance of goods by Western consumers, has meant that many global brands are scrutinizing the behaviour of their suppliers, fearful of the bad publicity that would be generated by another Rana Plaza disaster.

Key points

- The Rana Plaza disaster in Bangladesh resulted in many global companies reassessing their supply chain strategies and led to the increased scrutiny of suppliers' employment practices and the factory conditions of their workers.

- Supply chain audits were shown to be ineffectual. They should only be a starting not an end point.

- Modern slavery legislation has placed more pressure on global supply chain managers to eliminate employment malpractice.

- Short product lifecycles, seasonality and just-in-time schedules all create stresses in the supply chain that can be borne by workers in terms of their conditions.

- Retailers, manufacturers, governments and NGOs working in partnership can make a difference in some markets, although, especially in China, this should not be overstated.

References

BBC (2015) Bangladesh murder trial over Rana Plaza factory collapse, BBC, http://www.bbc.co.uk/news/world-asia-32956705

ETI (2015) *Corporate Approaches to Addressing Modern Slavery in Supply Chains: A snapshot of current practice*, Ethical Trade Initiative, London

Home Office (2015) *Transparency in Supply Chains: A practical guide*, Home Office, London

ILO (2012) 21 million people are now victims of forced labour, ILO says, International Labour Organization, http://www.ilo.org/global/about-the-ilo/newsroom/news/WCMS_181961/lang–en/index.htm

Intel (2012) Intel Corporate Responsibility Report, http://www.intel.com/content/www/us/en/corporate-responsibility/corporate-responsibility-report-overview.html

Knowthechain (2016) *ICT Benchmark Findings Report 2016*, Knowthechain, London

Tesco (2012) Corporate Responsibility Review 2012, https://www.tescoplc.com/assets/files/cms/Resources/Reporting/CR_Report_2012.pdf

Vander Stichele, M *et al* (2011) *Bitter Fruit*, Centre for Research on Multinational Corporations/SOMO, Netherlands

Ethical supplier relationships 12

THIS CHAPTER WILL FAMILIARIZE THE READER WITH

- How the relationship between supplier and customer carries the risk of unethical behaviour
- The balance of power in supply chains and how this can affect ethical behaviour
- The role of government regulation in the UK grocery retail market
- A code of conduct which governs supply chain relationships and good/bad practice
- The arguments over whether treatment of UK dairy farmers has been fair or not
- The potential for supply chain corruption in the supplier-customer relationship

Although much of this book has focused on how manufacturers and retailers must ensure ethical behaviour throughout their supply chain, with an onus on the suppliers to maintain certain standards, it is also important to recognize the ethical responsibility of the supply chain's 'economic owner' to its suppliers. Where there is a significant imbalance of power in the supply chain (for example, in the grocery supermarket sector in the United Kingdom) there is a risk that companies use their buying power in a way that is damaging to the suppliers' business or, indeed, their industry.

Business-to-business ethics have become increasingly sensitive over the last decade and this has led the UK's Chartered Institute of

Purchasing and Supply to advise their members that they 'must be aware of the compliance criteria they must meet; others may need to satisfy standards of ethical practice and look to organizational reputation' (CIPS, 2007). However, for many suppliers, concerns over the enforcement of rigid business terms and conditions, contracts that seem weighted in the customers' favour, late payment, payment required to fund promotions and other perceived 'unfair' practices have yet to be addressed. Of course, for many customers this is not about ethics but about commercial practice, and many would argue that by driving down costs and insisting on a range of specific requirements, consumers have benefited. Obviously there is a fine line between 'good business' and practices that smack of bullying tactics.

Use and abuse of supply chain power

The use of power in the supply chain is not necessarily a bad thing. For instance, UK retailers used their position in the supply chain to enforce 'factory gate pricing' (buying from suppliers on an ex-works basis and arranging the pick-up and delivery of goods themselves) on their suppliers. Although this was not in the economic interests of the suppliers that made money by bundling the cost of a product with their delivery charges, it has been widely credited with not only cutting the costs of the grocery supermarkets, but of significantly reducing carbon emissions through the consolidation of loads.

Another everyday use of power is the aggregation of order volumes in order to leverage greater value for money. This works in all sectors, not least the transport sector, where the biggest shippers are able to demand the lowest rates from carriers. While using scale as a competitive advantage may be acceptable, there are plenty of practices that would be considered unethical. The problem is identifying where good commercial practice ends and where the 'exertion of undue influence or the abuse of power' as CIPS (2007) puts it, starts. The dividing line looks very different depending on which perspective is taken – customers' or suppliers'.

According to the CIPS code of conduct, there are practices that should be regarded as unacceptable:

- *Paying to become an approved supplier.* Suppliers should be considered only on the merit of the services they provide, measured against an appropriate list of criteria. They should not be expected to pay a sum of money to gain entry to a list of approved suppliers.

- *Late payment.* In Europe, late payments are subject to EU legislation (Late Payment of Commercial Debts (Interest) Act 1998). Late payments undermine an organization's credibility, harming its long-term commercial interests.

- *Countertrade.* Although not illegal, the practice of insisting on reciprocal trading is generally seen as being unacceptable. There are circumstances where it can be mutually beneficial but only when there is no coercion, there is transparency and there is complete agreement between the parties involved.

- *Size of contract.* Purchasing professionals should take steps to understand the impact of the award of a contract on a supplier and its ability to meet the terms. What would happen to the supplier if the contract were terminated? Social factors (ie, what would happen to the supplier's workforce) may be taken into account, although the responsibility of the supplier's management should be primary.

In addition to these points, there has been criticism, specifically of retailers, of requiring payment to gain a better shelf position, ie one that attracts more consumers to buy their products (such as at eye-line level).

Groceries Code Adjudicator

The Groceries Code Adjudicator (GCA) is an independent adjudicator established in the United Kingdom in 2013 to oversee the relationship between the major grocery retailers and their suppliers. It rules on complaints and arbitrates over disputes, providing suppliers with reassurance and the threat of government sanction if a retailer has been proven to break a code of practice. The GCA has the powers to:

- investigate confidential complaints from any source about how supermarkets treat their suppliers;

- make recommendations to retailers if a complaint is upheld;

- require retailers to publish details of a breach of the code;
- in the most serious cases, impose a fine on the retailer;
- arbitrate disputes between retailers and suppliers.

The GCA has identified a number of key issues related to problems in the retailer-supplier relationship, as follows.

1. Delay in payments

- unilateral deductions relating to 'drop and drive' disputes;
- unilateral deductions for alleged short deliveries;
- duplicate invoicing, unilateral deductions for unknown or unagreed items;
- unilateral deductions for current and historic promotion fees; and
- delays in paying entire invoices where only part of an invoice is disputed.

2. Margin maintenance

Some retailers have required lump sum payments from their suppliers to ensure that their margins don't drop below a certain level. When imposed unilaterally and especially retrospectively this is clearly a breach of the code of conduct.

3. 'Pay to stay'

Also highlighted in the CIPS code of conduct is requiring payments to remain as a supplier, seen as unethical and poor practice.

4. Payments of better positioning

Some retailers may insist on suppliers paying for better positioning or more shelf space.

5. Payment for marketing costs

This is also considered a breach of the code of conduct and includes:

- buyer visits to new or prospective suppliers;
- artwork or packaging design;

- consumer or market research;
- the opening or refurbishing of a store; or
- hospitality for the retailer's staff.

6. Payments for wastage and shrinkage

The supplier should not have to pay for loss of inventory if it is the fault of the retailer.

7. Forecasting and over-ordering errors

If the retailer has knowingly provided a supplier with a forecast that is inaccurate and has led to the supplier making a loss, then the supplier should be compensated, unless there is an unambiguous agreement to the contrary.

8. Payments for customer complaints

The retailer must not charge the supplier an unjustifiable amount related to the settlement of a customer complaint.

In 2015 it was announced that the Groceries Code Adjudicator (GCA) would be launching an inquiry into Tesco's supplier practices. In particular it would be examining:

- delays in payment related to short deliveries;
- the imposition of penalties and delays in payment related to invoice discrepancies;
- the imposition of penalties and delays in payment related to consumer complaints;
- deductions for unknown or unagreed terms;
- deductions for incorrect promotional costs ('gate fees');
- deductions in relation to historic promotions that had not been agreed.

It seems that one of the major concerns is that payments by retailers are being halted for an entire order, even if only a small part of the order is being disputed.

During a separate investigation by the GCA into Wm Morrison Supermarkets plc, investigators found that the retailer had called a meeting of its largest suppliers in June 2015, with senior personnel present, and requested lump sum payments running into millions of pounds. The GCA found that Morrisons had breached the code of practice that establishes the principle of fair dealing and the retailer took immediate action to address the issue.

Milk: how ethical are supermarkets' supply chains?

The commercial relationship many of the world's largest retailers and manufacturers have with their farm suppliers is an important aspect of ethical supply chains. It has attracted considerable media attention given the power of the multiple grocery retail chains.

The issue came to a head in the United Kingdom with the inquiry by the House of Commons Environment, Food and Rural Affairs Committee into farm gate prices (HoC, 2016). Farmers' groups have, for many years, held the supermarkets responsible for unsustainably low prices for a range of products, not least milk. Their complaint is that they are being paid prices by the retailers that do not reflect the cost of production, and hence many are going out of business. In their defence, the retailers point to over-production and falling demand as the main problem on a regional and even global basis, which has made the industry vulnerable to price shocks. Weakening growth in China and an import ban by Russia of EU dairy products have had particularly severe effects.

The way in which supermarkets have used milk as a 'loss-leader' to attract customers has been the most controversial practice. The inquiry concluded that there should be no link between the consumer price and that paid to the producer. If a supermarket wanted to offer an unsustainably low deal to its consumers, it could; however if this meant a threat to the livelihood of farmers there were ethical as well as long-term strategic issues for the milk industry as a whole.

The milk supply chain: facts and misconceptions

The milk industry has endured a tough two years with many UK farmers being forced out of business. The issue revolves around the accusation by farmers that they are not being paid a 'fair' price for the milk they produce. The National Farmers' Union (NFU) has predicted that up to one in five dairy farmers in the United Kingdom could go out of business in 2016 and others face a rising debt crisis. Since 2006 it is estimated that the number of dairy farms has halved from 21,000 to just over 10,000 today. This figure could, according to some commentators, halve again in the next 10 years.

An example of the problem was cited in the national press (Anderson and Bury, 2016). According to the report, one farmer's income reduced from 32.69p per litre in 2013 to just 20.64p per litre in December 2015. His production costs were about 31p per litre. Government figures put the average dairy farmer's income at £46,500, down by 45 per cent in one year alone. Those farmers who are not in an 'aligned agreement' with one of the retailers have been hardest hit as they have no protection from market volatility. There have been demonstrations in London, at wholesalers' distribution centres and at retailers' premises themselves.

The situation in the United Kingdom is worse than in neighbouring European countries due to the fact that most milk produced is sold in liquid form – about 65 per cent. This makes it more difficult to store than if it had been processed as cheese or butter. In Europe, only approximately 30 per cent of milk is sold as a liquid, meaning that farmers are less exposed to sudden fluctuations in the milk price. Turning milk into cheese, butter and yoghurt at the point of origin also adds value that is otherwise lost to downstream processors.

Why do farmers blame retailers?

The grocery retail sector is very competitive, even more so now that 'hard discounters' such as Aldi and Lidl have aggressively targeted the UK market. Between them, Tesco, Asda, Sainsbury's and Morrisons account for 70 per cent of all sales in the United Kingdom. As a staple, everyday product, milk has been used by retailers to win new custom by reducing its price, and dairy farmers believe that they have suffered as a result. In written evidence to the House of Commons' inquiry, the NFU said: 'Ideally, all in the supply chain would commit to ensuring all food sold comes from a producer who has been paid a fair price. In practice, each retailer and processor has a different approach to sourcing policies.'

Despite headlines to the contrary, many of the country's largest retailers already have buying policies based on the cost of production, thereby ensuring a level of protection for those farmers supplying them. These retailers include Tesco, Sainsbury's, Waitrose, the Co-op and Marks & Spencer. Tim Smith, Tesco Group Quality Director, giving oral evidence to the farm gate prices inquiry, commented:

> We buy, we think, around a quarter of all the agricultural output in the UK, and when we are talking to our UK supply base – take milk, specifically – we know that where necessary, you have to decouple what the market is doing from the price that we need to pay those farmers, effectively to protect the investment they have put into the supply chain and their assets, which are built to supply Tesco. You have to keep doing that. That is why being close to the supply base and understanding the needs of those individual producers, even though some of that is going through processors, is absolutely vital. Being transparent and providing them with certainty about what the market is likely to do, while recognizing the volatility caused by the vagaries of currency and world commodity prices – those are an inevitable part of what we do.

Others (for example Asda, Morrisons, Aldi and Lidl) provide a minimum buying price. In the case of Morrisons, this policy was forced on them after a sustained campaign by disgruntled farmers in 2015. Prior to this the retailer bought all its milk from either Arla or Dairy Crest at a market rate, regardless of the impact on dairy farmers. After approaches from the NFU and the lobby group Farmers for Action, Morrisons agreed to provide a supplement to the price it paid and on top of that, a minimum floor price (at the time 26.5p). In addition it created a new product, 'Milk for Farmers', which was sold at a premium with the extra revenue raised returned to farmers.

Another issue is that only a relatively small number of farmers supply the supermarkets direct. Many supply buying groups which in turn supply the milk in various forms to a much larger number of retailers than just the main supermarkets. Many of these buying groups do not offer the same sort of safeguards that are available to those supplying the major supermarkets direct.

In the case of processed milk, the situation is even more opaque. A large proportion of the cheese bought by the supermarkets (50 per cent in the case of Sainsbury's Cheddar cheese products) comes from sources that are not protected from market volatility. However, the supermarkets have very little control over this situation as they are not allowed to stipulate where food manufacturers must source their ingredients from or indeed the price they pay for them.

Despite less attention in recent months by the media the issue has not gone away. A press release issued by the Tenant Farmers Association (TFA) in July 2016 claimed:

> Whilst we are seeing a reasonable distribution of returns within the liquid market, profits from the higher prices in milk powder and fats are not being passed down to farmers who have suffered major losses over the past two years and who desperately need their fair share of the return that the market is now delivering.

What are the solutions?

One of the solutions put forward by the UK Government has been the creation of producer organizations that would act as farmers' collectives. This would allow them to counter the oligopolistic nature of the market, presently dominated by a few giant supermarket chains, thus changing the balance of power in the supply chain.

Another suggestion has been the creation of a futures market in the industry. This would allow farmers to 'lock in' a forward commodity price, providing a more stable environment in which to invest.

Adding value at the point of production would be another supply chain initiative. As mentioned above, a higher proportion of milk is sold in liquid form in the United Kingdom than in mainland Europe. The United Kingdom imports a substantial amount of cheese, yoghurt and butter from other European countries, which suggests a significant opportunity for UK farmers and processors. For example, up to March 2016, Tesco used milk sourced from Germany for its yoghurt products.

The UK Government created the Groceries Code Adjudicator (GCA) in 2013 to regulate the relationship between the top 10 supermarkets (Aldi, Co-operative, Iceland, Lidl, Marks & Spencer, Morrisons, Asda, Sainsbury's, Tesco and Waitrose) and their suppliers. This necessarily covers the dairy sector. The agency does not seek to set or determine 'fair' prices, although it will theoretically curb any bullying of suppliers that may occur. It can investigate and where necessary fine retailers for behaviour such as late payments to suppliers.

For some this is not enough. The TFA has called for a reform of the GCA that would allow it to consider the entire supply chain, rather than just the relationship between the processor and the retailer. It would like to see the GCA report on the share of the retail price received at each point within the supply chain, which would then inform negotiations between farmers, processors and retailers.

Corruption in supply chain relationships

Although corruption is not a subject many companies are willing to discuss, there is no doubting its importance. Corruption has been identified as the leading barrier to conducting business in 22 out of 144 economies, according to the World Economic Forum's Global Competitiveness Report (WEF, 2013). In fact the WEF describes corruption – the widespread and deep-rooted abuse of entrusted power for private gain – as the single greatest obstacle to economic and social development around the world. This includes fraud, bribery and kick-backs but can also include, in other contexts, non-financial forms of corruption such as preferential treatment in the assistance or hiring processes of family members or friends, or even the intimidation of staff to turn a blind eye to illegal acts.

Corruption in the supply chain is a major issue that has attracted considerable attention from regulators and inter-governmental organizations. The problem has been particularly highlighted by the UN Global Compact, which summarizes the problem as follows:

The very significant corruption risks in the supply chain include procurement fraud perpetrated by suppliers, often in league with the customer's own employees, and suppliers who engage in corrupt practices involving governments and other public actors. (UNGC, 2010)

The Compact specifies the following as some of the most likely scenarios in the customer-supplier relationship:

1 Procurement manager demands kickback from supplier to secure contract or provide inside information on bidding process.

2 Supplier offers kickback to procurement manager to secure contract or provide inside information on bidding process.

3 Supplier offers gifts or entertainment to procurement manager.

4 Procurement manager selects supplier because of personal/family relationship.

5 Monopoly supplier demands that purchaser pay bribe or kickback to secure goods or services.

6 Customer employee demands that supplier purchase from company owned by or related to customer employee.

7 Supplier offers bribe to contract manager to overlook inferior goods or services.

8 Supplier submits false invoice for work done or employee work hours.

In recent years there has been a push by many administrations to clamp down on corruption in a range of anti-bribery, anti-corruption legislation. The United States and United Kingdom have been at the forefront of these moves, initiating far-reaching legislation.

The UK's Bribery Act 2010 makes companies accountable for the actions of third parties working on their behalf. It also applies to any British citizen either making or taking a bribe anywhere in the world. This is perhaps one of the main reasons why British ex-pats working in the supply chain and logistics sector are now very wary of becoming involved in import/export transactions in many developing countries.

A bribe doesn't necessarily have to be a direct payment under the terms of the Act. It could cover, for instance, a payment to an official's nominated charity if it were viewed as an inducement.

A controversial part of the Act is that a company can be held liable for an act of an employee or third party even if it had no knowledge of it unless it can show that it had implemented a robust compliance process. This could involve, for example, the appointment of a Compliance Officer and the development of policy documents related to proper behaviour.

In the United States, sanctions against bribery are contained within the Foreign Corrupt Practices Act 1977 (FCPA). The UK's Bribery Act is viewed as being more severe than the FCPA, which creates an exemption for facilitation payments; the Bribery Act makes no such exception. The UK Ministry of Justice guidelines on facilitation payments are as follows:

- Companies should have a clear and issued policy.

- Companies should have written guidance available to employees as to the procedures they must follow where a facilitation payment is requested or expected.

- It must be demonstrated that such procedures are being followed (monitoring).

- There must be evidence that gifts are being recorded at the company.

- Proper action, collective or otherwise, must be taken to inform the appropriate authorities in countries when a breach of the policy occurs.

- The company must take practical steps to curtail such payments.

One of the consequences of globalization has been the exposure to corrupt practices faced by companies establishing operations in emerging markets. This not only affects manufacturers but also the logistics companies they employ. This applies most to companies working with SMEs. As the UN Global Compact comments:

> In countries with a high degree of corruption, the supply chain for multinational companies very often consists of small and medium size local businesses. These businesses typically have more contact with corruption because they face both more temptation and more opportunity. As local entities, they may lack a global perspective and have less discomfort in participating in corruption, especially in a culture where such activity is the norm.

What can be done to limit corruption?

With legislation now in place, companies have a clear mandate to enforce anti-corruption policies throughout their organizations, especially when dealing with suppliers or customers. There are many guidelines and materials to help businesses and their employees deal with corrupt approaches. Best practice includes:

- Establishing a code of conduct and ensuring that employees understand its principles and sanctions.
- Implementing reporting procedures and mechanisms.
- Publicizing attempts to bribe employees.
- Establishing a reputation for zero-tolerance.
- Providing anti-corruption training (to own staff and suppliers).
- Remunerating staff at a level that will reduce their vulnerability to bribery.

Specifically within the purchasing process, best practice calls for more than one supplier being asked to tender for business. There should be objective tests in place, including pricing, quality and service attributes such as logistics, where appropriate. In addition, the financial status of the supplier should be checked. Importantly, internal checks should be in place. There should be multiple levels of management sign-off and reviews of bids by teams of employees rather than by individuals. These processes lessen considerably the chance that any individual with high levels of control could be corrupted by a single supplier.

Summary

In many industries, such as the UK grocery retail sector, a small group of companies exerts considerable power over their supply chains. Where this occurs there is the potential for the misuse of this power, which can lead to the imposition of unethical terms and conditions on a fragmented and weak supplier base. To make relationships 'fairer' there have been efforts to introduce self-regulation through codes of conduct and where these have been judged ineffective, subsequently through regulation such as the UK's Groceries Code Adjudicator (GCA). The UK milk industry has become a cause célèbre and characterizes many of the difficulties an oligopolistic market can face. In many parts of the world commercial relationships have the potential to transgress lines of legality and legislation has now been passed that deals firmly with bribery and corruption.

Key points

- Manufacturers and retailers can use their influence in the supply chain as a force for good, ie to push through ethical and environmental initiatives. However, it can also be used 'unfairly' to impose additional costs or stringent terms and conditions on suppliers.

- UK grocery retailers have been accused of exploiting suppliers, including asking for 'lump sum' payments to support their margins.

- The UK milk industry has been in the news due to the impact low prices paid by retailers have had upon farmers.

- Legislation in the United Kingdom and United States has been introduced to prevent supplier-customer relationships becoming corrupt.

References

Anderson, E and Bury, R (2016) Thousands of dairy farms face closure as debts reach crisis levels, *Daily Telegraph*, http://www.telegraph.co.uk/business/2016/02/21/thousands-of-dairy-farms-face-closure-as-debts-reach-crisis-level/

CIPS (2007) *Ethical Business Practices in Purchasing and Supply Management*, Chartered Institute of Purchasing and Supply, London

HoC (2016) *Farm Gate Prices*, Environment, House of Commons Food and Rural Affairs Committee, London

UNGC (2010) *Fighting Corruption in the Supply Chain: A guide for customers and suppliers*, UN Global Compact, Geneva

WEF (2013) *Global Competitiveness Report*, World Economic Forum, Geneva

Treatment of workers in the modern logistics sector

13

THIS CHAPTER WILL FAMILIARIZE THE READER WITH

- The issues surrounding the use of owner-drivers in the logistics sector
- The e-commerce pressures that have created the market environment for controversial working practices
- The confusing classification regulations that determine 'self-employed' or 'employee' status
- The circumstances involving the bankruptcy of City Link
- On-demand economy and its impact on couriers
- Working practices at the Sports Direct distribution centre in Shirebrook

Many logistics companies are rightly proud of the sustainability initiatives they have introduced within their warehousing and transport operations. Despite this, the fundamental business models and employment structures that many companies in the sector operate are coming under intense scrutiny due to the impact they have on logistics workers. Many of the issues relate to the highly sub-contracted nature of labour in the transport market and the use of agency workers in the warehouse sector.

The increasing use of owner-drivers

It may be surprising to many people, but a large proportion of drivers working in the European logistics industry are self-employed. Although the use of owner-drivers (self-employed transport workers who also provide their own vehicle) has been widespread for several decades, the demand for such workers has soared recently due to the spectacular growth of e-retail-related deliveries. While much of the logistics market has been stagnant due to economic weakness in much of the world, the volume of home deliveries has increased dramatically. This has brought a welcome source of revenue to many companies while at the same time raising a number of significant challenges.

Volatility in the market, with frequent peaks and troughs, has meant that the vast majority of parcels carriers have adopted an outsourced model, in effect de-risking their own operations. Sub-contractors bear not only the cost of investment in transport assets but also carry the risks associated with being paid 'by the drop'.

The e-retail market is such that 'free shipping' is a major selling point for many companies. Of course, much of the cost of this marketing device is pushed onto the carrier making the delivery, resulting in ultra-low rates of remuneration. This has raised ethical concerns. The low barriers to market entry and a plentiful supply of people willing to take on a low-skilled job have meant that the amounts paid by some carriers are barely enough to cover the cost of running a vehicle. There have been allegations that some carriers regard their sub-contractors (or owner-drivers as they are called) as 'disposable'. They can be utilized for a period of time at an unsustainable rate, knowing that they will eventually be forced to give up due to the lack of economic viability. The carrier will then replace the owner-driver from a plentiful pool of new market entrants.

Of course many would argue that this state of affairs is merely derived from the healthy operation of a free market. In the United Kingdom, many owner-drivers are migrants from Eastern Europe who have been attracted to the country by full employment and wages much higher than those in their own countries. A large pool of new migrants has meant that the UK economy has benefited from a lower cost base. If this labour pool were reduced, supply chain costs would rise throughout industry.

The status of owner-drivers provides them with fewer entitlements than people who are legally defined as employees. For example, they have none of the protection rights of employees, sick pay, maternity/paternity leave, pensions, etc despite fulfilling a role that, it could be argued, is identical to that of an employee. Also, due to the likelihood in the parcels sector that owner-drivers will be providing and driving a van rather than a Large Goods Vehicle (LGV), they do not have to comply with European drivers' hours legislation, placing a limit on the length of time they can drive. Consequently workloads are often high and hours very long and, as discussed above, rates of pay very poor.

Self-employed or not?

Whether a person is an 'employee' or 'self-employed' is a grey area. According to the UK Government, someone is probably self-employed and should not be paid through the pay-as-you-earn (PAYE) taxation system if most of the following are true (HMRC, 2014):

- they're in business for themselves, are responsible for the success or failure of their business and can make a loss or a profit;
- they can decide what work they do, and when, where or how to do it;
- they can hire someone else to do the work;
- they're responsible for fixing any unsatisfactory work in their own time;
- their client/employer agrees a fixed price for their work – it doesn't depend on how long the job takes to finish;
- they use their own money to buy business assets, cover running costs, and provide tools and equipment for their work;
- they can work for more than one client.

On top of this, guidance asserts that workers won't have employment rights if they are exempt from PAYE and most of the following are also true:

- they put in bids or give quotes to get work;
- they're not under direct supervision when working;

- they submit invoices for the work they've done;
- they're responsible for paying their own National Insurance and tax;
- they don't get holiday or sick pay when they're not working;
- they operate under a contract that uses terms like 'self-employed', 'consultant' or an 'independent contractor'.

Consequently, although it may seem evident that a full-time delivery driver, working exclusively for a single transport company, wearing a liveried uniform and driving a liveried vehicle would be an 'employee', this is often not the case. The guidance does not provide a definitive test for self-employment, which is allowing the status to be challenged in the courts.

This is not just a UK issue, as legal challenges have been ongoing in the United States for many years. In 2015 FedEx paid $228 million to settle a court case in California related to the 'misclassification' of thousands of drivers as self-employed. Start-ups Uber and Lyft face the same challenge. The US Government believes that across the economy as a whole 30 per cent of employers misclassify staff, costing $2.7 billion in unpaid taxes.

For US legislators, the issue is one of overall control. If the majority of control over an operation is being exerted by a single company, then the worker is likely to be deemed as employed.

CASE STUDY City Link's failure shines light on owner-driver predicament

On Christmas Eve in 2014, major UK express parcels carrier City Link called in the administrators. The carrier was owned by private equity company, Better Capital, which acquired it in 2013 from Rentokil plc for £1. Despite investing a reported £40 million in the business it was unable to make a profit and its failure led to the loss of 4,000 jobs.

City Link used over 1,000 so-called 'service delivery partners' none of whom had guaranteed hours, sick pay, holiday pay or redundancy entitlements. Owner-drivers typically had to arrange their own holiday or sick cover, including arranging for payments. If they did not they would be fined in the region of £150 per day for breach of contract.

Delivery drivers were paid about £1.65 for each delivery. If there were multiple deliveries to the same location this would still only count as a single delivery. Working hours could extend from 4.30 am to 7.30 pm on any one day. Being self-employed they were not eligible for the minimum wage. According to the *Financial Times* report (Barrett and Shubber, 2015), financial projections for owner-drivers were worked out on the assumption of 103 drops per day, although the company made it clear it could not guarantee that level. While City Link paid by the drop, some companies pay by the loaded mile – this could be as little as 50 pence per mile, regardless of the time taken.

Although City Link drivers could be paid as much as £43,000 a year this would not include fuel, insurance, uniform or a weekly charge for the van. The net amount the driver would take home was probably less than half of that, from which income tax and National Insurance would be payable. Drivers would lease the van from City Link at a cost of around £6,240 a year, paid in monthly instalments. It was possible to use their own van if it met certain standards, but it would have to be painted in the City Link livery. Uniforms cost £88.

When the company collapsed many of the sub-contractors (as unsecured creditors) were not paid, having worked through the busy Christmas period. However, employees were paid up until the end of the month.

The outcry over the collapse was such that the UK Parliament's Business, Innovation and Skills and Scottish Affairs Committee undertook an inquiry into the whole affair. In its report in March 2015 it commented:

> We are dismayed that, although it was clear for some time there were serious questions over the ability of City Link to continue trading after December 2014, small businesses and self-employed drivers working for City Link were encouraged to take on additional costs despite a strong possibility that they would not receive payment for a significant part of their work in December. (HoC, 2015)

It went on to say: 'There is no doubt that contractors were deliberately deceived as to the true state of the business. City Link and Better Capital are morally, if not legally, responsible for the difficulties that many of these individuals and small business now find themselves in.' The Committee added that it welcomed the Secretary of State for Business, Innovation and Skills' review of 'how to tackle the problem of bogus self-employment'. Even the owner of Better Capital recognized the potential problem of self-employment. He told the Committee that self-employment could be either 'a panacea or a terrible evil' and that for some City Link employees who became self-employed City Link drivers, 'in some cases it would have been to their benefit, and in some cases it would have been to their detriment: no question'.

The Government's response to the issue of 'bogus' self-employment was to stress that the status of a worker depends on the reality of the working relationship with the employer, and not on what the employer chooses to call the worker (ie either employee or sub-contractor). However, it did admit that in many cases it was difficult to determine employment status (BIS, 2015). Of course in the case of City Link the self-employed workers would have had a commercial contract with the company regarding the lease of a transport asset even though the relationship was exclusive. This perhaps complicated the issue further.

The on-demand economy – unethical or new employment model?

The business models of many companies operating in the 'on-demand' economy (also called 'gig' economy) in the transport sector, at least, are coming under intense scrutiny due to the treatment of suppliers.

Start-up restaurant meal delivery company Deliveroo is facing challenges to its sub-contracted labour model from both regulators and the sub-contractors themselves. The company has a network of 5,000 drivers and riders across the United Kingdom who collect and deliver meals from a range of food outlets that do not have their own delivery capabilities. At present the company pays its sub-contractors £7 an hour, plus £1 per delivery. However, management has introduced a new pay structure that has resulted in demonstrations by its drivers. The company wants to change the remuneration to a simple £3.75 per delivery. Although this may result in higher payments during peak times, overall there is concern that the new system will result in contractors receiving less than the minimum wage across the day as a whole.

Rival start up, UberEats, is facing similar dissent among its contracted workforce. The casual basis of employment for couriers means that although there are opportunities to earn around £9 an hour, on some occasions few, if any, jobs will be allocated. Management counter that couriers don't have set shifts, minimum hours or delivery zones that they must keep to. Many have other jobs as well.

Although some of the sub-contractors may see the on-demand model as unethical, the arrangement suits some: both Deliveroo and UberEats have attracted many thousands of couriers to sign up to their business models. However, there have been legal challenges to whether self-employed workers should be given access to the same rights as other employees. In the contract that Deliveroo requires its drivers to sign, contractors must sign away their right to challenge their status, although legally this may be unenforceable. Employees would have rights such as pensions, holiday pay and sick pay, plus a minimum wage.

In a case related to the sacking of two workers by private hire company Addison Lee, the legal representative of the GMB union commented:

> Employers cannot be allowed to have all the financial benefits of employees and none of the responsibilities to these people's livelihoods. The attempt to reframe normal employment as part of the gig economy is a serious threat to the financial security of thousands of hard working people and will end up costing the tax payer huge sums whilst companies take all the profit. (GMB, 2016)

One of the main issues, it would appear, is that barriers to less formal employment will need to be overcome if the on-demand economy is to become mainstream. It is likely that employment status will become even more contentious in the future as labour organizations try to prevent the prevalence of more informal working structures and governments try to mitigate the loss of tax receipts. Both sets of vested interests are likely to be left behind by developments in the sector.

Ethical work practices in the warehouse

Distribution centres often require large numbers of staff to undertake warehousing functions such as put-away, picking and packing. In addition a number of manufacturing tasks can be undertaken, such as product customization or returns testing. These manual roles are likely to attract low wages and draw on agency staff, often immigrants, especially when there are high levels of employment in an economy. This has, on occasion, made the sector vulnerable to accusations of exploitation.

CASE STUDY   Conditions and practices at Sports Direct's warehouse

The UK sportswear and equipment retailer, Sports Direct, came under scrutiny from the House of Commons Business, Innovation and Skills Select Committee in 2016 after accusations of employee abuse (HoC, 2016). The retailer is led by the charismatic owner Mike Ashley who for several months refused to cooperate with the Committee's inquiry before eventually testifying.

Although accusations related to all aspects of Sports Direct's employee relations, particular attention was paid to terms and conditions at its Shirebrook warehouse, an 800,000ft^2 distribution facility. The inquiry shone a light on some of the poor practices that can take place even in a developed economy.

Agency workers

Sports Direct pays around £50 million a year to two agencies to supply staff to undertake a range of warehouse functions. Most of the staff supplied are of East European origin and are guaranteed seven weeks work a year (336 hours). According to the company, pay is just above the minimum wage (although this assertion was challenged in the Committee).

One of the issues the inquiry flagged up was that while the agencies had no responsibility to provide employment for the staff beyond the seven weeks a year, should a staff member not be able to provide a reasonable excuse for not turning up to work he or she was liable to be sacked. This was seen by the Committee as an unfair and unbalanced relationship, as the worker would not be able to seek work elsewhere as he or she always needed to be available to work for Sports Direct.

Of course, from an operational perspective, such flexibility is important to be able to meet the peaks and troughs of demand. 'Zero hours' (no guaranteed hours) and 'short hours' are common throughout the industry as a whole. As Mike Ashley commented at the inquiry, it would have been impossible for him to have been able to grow the business at the rate he did without using agencies. The role of agencies has developed largely due to the e-retail revolution that has generated the need for large numbers of flexible staff to meet volatility, seasonality and high volume growth rates.

Working practices

A 'six strike' policy was in force at the warehouse. A 'strike' would be issued for such misdemeanours as taking too long a toilet break, taking time off if dependants were ill or over-long chatting in the workplace. Sport Direct's management denied that they had put the policy in place and it seemed that the agency was responsible. However, of course, ultimate responsibility must lie with the retailer itself.

Health and safety

The inquiry found that between January 2010 and April 2016 there were 115 accidents in the Shirebrook warehouse, which included a finger amputation, fractured neck and a crushed hand as well as a range of other injuries to backs, arms and legs. Twelve of these injuries were considered serious. Between 2013 and 2016, 110 ambulances or paramedic vehicles were dispatched to the facility. The inquiry said that it was concerned with the number of cases and health and safety breaches.

Impact on the community

There have been complaints by the local community on the impact the warehouse has had upon its social fabric, transport and housing. Due to the influx of workers to the local region (there are 3,500 staff employed at the facility), housing resources have come under huge pressure. Many houses have been divided into flats, resulting in overcrowding and poor housing conditions including insufficient fire safety measures (Willgress, 2016). Although the actions of landlords cannot directly be attributed to Sports Direct (and employment opportunities are generally welcomed), this is an example of a lack of planning both by the retailer and the local authority that would have sanctioned the building of the warehouse in the first place.

Response by Sports Direct

Stung by criticism from the House of Commons Select Committee, the media and trade unions, Sports Direct undertook to make changes to its operations. Management committed to:

- offer directly-employed casual employees either zero hours contracts or a permanent contract with 12 hours a week guaranteed;
- suspend the 'six strikes' policy;
- agree back payments to staff to compensate for unpaid time spent queuing to get through security checks;
- increase medical support on site.

The response to Sports Direct's undertakings has not been wholly positive. Critics pointed out that only 400 staff in the warehouse qualified for permanent contracts. Those employed through the agencies fell outside the new offer.

Summary

The failure of express parcels company City Link in Christmas 2014 shone a light on the established working practices that exist throughout the industry – the widespread use of owner-drivers within a transport network. Many people would expect that the liveried drivers representing parcels companies would be their employees, but for many operators this is not the case. Parcels companies use flexible resources that are often paid by the delivery in order to balance peaks and troughs of demand. It doesn't make economic sense for couriers to employ their own staff and invest in their own fleet of vehicles. However, this business model has come in for criticism due to the very low rates of pay and the long hours entailed. Similarly, the low rates of pay in the warehouse sector have also been highlighted, most recently by the furore caused by practices at Sports Direct's Shirebrook distribution centre. The majority of employees are low paid migrants living in very poor conditions.

Key points

- The growth of the e-commerce sector, with associated variable peaks and troughs of demand, has led to the widespread use of owner-drivers by delivery companies.
- Owner-drivers, being self-employed, have none of the legal rights of employees.
- The UK Government admits that in many cases it is difficult to determine the employment status of a worker.
- The on-demand economy is adding to the demand for owner-drivers, but many are protesting at the conditions and rates of pay.
- The warehousing sector is characterized by low pay, and recruitment is often handled by agencies.

References

Barrett, C and Shubber, K (2015) City Link collapse reveals sector's systemic problems, *Financial Times*, http://www.ft.com/

BIS (2015) Government response to the joint House of Commons committee's report on the impact of the closure of City Link on employment. Presented to Parliament by the Secretary of State for Business, Innovation & Skills, London

GMB (2016) GMB launches Addison Lee legal proceedings, http://www.gmb.org.uk/newsroom/gmb-launches-addison-lee-legal-proceedings

HMRC (2014) Employment status: employed or self-employed? HM Revenue & Customs, https://www.gov.uk/government/collections/employed-or-self-employed

HoC (2015) First joint report impact of the closure of City Link on employment, Business, Innovation and Skills and Scottish Affairs, House of Commons, London

HoC (2016) Employment practices at Sports Direct, Business, Innovation and Skills Committee, House of Commons, UK

Willgress, L (2016) Police investigate safety of houses in Derbyshire town where Sports Direct employs 3,500 workers after they were divided into flats and packed with migrants, *Daily Mail*, http://www.dailymail.co.uk/news/article-3457441/Police-investigate-safety-houses-carved-flats-packed-migrants-home-town-Sports-Direct.html

INDEX

Note: The index is filed in alphabetical, word-by-word order. Numbers within main headings are filed as spelt out. Acronyms are filed as presented. Page locators in *italics* denote information contained within a Figure or Table.